INTRODUCING THE WOMEN'S HEBREW BIBLE

INTRODUCING THE WOMEN'S HEBREW BIBLE

Feminism, Gender Justice, and the Study of the Old Testament

Susanne Scholz

Bloomsbury T&T Clark
An imprint of Bloomsbury Publishing Plc

B L O O M S B U R Y
LONDON · OXFORD · NEW YORK · NEW DELHI · SYDNEY

Bloomsbury T&T Clark

An imprint of Bloomsbury Publishing Plc

Imprint previously known as T&T Clark

50 Bedford Square	1385 Broadway
London	New York
WC1B 3DP	NY 10018
UK	USA

www.bloomsbury.com

BLOOMSBURY, T&T CLARK and the Diana logo are trademarks of Bloomsbury Publishing Plc

First published 2007
This version published 2017

Library of Congress Cataloging-in-Publication Data
A catalogue record for this book is available from the British Library.

ISBN: HB: 978-0-5676-6337-5
PB: 978-0-5676-6336-8
ePDF: 978-0-5676-6338-2
ePub: 978-0-5676-6339-9

Library of Congress Cataloging-in-Publication Data
A catalog record for this book is available from the Library of Congress.

Cover image © Zvonimir Atletic/Alamy Stock Photo

Typeset by Fakenham Prepress Solutions, Fakenham, Norfolk NR21 8NN

In Memory of
Frau Friedel Süß
(1910–1987)

And to
Rev. Dr. Peter Sauer

CONTENTS

ACKNOWLEDGMENTS OF THE FIRST EDITION

The writing of this book enjoyed the support of many people and I am grateful to all of them for their collegiality, friendship and expertise. Let me begin by thanking Lisa Isherwood, one of the series editors, who invited me to write this volume when we attended the international conference of the European Society of Women in Theological Research (ESWTR) in Salzburg, Austria, in 2001. Her invitation meant a great deal to me. I also want to thank the Faculty Development Committee at Merrimack College for supporting the writing of this book with two grants, one for a course release in Fall 2005 and another for a summer grant in 2006. Thanks also to the following colleagues, friends, and family members—to Merrimack Women's Studies Program Board for feminist laughter, support and company: Marie Plasse, Elaine Donavan, Cinzia DiGiulio and Monica Cowart. To my faculty mentor, David Raymond, whose time, energy and support will never be forgotten. To members of my department: Warren Kay, Elaine Huber, Padraic O'Hare, Rebecca Norris, and Mark Allman. To my colleagues Ray Dorney, Charlie Tontar and Larry Gillooly. Also many thanks to Chris Royer, Jean van Riper, Laurie Alexander-Krom, and Gary Feldman for their expert advice. I thank my colleagues in biblical studies: Athalya Brenner, Ed Greenstein, Greg Mobley, Rich Weiss, and Gale Yee. With gratitude to my friend and editor, Chris Herlinger. Thanks to my theological "sisters": members of the NA ESWTR and the ESWTR, Gabriella Lettini, Katharina von Kellenbach, Carleen Mandolfo, Janet Parker, Teresa Berger, Renate Rose, Jane Webster, Diemut Cramer, Kathinka Kaden, Gabi Schröder, Annemarie Kidder, Monika Jakobs, and Hanna Dieckmann. Thanks to my dear mother, Witha Scholz-Ardebili, who was not deterred by English. To Ekkehard and Gabi Knobloch who travelled far to visit. To Bernd and Ursula Deißler for the gift of homeopathy. To my first reader, Lorraine Keating, for her good judgment, honest and engaging feedback, serious commentary, and delicious dinners in the City. The book is dedicated to two teachers who shaped my life: Frau Süß who introduced me to the joys of good tea with intellectual conversation, and Peter Sauer, my religion teacher in the *gymnasialen Oberstufe* who was the first to introduce me to feminist theology and the world of academic (feminist) theology.

North Andover, MA
August 2006

ACKNOWLEDGMENTS OF THE SECOND EDITION

Ten years have passed since the first edition appeared in 2007. During this time T&T Clark, the original publisher of the volume, was acquired by Bloomsbury Publishing. I am most grateful to the Bloomsbury acquisition editor, Dominic Mattos, for his suggestion to publish a second revised and expanded edition of *Introducing the Women's Hebrew Bible*, especially since I have noticed that mergers and acquisitions in the academic book publishing world in religious and theological studies often make some titles hard to find, if they do not disappear altogether.

I also thank the four anonymous reviewers for their careful, nuanced, and valuable suggestions regarding my ideas for revising the first edition. Although I did not include all of their suggestions, the second edition has benefited from many of them. I expanded the history chapter and I added two new chapters: one about queer and masculinity bible hermeneutics, and another about Christian right's interpretations on women in the Bible. When I wrote my manuscript for the first edition, I wondered what the next ten years of feminist Hebrew Bible scholarship would bring. At the time I ended with a chapter on postcolonial feminist Hebrew Bible scholarship because it seemed the most vibrant, innovative, and exciting new development to me. While this is still the case, the second edition no longer ends with postcolonial feminist biblical studies because, in my view, two additional areas of feminist biblical hermeneutics have come to produce great interest in the field. Chapters 6 and 7 discuss these developments, as I have come to think of them during the past ten years. It will be fascinating to find out how the field will have developed by 2027! The way I see it, feminist Hebrew Bible studies ought to develop, shift, move, and expand into all kinds of directions so that the early beginnings—whenever we pinpoint them—will not have been in vain but flourish into an exciting, comprehensive, and advanced field of academic study that also stays connected to the material and intersectional gender conditions of the world.

More gratitude needs to be expressed. I thank my courageous, thoughtful, and honest Christian theology students at Perkins School of Theology who signed up for the two installments of the course entitled "OT8317 Queer Bible Hermeneutics" in Fall 2014 and Spring 2016. Our reading lists were extensive, our conversations profound, and our learning about the theo-political connections and implications of genderqueer exegesis enormous. I also thank the Associate Dean for Academic Affairs at Perkins School of Theology, Evelyn Parker, for granting me research assistance for the preparation of this manuscript in the summer of 2016. I thank my research assistant, David Schones, doctoral student in the Graduate Program in Religious Studies at SMU, for his tremendous help in getting the bibliography into a publishable format and for his reliable proofreading assistance. I thank the librarians of Bridwell Library at Perkins School of Theology for their reliable and speedy help. It is always a pleasure to work with the Bridwell staff members, with special thanks to Jane Lenz Elder, Reference Librarian, and Sally Hoover, ILL & Reserves Assistant. It is a great privilege to have access to this gem of a theological library right where I have been teaching and researching since 2008.

I also want to thank my Iyengar yoga teachers, George Purvis, and Marj Rash, for helping me stay physically and mentally relaxed since I moved to Dallas so that I can teach, sit in committees, research and write with ease and joy. I thank my Dallas friends and colleagues, especially Pat Davis and Jeanne Stevenson-Moessner for our estate-sale expeditions, a local Dallas pursuit that brings us great pleasure and feminist companionship. Last but not least, my gratitude goes to my enduring first reader, Lorraine Keating, whose astute theological observations strengthen my argument every single time.

Thanks y'all!

Dallas, Texas
July 2016

INTRODUCTION

Personal Beginnings

"Who is Moses?" I asked my mother when I was twelve years old after I came home one afternoon from my confirmation class. Attending secular schools in West Germany and raised by parents who had sworn to themselves not to force religious education onto their children, I had grown up like most of my friends. Nominally, we belonged to the Protestant or Catholic Church because we were baptized, in my case into the Protestant Christian faith, but we did not go to church, rarely prayed at home, and did not have religion courses in school. Like many Germans of my generation, therefore, I had grown up secular without religious talk and language anywhere.

At age twelve, however, I wanted to go to confirmation class because I had heard—I do not remember where—that during this process one goes to church and learns more about one's faith. I wanted to go badly, to the big surprise of my parents and extended family. Even the Protestant minister, Rev. Büttner, had some initial hesitations, mostly because I was a year younger than everybody else. Yet my mother, wise in these matters, explained to the minister who even made a home visit for the occasion that she approved of my wish to attend confirmation class now rather than later. She anticipated that I might change my mind if delayed. So I went, not knowing anything about the Bible or Jesus, no less about Moses. I started as a *tabula rasa* in terms of my religious knowledge, and my ignorance was perhaps worse than that of other children who had the benefit of religious practice at home. Many years have passed since that time, and by now I believe that it was not an accident that I felt the need to attend confirmation class as soon as I had heard of its existence. What I lacked most shaped my path so far. Strange how these things sometimes work out! I delved into a field that most people do not even know exists as a serious academic subject matter. Since I grew up secular, I understand secular people. Their ignorance about religious matters was once mine, and I feel sympathetic although at the same time I want them to recognize that the loss is theirs. In my view, the Bible and its academic study help to understand oneself and the world. Not faith but a desire to understand is the requirement.

In today's Germany most people under forty have at best a fragmentary religious education and know little of the extensive theological discussions that have taken place in the scholarly world. Sure, they listen for a moment when archaeologists claim to have found the coffin of the brother of Jesus. Yet they quickly turn to other things, sometimes even to church concerts that are regularly offered with great success in German cathedrals. Germany of the early twenty-first century is a post-biblical country, as is much of Europe. I know the feel of it but my path has led me into a different direction. During the last three years in *Gymnasium*, I had the opportunity to take religion courses and my teacher, Dr Peter Sauer, left little doubt in my mind that "religion" is a most serious academic subject that includes everything necessary to understand the world: history, political science, literature, art, philosophy, psychology, even science, and once I understood this, I wanted to know more about the field that seemed so all-embracing, so all-illuminating and absolutely mind-opening to me. I decided to study Protestant Theology at the university level. Everybody was stunned: my parents, family, and friends. They could not understand why I would not go into a secular profession as the secular person I was who went dancing, played sports, was dynamic, smart, and definitely not pious enough in the expected ways to become a Christian minister, the standard professional goal for a student of Protestant Theology in Germany at the time.

But determined as I have always been, I knew exactly what I wanted and was not deterred by people's comments. I enrolled at the University in Mainz in the full-fledged Protestant Theology program and was immediately pushed toward the Hebrew Bible. Every student in the Master of Divinity degree (*Kirchliche Examen*) was required to first pass rigorous language exams in biblical Hebrew and classical Greek before we were eligible for many other courses. Luckily, I loved my biblical Hebrew class, taught by Dr Gross who was already retired at the time and hard of hearing. A class of a hundred students, we met during the early morning hours in a tiny lecture classroom while Herr Gross rattled down stem forms and verbal roots. I also registered for a lecture course on Second Isaiah. I was a first-semester student and did not understand why the professor, Horst Seebaß, spent the entire semester on parsing verses, even half- and quarter-verses, from one place to another in the book of Isaiah, as if his life depended on it.

Yet I was committed to the field I knew very little about. I took almost every course offered in "Old Testament": Kohelet, Jeremiah, Genesis, the obligatory introduction courses on the Old Testament and exegesis, as well as biblical archae-ology. I also ventured into a course on Ugaritic in which the professor, Diethelm Michel, learned the language with his students and we translated texts from a time and place I had never known anything about. I wanted to study everything, even participated in an archaeological dig in Israel, and passed a challenging Bible content exam. For the latter I studied day and night because I was deeply worried that I might fail due to my limited Bible knowledge. Who was Moses? After the Bible content exam, this was not my question anymore. Moses, Miriam, Abraham, Sarah, Hagar, and Keturah—I knew about them and all the other biblical narratives, poems, legal texts, songs, and genealogies, both in the Hebrew Bible and the New Testament. My desire to know more was huge, and when I had the opportunity to go abroad, to Israel, to the Hebrew University in Jerusalem, I went. I studied Torah, Talmud, and Midrash in modern Hebrew and was part of a program for students of Theology from German-speaking countries, called "Studium in Israel." And I loved it.

I was also a feminist and had read books on feminist theology, but biblical feminist courses were not offered anywhere at the time, neither in Germany nor in Israel. I knew that an academic discourse on the link between feminism and religious-theological studies existed, mostly in the United States, and it was in Israel that I decided to go there and learn more about this approach to theological and biblical studies. Why did I not ask about Miriam when I was a child? Androcentric bias was clearly omnipresent in all of my theological training, and it was present in the world at large. One of my New Testament professors in Mainz had been Luise Schottroff, the only woman professor I ever had in Germany, and so, thanks to her courses and publications, I was aware of patriarchal and anti-Jewish biases in much of German Protestant exegesis, history, and doctrine.[1] I will never forget the dubious advice of a male New Testament professor after he had examined me on my topic, "Women in the Early Christian Movement." He said: "Just make sure you don't get pushed onto the feminist track—that would be a pity!"

After I graduated with the German equivalent of the Master of Divinity (M.Div.) from the University in Heidelberg, I was lucky to be awarded a scholarship of the World Council of Churches for a one-year program at Union Theological Seminary in New York City. My goal was to focus on feminist biblical studies and theologies, and I took courses with pioneers of feminist biblical studies and ethics, especially with Phyllis Trible and Beverly W. Harrison. At Union we read books of major feminist theologians from the U.S.A. and elsewhere. To me, the "feminist track" illuminated one of the most important injustices in the world and in theological studies: gender discrimination, bias, and oppression. Encouraged in my Union courses, I found the inclusion of other forms of social, political, economic, and religious oppression the logical next step. Back in Germany the feminist theological community had already debated the significance of anti-Jewish bias in feminist theological work.[2] In womanist, *mujerista*, Black, liberation theologies—Jewish and Christian, Latin American, African, and Asian—I found the intellectual and social challenges of a multi-dimensional analysis theologically invigorating and ethically necessary.

In addition, it was always clear to me that biblical and theological studies need to make connections with the contemporary world. The feminist study of the Hebrew Bible was therefore a perfect fit in my mind. For sure, the Bible as the sacred text of Christianity and Judaism provides central clues about the cultural,

---

1. An influential anthology on the topic is Lenore Siegele-Wenschkewitz (ed.), *Verdrängte Vergangenheit, die uns bedrängt: Feministische Theologie in der Verantwortung für die Geschichte* (München: Kaiser Verlag, 1988). It includes an essay by Luise Schottroff.

2. For a brief summary in German with bibliographical resources, see, e.g. Marianne Grohmann, "Feministische Theologie und jüdisch-christlicher Dialog," available at http://www.jcrelations.net/Feministische+Theologie+und+christlich-j%FCdischer+Dialog.1273.0.html?&L=3 (accessed December 12, 2016).

political, economic, social, and religious dynamics of past and present gender oppression. My early question, "Who is Moses?", for instance, illuminates the pervasiveness of gender bias. It was not an accident that I learned about Moses and not Miriam in my German Protestant confirmation class, and feminist biblical studies helped me to understand the history and politics of this deep-seated bias.

Why Moses and not Miriam? A post-biblical society such as Germany does not know why the question matters. If one does not know who Moses is, Miriam does not even come up. To make both biblical characters relevant, to introduce the accomplishments of feminist biblical studies to a Bible-illiterate audience is needed now more than ever before. I have always loved learning about religion, theology, and the Bible, perhaps thanks to my parents who felt so burned by their own religious upbringing that their decision protected me from some of the damage that childhood faith can bring. I am most grateful to the feminist professors I was lucky enough to have at Union, but I also appreciate the andro-centric ones. Unbeknownst to them, they too added to my firm conviction that feminist biblical studies are making significant contributions to academia and society, and the results have to be made available to the lay public. I was lucky that my personal theological beginning was nurtured by the collective labor of feminist theologians who have surrounded me during much of my theological education and career as a biblical scholar and teacher, especially since I have come to the United States. They have made it possible for their students to join them and to explore the long history and the many traditions of theological and biblical gender bias. This book introduces their accomplishments, as well as their ongoing efforts of dismantling the master's tools and of developing our own paths.[3]

Forging a Path in Feminist Biblical Studies

During the past four decades a quiet revolution has occurred. Certainly, it is far from completed and sometimes it seems that it has barely begun at all. Yet this revolution has made it possible for women—black, white, and brown, from previously colonizing and colonized countries, rich, wage-earning, and poor, from the North, South, East and West, younger and older—to be heard and, if they wish and can, to join the academic study of the Hebrew Bible.

Unlike ever before in the history of biblical studies women now participate actively and vigorously in research and teaching of the Bible. Although discriminatory theories and practices against women still exist in abundance almost anywhere worldwide, this is a sign of hope. During the past forty years, women have enjoyed relative ease of access as students and professors to academic programs in theology and religious studies. Employed by universities, colleges,

---

3. See Audre Lorde, "The Master's Tools Will Never Dismantle the Master's House," in *Sister Outsider: Essays and Speeches* (Berkeley, CA: Crossing Press, 2007; originally published in 1984), 110–14.

and, seminaries, women have been able to produce important and new knowledge in the field of biblical studies.

By now, the plethora of feminist publications on the Hebrew Bible is staggering. Investigations on almost any topic and text are abundantly available and it is no longer possible to read every published work since there are just too many. Specialization is a must, and years of study are necessary to know one's way around in feminist biblical scholarship. The success of feminist biblical studies is especially impressive considering the fact that many academic institutions are still hesitant to support feminist research. There are also some women scholars who do not want to be connected with feminist work because they fear diminished career opportunities in an androcentric world. Determination, courage, and persistence have therefore been required by those who committed themselves to feminist biblical research. Their examples have inspired others to join the new field, and as a result their research has created a mature area of study.

For beginners and even for seasoned specialists of other fields it can be intimidating to pick up a book on feminist biblical studies. Where shall one begin to enter the conversations which have grown, deepened, and expanded so considerably during the past four decades? This book aims to help in the process of forging a path through the maze of feminist work on the Hebrew Bible.

About the Contents of this Book

This book introduces readers to the diverse field of feminist studies on the Hebrew Bible. Not organized as a traditional introduction to the "Old Testament," the chapters do not follow a biblical book-by-book structure, but instead they provide an introductory survey on the history, participants, methods, and main topics related to the feminist biblical scholarship. Accordingly, feminist scholars and their careers, and biblical texts, characters, and themes stand at the forefront. The discussion is biased toward "Western" feminist research because of the historical developments of feminist scholarship in general and biblical studies in particular. Yet the chapters also include many African, Asian, and Latin American perspectives. In short, then, the book offers an overview on the historical, social, and academic developments of reading the Hebrew Bible as the "Women's Hebrew Bible" during the past forty years.

A first chapter, entitled "From the 'Woman's Bible' to the 'Women's Bible': The History of Feminist Approaches to the Hebrew Bible," outlines the Western history of women interpreting the Hebrew Bible. The account begins with examples from Christian medieval women who argued for women's equality on the basis of selected biblical texts. The chapter then focuses on the arguments of nineteenth-century U.S.–American suffrages, especially Elizabeth Cady Stanton, who regarded religion and the Bible as a major detriment for women's rights. A discussion on early and mid-twentieth century women's interpretations of biblical women follows. The chapter culminates in a discussion on feminist biblical scholarship since the 1970s, and it ends with some considerations on feminist hermeneutics.

The last section touches on important questions affiliated with feminist biblical study, such as: Is the Hebrew Bible thoroughly patriarchal and is its androcentrism "redeemable"? And what makes a reading of the Bible "feminist"?

A second chapter, "A Career as a Feminist Biblical Scholar: Four Stories," describes why and how four feminist scholars of the Hebrew Bible became biblical scholars. The four scholars are Phyllis Trible, Athalya Brenner, Marie-Theres Wacker, and Elsa Tamez. Their stories offer diversity in terms of generation (pioneering and second generation), religion (Protestant, Jewish, Catholic), nationality (American, Israeli-Dutch, German, Mexican) and scholarly approach (historical, literary, cultural). Based on personal conversations with them, the chapter establishes that "real" women stand behind the developments of feminist biblical work. The chapter also makes connections between their lives and career choices, addresses some of the difficulties they encountered as feminist scholars, and describes their major scholarly contributions.

A third chapter, entitled "Gendering the Hebrew Bible: Methodological Considerations," discusses the main methods with which feminist scholars have interpreted the Hebrew Bible during the past decades. The chapter begins with a brief description of the three major methods, "Historical Criticism," "Literary Criticism," and "Cultural Criticism," and then illustrates each method with feminist biblical research. One section, illustrating historical criticism, discusses how feminist historians describe the patriarchal living conditions of Israelite women and how androcentric structures developed over time in ancient Israelite society. Another section, addressing literary criticism, depicts how feminist literary critics focused on the study of biblical mothers and these characters" status, role, and function in biblical narratives. Still another section describes feminist interpretations that investigate gender issues in contemporary art such as movies and paintings, and so it demonstrates how feminist biblical scholars use effectively cultural criticism.

A fourth chapter, entitled "Rape, Enslavement, and Marriage: Sexual Violence in the Hebrew Bible," examines the topic of rape in biblical texts to illustrate some of the hermeneutical problems with which feminist biblical scholars wrestle. Organized into two main sections, "Raped and Enslaved: Sexual Violence in Biblical Narrative" and "The City as a Raped Woman: Sexual Violence in Biblical Poetry," the chapter refers to selected biblical narratives and poems that contain metaphors on sexual violence. Among the narratives included are the stories of the enslaved women, Bilhah and Zilpah, in Genesis 29:31–30:24 and Genesis 35:22. The poetic literature comes from a variety of prophetic texts that present Israelite and ancient Near Eastern cities as women. They are among the most disturbing poems of the Hebrew Bible because the metaphoric speech includes God as sexual violator and rapist. The chapter takes for granted feminist theories on violence against women, as they inform feminist interpretations of these and other "texts of terror."[4]

---

4. For this expression, see Phyllis Trible, *Texts of Terror: Literary-Feminist Readings of Biblical Narratives* (Philadelphia: Fortress Press, 1984).

A fifth chapter, entitled "Ruth, Jezebel, and Rahab as 'Other' Women: Integrating Postcolonial Perspectives," takes seriously a recent development in feminist biblical studies, the emergence of feminist postcolonial perspectives. Since the late 1990s, feminist biblical scholars, mostly originating from Two-Third World countries, have begun integrating biblical gender analysis with postcolonial theory. The chapter reports on pertinent studies as they relate to feminist and postcolonial theoretical discourse in general. An introductory description of postcolonial theory outside and inside biblical studies begins the discussion, followed by a detailed and illustrative presentation of feminist biblical interpretations. It summarizes important examples from feminist postcolonial studies on the Hebrew Bible that compare biblical women, such as Ruth, Jezebel, and Rahab, with the situations of Two-Third World women, emphasize the significance of ordinary women, and insist on connecting biblical interpretations with colonial histories, cultures, and traditions.

A sixth chapter, entitled "Denaturalizing the Gender Binary: Queer and Masculinity Studies as Integral to Feminist Biblical Hermeneutics," presents the hermeneutical-exegetical developments that have redefined the Bible as queer literature. It discusses the emergence and significance of queer theories in general and explains why and how queer Bible scholars have contested methodological and hermeneutical heteronormativity of mainstream Bible meanings. Central in the debate is the problem of normativity and neoliberal assimilation in all gender discourse, biblical or not, as it is co-opted into serving the structures of domination and failing in its goal to transform society toward gender justice. Examples from clobber passages, such as Leviticus 18:22, and innovatively interpreted biblical passages, such as Judges 3:12-30 illustrate the hermeneutical claim that the Bible is a queer book. This chapter also elaborates on the hermeneutical development of studying the positionality of males and maleness in the Hebrew Bible. Related to the larger scholarly enterprise of investigating hegemonic masculinity in society, culture, and religion, exegetes in biblical masculinity studies have begun to take another look at many of the male-identified biblical characters such as the men in Genesis, King David, or even God. The chapter indicates how wide-ranging feminist and gender studies in Hebrew Bible scholarship can be, sometimes venturing out into hitherto unknown territories and sometimes continuing the long-standing tendency in biblical studies to adapt biblical interpretations to the ruling hegemonies in the field and in society.

The seventh chapter, entitled "Essentializing 'Woman': Three Neoliberal Strategies in the Christian Right's Interpretations on Women in the Bible" elaborates further on the problem of reinforcing the socio-religious status quo when interpreting the Bible. Although technically Christian Right's books on women in the Bible cannot be classified as "feminist," they are often confused as being part of the Second Feminist movement that has led to a focus on women and gender. After all, the abundance of the Christian Right's publications on women in the Bible also deal with the same topic, or so it seems. This chapter discusses this important development that makes it difficult for many lay and academic Bible readers to differentiate between feminist and Christian Right's approaches to the

Bible, women, and gender, especially since sometimes feminist Bible scholarship and the Christian Right's interpretations on biblical women rely on similar hermeneutical assumptions. Thus, this chapter organizes the analysis according to three neoliberal strategies that Esther Fuchs identifies in feminist biblical scholarship. The organization helps in making the central point that the Christian Right's assertion of offering "common sense, natural, and straightforward reading of the Bible,"[5] whether in the case of biblical women or biblical literature in general, is a hermeneutical fallacy. Since this fallacy is also found in academic feminist works, this chapter reminds every feminist interpreter of the serious need to integrate intersectional feminist, gender, and queer theories into biblical exegesis as a way out of the essentializing, naturalizing, and universalizing gender discourse so pervasive in Christian Right and academic works.

The conclusion provides a provocative reflection on the future of feminist biblical research from my German/European diasporic and U.S.–American perspective. The chapter considers questions raised by the weakening of the "Dead White Male" (DWM) Western paradigm in biblical research. Among the questions discussed are: What are the weaknesses and strengths of feminist biblical readings as currently carried out? How does feminist work on the Hebrew Bible relate to feminist research on the New Testament and early Christian literature? How do feminist biblical studies interact with religious studies in general? What are the institutional dangers and possibilities for a gendered approach to the Hebrew Bible in the academic world of today? The conclusion also considers the relationship between feminist biblical studies and movements of socio-political and economic transformation. We have to consider the future of feminist biblical studies from global perspectives and in increasingly interreligious and religiously diverse contexts that sometimes advance stridently secular ideologies, such as human rights and neoliberalism, and often also include numerous proponents of religious fundamentalism and political conservatism. The conclusion thus invites readers to think about feminist biblical research as an ongoing effort to relate the "Women's Hebrew Bible" to the socio-political, academic, and religious developments in the world.

Purpose and Limitations of this Volume

This book introduces some of the main issues, debates, and accomplishments of feminist studies on the Hebrew Bible during the past four decades. Much research had to be omitted, mostly due to space limitations but also due to my assessment of the field and the goals of this introductory volume. Accordingly, this book does not claim comprehensiveness but it presents a general view of the field as I see it after being involved in the feminist study of the Hebrew Bible during the past two

---

5. Esther Fuchs, "The Neoliberal Turn in Feminist Biblical Studies," in *Feminist Theory and the Bible: Interrogating the Sources* (Feminist Studies and Sacred Texts; Lanham, MD: Lexington Books, 2016), 66.

decades. As a German and U.S.–American Protestant feminist scholar and teacher of the Hebrew Bible who received her theological training at German universities and pursued doctoral work in the United States, where I have lived and worked for the past two decades, I emphasize international contributions to feminist biblical research. Readers will come away from this book with a clear sense of what they need to read and what areas of feminist biblical studies they will want to pursue next.

I decided to begin the survey where Western feminist scholars usually begin the history of women reading the Bible, namely in Europe and then in the United States, starting with the Christian mystical and religious traditions in which women played a crucial role, continuing with Elizabeth Cady Stanton in nineteenth-century America, and then moving into the twentieth century and the Second Feminist Movement. The pre-twentieth-century history was unknown when the pioneering generation of feminist Bible scholars began their work in the 1970s. The tradition of Western women reading the Bible who tried so desperately to eliminate androcentric bias in Western women's lives had been forgotten. When these women and their works were rediscovered, it felt enormously uplifting, energizing, and also infuriating to feminists in the 1970s. The rediscovery was Western-oriented because it dealt with European and U.S.–American, initially mostly white women's history. The geographic limitations of these early voices as well as their socio-theoretical limitations are obvious to today's feminist historians, theorists, and Bible scholars who recognize the value of employing multi-dimensional gender analyses.

Still, I introduce the collective beginnings of women reading Hebrew Scriptures in this line of historical memory because it has played such a central role for feminist biblical studies since the 1970s. To my knowledge, our research has not yet led to compelling alternatives which locate the early history of women reading the Bible elsewhere. This may still happen since Two-Third World feminist scholars have joined the conversation in recent years, and their findings might expand the historical traces of women reading the Bible, and it will be a happy day when it happens. The quiet revolution that began forty years ago is far from over, and this introductory volume serves only as an appetizer inviting readers to join the unfolding conversations in feminist biblical studies.

Nowadays, academic women readers of the Hebrew Bible are a diverse group of people from many countries and continents, although Western nationalities still dominate. They come mostly from Christian traditions, yet some are also Jewish, secular, or a combination of both religious and secular identities. All of them are committed to reading the Hebrew Bible from feminist perspectives and they take seriously the social category of gender in their work. It is an exciting time to learn about feminist biblical studies because the conversations are numerous, and newcomers are invited to join them.

And the Next Generation ...

Forty years is a biblical time period. For instance, the Israelites walked in the desert for that many years. At the end of four decades their leaders were in the process of changing. The pioneering generation had led them as far as they could and it was time for the next generation to take over. In the case of the Israelites, one of the male leaders, Moses, was replaced with another male leader, Joshua, who went on to occupy and settle the new, the so-called Promised Land. The biblical account presents a story of war at this point in Israel's history. According to the book of Joshua, the Israelite invasion of the land brought on the killing of the indigenous Canaanite population. Was it not better for the Israelites to wander in the desert for forty years? Should they have stayed in Egypt and suffered their fate as an enslaved people if their liberation meant the murder of others?

These are serious questions, and many will probably prefer an imperfect liberation from slavery to oppression in silence. The questions also apply to the current state of feminist biblical studies. Athalya Brenner asked poignantly:

> *Quo vadis*, feminist biblical scholarship? ... What is beckoning? Where do you want to go? Is the Master's House still the house you long to possess, only that you would like to become its legitimate(d) masters and mistresses instead of marginal(ized) lodgers? ... Should we not simply demolish the house instead of merely deconstructing it and its inhabitants, in order to build a completely new one instead? And if so, who will get right of occupation in the new house, and on what terms?[6]

After almost forty years of feminist biblical studies it is time to make widely available to new students of the Bible and readers interested in feminist biblical work what has been going on during the past few decades. The pioneering generation is in their seventies and eighties and almost ready to let the next generation take over. We need to catch up everyone and tell them what has been accomplished so far. We also need to talk about what will be next and where we want to go, certainly without murder and violence, and in support of social, political, economic, and religious changes for justice and peace to women and men and people beyond the gender binaries, black and white and brown, straight and gay, from the North and South as well as the East and West of our planet, of modest means and endowed with financial wealth. Much has happened in feminist biblical studies in only four decades and certainly much will emerge in the next few decades.

Yet there are considerable road blocks that the pioneering generation did not need to face. Religious and political conservatism is rampant in the United States

---

6. Athalya Brenner, "Epilogue: Babies and Bathwater on the Road," in Caroline Vander Stichele and Todd Penner (eds), *Her Master's Tools? Feminist and Postcolonial Engagements of Historical-Critical Discourse* (Atlanta, GA: Society of Biblical Literature, 2005), 338.

and elsewhere. In fact, religious fundamentalism is growing in many countries.[7] Gone are the days of the Civil Rights Movement and the economic opportunities in Western societies of the 1960s and 1970s. Nowadays, young people in Western countries have mostly lived through politically and culturally conservative times and they worry about their employment options, but in recent years the Occupy and Black Lives Matter movements have also galvanized politically progressive people into the limelight. The backlash towards feminism has been steady and many young women acquiesce to the heteropatriarchal status quo, assuming everything is fine for them. But these are also signs of feminist hope, as indicated in the Title IX movement that has brought to national attention the continuing pervasiveness of sexual violence and rape. There is also the serious threat that much of the feminist work in biblical studies and in other fields may be forgotten again. The dissemination of the intellectual and political-cultural feminist accomplishments remains an urgent task so that the next generation does not settle for the many compromises that are being made even today.

This book, then, introduces some of the work done during the first forty years of feminist biblical scholarship that can no longer be ignored. The hope is that the next generation will join and make their own contributions, standing in the footsteps of their foremothers and moving forward with hitherto unknown interpretations, hermeneutical discussions, and hybrid connections among biblical texts, histories of interpretation, and our world. Let the explorations in feminist biblical studies continue.

---

7. See, e.g. the discussions in Philip Jenkins, *The New Faces of Christianity: Believing the Bible in the Global South* (New York: Oxford University Press, 2006).

Chapter 1

FROM THE "WOMAN'S BIBLE" TO THE "WOMEN'S BIBLE": THE HISTORY OF FEMINIST APPROACHES TO THE HEBREW BIBLE

The history of women interpreting biblical literature is not well known, neither in the academic field of biblical studies nor among lay people. Nevertheless, the interpretation of the Bible by women is not new but grounded in a centuries-long tradition. Indeed, as long as women have lived in Bible-dominated societies and participated in the religious life of Christianity and Judaism, they actively and independently read biblical texts. Many, it is true, were the recipients of biblical meanings as handed down and interpreted by androcentric institutions such as church and synagogue, and it was often dangerous for women to speak publicly in front of women and men. Yet alongside this baleful tradition was an alternative experience: again and again, women of high intellect, great independence, and strong conviction challenged male political and religious leaders to accept women's equality with men not only before God but also in society. By raising their voices, these women, often situated in religious orders and in the upper class, tried to defeat entrenched structures of sexism and misogyny. Sometimes, especially when they came from the underprivileged strata of their society, these lone voices connected the discrimination of women with other structures of oppression, such as racism, and demanded to abolish them.

This chapter traces the emergence and developments of feminist Hebrew Bible studies. It begins with a cursory survey on the proto-feminist era of women reading the Bible since the Western Middle Ages. It then outlines developments in the nineteenth century with a focus on the U.S.–American scene. It continues with a discussion of the cultural-political situation in the early to mid-twentieth century, during which a number of books on women in the Bible were published. It then discusses comprehensively the emergence and diversification of feminist studies in the Hebrew Bible since the Second Feminist Movement in the 1970s through the early twenty-first century.

"In the Image of God": Individual Women's Voices in Western Societies from the Middle Ages to the Nineteenth Century

Biblical interpretations of individual medieval women never gained much influence in the religious institutions and societies of their times and remained on the margins of intellectual, religious, and social discourses and practices. Bold, courageous, and outspoken women came and went, and they were quickly forgotten when they passed away. Each woman believed that she reinvented the arguments, but one after another claimed her right to read and to interpret the meaning of biblical literature. We only have knowledge of a few, usually of those who published their work. Many others who were unable to write or publish their views remain unknown, although such women probably existed.[1] Indeed, women have always participated at the grassroots level in the interpretative process, and so it seems likely that the next generation will continue holding on to their Bibles. It is therefore crucial to remember the many women who created biblical meanings in opposition to androcentric theories and practices prevalent in their lives. Their voices and insights will surely inspire their daughters and granddaughters to do the same.

Before the first feminist movement in Western societies during the nineteenth century, which brought about the first systematic wave of women struggling for equal political, economic, social, and religious rights, women interpret the Bible independently and in isolation from each other. They follow their conviction that women are not second-class citizens, and they read biblical texts in support of women's equality in society and before God. For instance, the twelfth-century Christian mystic Hildegard von Bingen repeatedly emphasizes the significance of Genesis 1:26-7. This verse introduces the notion of female and male as created in the image of God and does not limit any aspect of the *imago Dei* to women, as Bingen's contemporary male medieval colleagues maintain. They accord the full *imago Dei* in terms of memory, intelligence, and will (*memoria, intelligentia, voluntas*) only to men and deny women the capacity of intelligence. Bingen does not accept this view and defends women as fully created in the image of God.[2] Her inner conviction of women's equality characterizes her interpretation of Genesis 1:26-7 and she criticizes the androcentric status quo of her time in which women are considered as lesser human beings than men. Yet her position that the biblical text asserts women's full and equal inclusion in God's creation is an isolated phenomenon and does not enjoy the support of a whole movement pushing for change.

Hildegard von Bingen, however, was not alone in her belief in women's equality. Later on, fourteenth-century Christian writer, Christine de Pizan, defends women's

---

1. For more information on select premodern and early modern women Bible readers, among them Argula von Grumbach (1492–1568) and Marie Dentière (1495–1561), see Joy A. Schroeder, *Deborah's Daughters: Gender Politics and Biblical Interpretation* (Oxford and New York: Oxford University Press, 2014).

2. For a more comprehensive description, see Elisabeth Gössmann, "History of Biblical Interpretation by European Women," in Elisabeth Schüssler Fiorenza (ed.), *Searching the Scripture: A Feminist Introduction* (New York: Crossroad, 1993), 29–32.

equality on the basis of Genesis 1–2. She maintains that woman, like man, is not only created in God's image but also consists of much better material than man. Woman is taken from human flesh whereas man is made from soil. Moreover, the location of woman's creation is better than man's. Woman was created in paradise, de Pizan argues, and as a result her noble nature is guaranteed by God.[3] De Pizan regards the first woman as God's masterpiece because she appears last in the creation process in Genesis 2. Woman thus is the culmination of divine creation, a conviction that later feminist readers repeat.

Other proto-feminist interpreters who affirm women's equality before God and in society are the medieval mystics Mechthild of Magdeburg, Gertrud von Hackeborn, and Gertrud the Great, the fifteenth-century Italian Isotta Nogarola, the seventeenth-century radical Italian nun Arcangela Tarabotti, the early seventeenth-century interpreters Lucretia Marinella and Suzanne de Nervèze, the seventeenth-century founder of Quakerism, George Fox, as well as his wife, Margaret Askew Fell Fox; the eighteenth-century sisters Sarah and Angelina Grimkè, the early nineteenth-century Lucretia Coffin Mott and African–American abolitionist and women's rights activist Sojourner Truth. They and many others find full equality of women inscribed in the biblical text in a time when women do not even have the right to public speech. Their courageous and bold individual voices challenge androcentric primacy, and eventually their efforts lead to a full choir in the nineteenth century, when a systematic approach to the Christian canon of the Bible is published for the first time in the Western history of interpretation.

"Inspired by Mrs God": Nineteenth-Century Women's Voices of the First Women's Movement in Western Societies

During the nineteenth century many women, black and white, U.S.–American and European, lifted their voices against male-dominated patriarchal structures of oppression in Western societies. Known as the suffrage movement, this socio-political effort found success in the early decades of the twentieth century, although most of the suffragettes did not live long enough to enjoy the fruits of their persistent labor, determined patience, and unwavering commitment to women's rights. Their names are many although some of them have been lost to the vagaries of time and history. Yet those whom we know are now famous, and women owe them a great deal. U.S.–American women devoting their working lives to women's rights include Marie W. Miller Stewart, Anna Julia Cooper, Sojourner Truth, Antoinette L. Brown Blackwell, Susan B. Anthony, and Elizabeth Cady Stanton. All of them read the Bible against the status quo of patriarchal order and social hierarchies. While African–American women combined the problem of sexism with a call to abolish slavery and racism, white women emphasized

---

3. Ibid., 34.

women's lack of civil rights and did not always confront the complexities of racism and class oppression.[4]

Most renowned among those women is Elizabeth Cady Stanton, who has been severely criticized for ignoring issues of racism during her lifetime.[5] The editor of *The Woman's Bible* (1895 and 1898),[6] Stanton asked other qualified women from the United States and Europe to contribute to a critical examination of the Bible. At the time she is over eighty years old and spent her entire life fighting for women's right to vote. She insists that religion and more specifically the interpretation of the Bible are the crucial reasons for her lack of success. She considers the Bible as the original cause of women's oppression, and is convinced that only a systematic study of the oppressive biblical passages would dismantle the sexist forces in society and lead to women's equality. She also wants to dispel women's attraction to religion by exposing its deep complicity in androcentric domination. Stanton is a radical feminist, and the older she becomes the more radical she turns. She also views women as complicit in their lack of rights and their religiosity as nurturing this complicity. It is, therefore, the next logical step for Stanton to demonstrate that religion is the real cause—the fundamental cause of women's oppression.

In arguing that religion is the chief culprit of women's oppression, Stanton receives much criticism, both from contemporary fellow suffragettes and clergy members. Feminist thinkers and theologians of the second feminist movement that emerges in the 1970s also find this argument flawed. They advance a systemic feminist analysis that interrelates sexism with racism, classism and other sociopolitical, and religious forces. To them, Stanton's monolithic explanation about religion is too narrow, even provincial, and a product of her white, upper-class, Protestant background.

Nevertheless, Stanton's determination and unwavering commitment to women's rights remain unsurpassed and her views provoke people even today. She was profoundly frustrated with organized religion and not afraid to say so. For instance, she tells a collaborator of *The Woman's Bible*: "If we who do see the absurdities of old superstitions never unveil them to others, how is the world to make any progress in the theologies? I am in the sunset of life, and I feel it to be my special mission to tell people what they are not prepared to hear, instead of echoing worn-out opinions."[7] She feels the need to criticize religious conviction, and as a Protestant she goes straight to the Bible because, as she explains, "It

---

4. For a focused discussion on this dynamic, see Nyasha Junior, *An Introduction to Womanist Biblical Interpretation* (Louisville, KY: Westminster John Knox, 2015).

5. For a discussion on this issue, see Elizabeth Schüssler Fiorenza, "Transforming a Legacy," in Elisabeth Schüssler Fiorenza (ed.), *Searching the Scripture: A Feminist Introduction* (New York: Crossroad, 1993), 2–8; Kathi Kern, *Mrs. Stanton's Bible* (Ithaca and London: Cornell University Press, 2001), 22–30.

6. Elizabeth Cady Stanton, *The Woman's Bible* (Boston: Northeastern University Press, 1993).

7. Quoted in Kern, *Mrs. Stanton's Bible*, 19.

requires no courage now to demand the right of suffrage ... But it still requires courage to question the divine inspiration of the Hebrew Writings as to the position of women."[8] This debate, namely the search for biblical authorship, is indeed the central topic at the end of the nineteenth century in academic and religious institutions in the United States, as well as in Europe. Although Stanton's work does not contribute to this debate—after all, she is not an academic or a trained biblical scholar, the commentaries in *The Woman's Bible* reject divine inspiration of many biblical texts and dismiss them as valid justifications for women's secondary status in nineteenth-century society.

The Woman's Bible *Commentary*

The Woman's Bible was never popular, neither when Stanton published it in the late 1880s nor in the following decades.[9] In fact, it is quickly forgotten and only rediscovered in the early 1970s when feminists of the second feminist movement stumble upon it by chance. But *The Woman's Bible* is a radical piece of work for it insists on the liberation of women from Christian androcentrism rooted in biblical literature. Stanton asserts that a critical and systematic examination is a necessary step to prove the Bible's oppressive nature for women and their roles in society and church. She writes: "So long as tens of thousands of Bibles are printed every year, and circulated over the whole habitable globe, and the masses in all English-speaking nations revere it as the word of God, it is vain to belittle its influence."[10] Her interpretative results are predictable. Section after section and commentary after commentary, Stanton elaborates on the negative influence of the Bible on women's status throughout Western history.

The commentaries, written by Stanton and other women colleagues and friends, follow the chronology of the Christian canon but select only passages relevant to issues of women's equality. The book begins with Genesis 1, the seven-day creation account, and selects for commentary vv. 26-8, the famous passage on humans created in the image of God. Stanton's comments do not indicate that she knows about the long history of Christian women addressing these verses. Yet her interpretation is similar to earlier women's conclusions. Stanton notes: "The above texts plainly show the simultaneous creation of man and woman, and their equal importance in the development of the race."[11] Thus woman is "an equal factor in human progress." Yet what is more, Stanton also argues that "these texts [contain] a plain declaration of the existence of the feminine element in the Godhead, equal in power and glory with the masculine."[12] Remarkably, based on her reading of

---

8. Ibid., 49.

9. For more details on this sad historical development, see Kern, *Mrs. Stanton's Bible*, 2–6.

10. Stanton, "Introduction," in *The Woman's Bible*, 11.

11. Stanton, "Comments on Genesis," in *The Woman's Bible*, 15.

12. Ibid., 14. See also 21.

Genesis 1.26-8, Stanton applies inclusive language to the divinity and views God as "The Heavenly Mother and Father." Clearly, Stanton is a radical thinker who went far beyond the gender stereotypes and expectations of her time and place.

Stanton points again to the equal gender qualities of God when she discusses the second creation account with an emphasis on Genesis 2:21-5. As many feminist interpreters before and after her, Stanton praises the first account in Genesis 1. It "dignifies woman as an important factor in the creation, equal in power and glory with man" whereas "[t]he second makes her a mere afterthought."[13] It is obvious to her that "some wily writer, seeing the perfect equality of man and woman in the first chapter, felt it important for the dignity and dominion of man to effect woman's subordination in some way."[14] The bias of the biblical writer and not the divinely ordained order, she maintains, leads to woman's secondary status in this creation account. As a result, Genesis 1 is Stanton's preferred narrative, and in typical Christian fashion Stanton cites Galatians 3:28 to underline the validity of Genesis 1. She also uses the texts to criticize church policy. "With this recognition of the feminine element in the Godhead in the Old Testament, and this declaration of the equality of the sexes in the New, we may well wonder at the contemptible status woman occupies in the Christian church to-day."[15] Stanton never tires of connecting biblical androcentrism with contemporary church and society.

Her comments, perhaps more so than those of her co-contributors, continually challenges contemporary church practice. Her tone is harsh and direct, and it is therefore little wonder that other women and suffragettes are afraid to promote *The Woman's Bible*. Stanton offers views about women's place in the world that still cause discomfort among many people even today. For instance, Stanton notices that in Exodus 2, most women remain unnamed in the narrative on the birth of Moses and his rescue by Pharaoh's daughter whereas Moses receives a name. Stanton states sharply:

> If we go through this chapter carefully we will find mention of about a dozen women, but with the exception of one given to Moses, all are nameless. Then as now names for women and slaves are of no importance; they have no individual life, and why should their personality require a life-long name? To-day the woman is Mrs Richard Roe, To-morrow Mrs John Doe, and again Mrs James Smith according as she changes masters, and she has so little self-respect that she does not see the insult of the custom.[16]

Her critique has not lost its sting—or for that matter its validity: even now many women still give up their names in marriage or for their children. Stanton is not content to leave things at that but continues: "Women have had no voice in the

13. Ibid., 20.
14. Ibid., 21.
15. Ibid.
16. Ibid., 73.

canon law, the catechisms, the church creeds and discipline, and why should they obey the behests of a strictly masculine religion, that places the sex at a disadvantage in all life's emergencies?"[17] She points to the relentless omission of women in all affairs of society, and this angers her greatly. At over eighty years of age, she cuts through politeness and political strategizing. To her, the problem of women's secondary status is clear and simple: "As long as our religion teaches woman's subjugation and man's right of domination, we shall have chaos in the world of morals."[18] Because of her feminist wit and cutting analysis, some contemporary feminist theologians suggest that we might still benefit from "enter[ing] into dialogue with those nineteenth century sisters who refused to believe that their oppression was divinely ordained."[19]

What emerges from Stanton's comments in *The Woman's Bible* is a strong commitment to deconstruct the biblical text as an androcentric product, which has to be demolished and left behind in order to free women from male domination. As such, *The Woman's Bible* is thoroughly devoted to women's liberation and often sounds refreshingly bold and proud. It is a product of women who subscribe to the notion of reason and the intellect, unbound by the traditional authorities of religion and state power. Stanton's final recommendation stands in line with the entire project when she writes: "Verily, we need an expurgated edition of the Old and the New Testaments before they are fit to be placed in the hands of our youth to be read in the public schools and in theological seminaries, especially if we wish to inspire our children with proper love and respect for the Mothers of the Race."[20] Her wish has yet to be realized and an "expurgated edition" of the Bible does not exist even today. For her views on religion Stanton is buried "alive" by her contemporaries, and nowadays she is criticized for her views on race and class.[21] Still, the impetus to examine biblical texts for information about women's status then and now has not disappeared, and for that Stanton deserves praise and credit. In the first decades of the twentieth century other writers emerge examining the Hebrew Bible with a focus on women and gender, but they live in a time far less receptive to issues related to gender discrimination in society, religion, and the Bible.

"Nothing in Common Save Their Sex": Early and Mid-twentieth Century Women's Voices

When women in Western countries gain the right to vote shortly after the First World War, a period of slow, if not stalled, progress for women's rights begins. It lasts until the late 1960s when the second feminist movement emerges. During

17. Ibid., 74.

18. Ibid., 79.

19. Elaine C. Huber, "They Weren't Prepared to Hear: A Closer Look at *The Woman's Bible*," *Andover Newton Quarterly* 16 (March 1976): 276.

20. Ibid., 184.

21. See, e.g. Kern, *Mrs. Stanton's Bible*, esp. 8–11.

these decades many of the arguments and accomplishments of the suffragettes are quickly forgotten. Publications that deal with biblical women never mention Stanton's *The Woman's Bible*. Few women are admitted to the ranks of academia and even less make it as biblical scholars, and those who work in isolation enjoy little academic support and collegiality. Some manage to publish treatises on women and the Hebrew Bible, among them Hedwig Jahnow, Lee Anna Starr, Margaret Brackenbury Crook, Isabella Reid Buchanan, Norah Lofts, Edith Deen, Annie Russell, and Helga Rusche. During this time some men also write books on the topic. Among them are Max Löhr, H. V. Morton, Herbert Lockyer, and John Whitford.

These works share something in common: they lack the intellectual fervor and political zeal that characterize the work of Stanton and her co-writers. Although later studies signal religious-conservative interests, many attempt to establish investigations on biblical women as a legitimate historical pursuit rather than as a topic with contemporary socio-political implications. An example of the less-politically driven ambition is an essay by the German theologian Hedwig Jahnow, which was originally published in 1914, then forgotten, and rediscovered only in the 1990s.[22] The only female German Bible scholar at the time, Jahnow presents the various stages and societal roles of Israelite women in her essay. The article begins with a description of the Israelite woman as daughter and then discusses her role and responsibilities as mother, her position as widow and enslaved woman, and her legal rights in matters of divorce. The essay also includes references to a biblical woman's physical appearance and emotional life as lover, wife, mother, and smart or foolish woman. Jahnow concludes with two Israelite heroines, Esther and Judith, whom Jahnow lifts up as remarkable women. She points to their lacking "simplicity and straightforwardness of intent" that "German sensibility" admires,[23] but she nevertheless ends her study with them. Today some feminist interpreters remind us that Jahnow's choice is quite progressive in the context of her time.[24] Jahnow closes her description with strong and independent biblical women who do not represent the motherly and family-oriented ideals of her German context. Indirectly, at least, Jahnow's description of female life in ancient

---

22. Hedwig Jahnow, "Die Frau im Alten Testament," in Hedwig-Jahnow Project (ed.), *Feministische Hermeneutik und Erstes Testament: Analysen und Interpretationen* (Stuttgart: W. Kohlhammer, 1994), 30–47. The essay was originally published in the non-scholarly journal *Die Frau* 21 (1914): 352–8, 417–26. Interestingly, the journal was edited by the German suffragettes Helene Lange and Gertrud Bäumer, but Jahnow's essay does not make explicit connections between the Israelite and the contemporary German women's roles. It is a historical treatise.

23. Ibid., 47: "Das spätere Judentum hat zwei Frauengestalten aufzuweisen, die nach Absicht der Erzähler als Nationalheldinnen aufgefaßt werden sollen, denen aber für unser deutsches Empfinden zur Heldenhaftigkeit vor allem die Einfachheit und Geradlinigkeit der Gesinnung fehlt: Esther und Judith."

24. See Ulrike Bail und Elke Seifert in the introduction to Jahnow's essay in Jahnow Projekt (ed.), *Feministische Hermeneutik*, 28.

Israel hints at an implicit attempt to go beyond the status quo of her time—though Jahnow is clearly not as candid as Stanton several decades earlier.

There is also an unusual little book of a proto-feminist spirit, entitled *Career Women of the Bible*, published in 1951. It portrays biblical women as professional women.[25] Elizabeth Williams Sudlow, the author, attributes a career to each chosen biblical woman, and so, for instance, Deborah appears as "The Judge," Rahab as "An Undercover Agent," Ruth as "The Farmerette," and the daughters of Zelophehad as "The Suffragettes." Sudlow explains that "[h]ad [these women] lived in this age their qualifications would have placed them in one of the several classifications of work being done by women today."[26] Appearing after the first and before the second feminist movement and placing biblical women in the long history of the struggle for women's equal rights with men, this unique little book does not entirely forget the accomplishments of women living in earlier centuries.

Yet most publications of the post-suffragette period are less politically motivated and socially aware. In fact, in the 1920s Annie Russell Marble openly criticizes such tendencies in books on biblical women. Her volume, entitled *Women of the Bible: Their Services in Home and State*,[27] presents a potpourri of biblical women organized in thematic sections such as "The Hebrew Woman in Her Home," "Wives of the Bible: Some of Them Were Wise and Some Were Foolish," "Mothers in Israel" and "Women in Patriotic and Religious Service." Marble wants to "vitalize women who are mentioned in biblical literature, as fully as is possible from historical sources and sympathetic imagination."[28] Yet she also hopes to avoid "the too general mistake of 'reading back' into their lives the standards and customs of far later periods," and thus her descriptions "recognize their essential qualities of womanhood."[29] Only a few sentences indicate that she wrestles with correlating

25. Elizabeth Williams Sudlow, *Career Women of the Bible* (New York: Pageant Press, 1951).

26. Sudlow, "Preface," in *Career Women of the Bible*.

27. Annie Russell Marble, *Women of the Bible: Their Services in Home and State* (New York and London: The Century Co., 1923). See also Helga Rusche, *They Lived by Faith: Women in the Bible* (Baltimore: Helicon, 1963). Rusche begins with a chapter on "father" Abraham from whom in her view biblical women of faith emerged. The chapters present stories on selected female characters from the Hebrew Bible and the New Testament such as "The Women in the 'Genealogy of Jesus,'" "Give Praise, O Thou Barren," and "The Wives of the Prophets."

28. Ibid., vii.

29. Ibid., 3–4. Other books oppose more explicitly a politically motivated interpretation of biblical women, such as Herbert Lockyer, *All the Women of the Bible* (Grand Rapids, MI: Zondervan, 1967), 8–9: "As long as history continues, women remain women, in spite of their present effort to become more masculine. Looking into the mirror of Scripture, women of today can see their counterparts both in the women whose names remain and in the lives of those who are anonymous … Woman is an integral part of humanity, and if humanity is to be purified and Christianized to a far greater extent, it is imperative to have an enlightened, spiritual womanhood." See also pp. 159–160 in the present book.

biblical and contemporary women. For instance, in a chapter on "The Hebrew Woman in Her Home," Marble asks: "Does she not fulfill all the aspirations of the well balanced home-maker of the twentieth century?"[30] The comparison focuses on a traditional woman's role, that of a homemaker, and not, as in Jahnow's essay, on Israelite heroines who kill and trick enemy men to reach national liberation. As a result, Marble's book assumes the patriarchal status quo, claiming historical accuracy and an unprejudiced agenda. This, of course, is hardly the case.

A descriptive interest in biblical women is also apparent in two other books penned by Norah Lofts and Edith Deen.[31] In these and other books, specific chapters are named for biblical women, giving the publications an aura of objectivity. Among the biblical women described are well-known female characters, such as Sarah, Rebecca, Deborah, or Bathsheba. Lofts stresses the wide range of her discussion when she writes: "They [the biblical women] range from simple nomadic desert women to palace-bred princesses; here are women of sound practical sense and mystics; prudes and harlots: women who have attained immortality because some men once looked upon them with love, and women who by their own actions influence the history and thought of their times."[32] Interestingly, Lofts does not include Eve, the biblical figure who has traditionally inspired writings about the Bible by women. Instead the volume begins with "Sarah and Hagar," and Lofts also explains that she is not interested in past theological and political writings. She maintains that her book is "written by a woman, about a group of people who have nothing in common save their sex and the fact that their names or their stories happen to be included in what is one of the most significant pieces of history in the whole of literature ... ."[33]

Such a cautious tone in a book published in 1950 is not dissimilar from Edith Deen, who also views biblical women from a conservative perspective. Her book begins with Eve, whom she characterizes as one of the "women of the dawn."[34] Deen, an editor of a newspaper and writer of a daily woman's column, tries "to understand and interpret their [biblical women's] spiritual experiences, their faith and their relationship with God."[35] Her goal is religious, and her interpretations are undergirded by this agenda. For instance, Deen emphasizes that God creates Eve, and so Eve has a "unique relationship to God, the supreme power in the universe."[36] Deen also explains that "Eve fell far short of the ideal in womanhood" but "rose to the dream of her destiny as a wife and mother" and "despite her later transgressions, Eve still stands forth as a revelation of the Father, and as

---

30. Ibid., 41.

31. Norah Lofts, *Women in the Old Testament: Twenty Psychological Portraits* (New York: Macmillan, 1950); Edith Deen, *All the Women of the Bible* (Edison, NJ: Castle Books, 1955).

32. Lofts, *Women in the Old Testament*, x.

33. Ibid., ix–x.

34. See Deen, *All the Women*, ix.

35. Ibid., xxi.

36. Ibid., 3.

one who can rise above her transgressions."[37] Long forgotten is Stanton's radical claim of God as "Father and Mother." The ideals of the conservative 1950s, in which women are seen to fare best as wives and mothers, dominate this and other similar works. Even though the focus of these books was explicitly on women, the Eisenhower-era patriarchal status quo appears on every page.

This preachy and religiously limiting characterization of biblical women is also apparent in male-authored presentations. Clarence Edward Macartney's book on *Great Women of the Bible*, conceptualized as a guide for sermon topics, is a case in point. Macartney frankly admits that initially he is not particularly interested in the plight of biblical women because their narratives seem not to have "enough of the personal and dramatic element in them to make them the subject of successful and popular sermons."[38] Yet interestingly, he also explains, his congregation kept requesting sermons on biblical women, and so he has preached about women and their lives. (According to a vote by his congregation, Ruth is the most popular among the biblical women, while Eve ranks last.)

Macartney's resulting book reflects the broad interests and questions his congregation has about women: it consists of thirteen summary discussions on various women of the Christian canon and begins with a chapter on Ruth entitled "The Woman Who Got Her Man," which Macartney characterizes as "a sweet interlude of peace and love in a fierce, wild chorus of war and passion."[39] Among the other chapters is one about Esther ("The Woman Whose Beauty Saved a Race"), Rahab ("The Woman Who Was Better Than Her Job"), and Lot's wife ("The Woman to Remember"). Each chapter summarizes the story of the particular woman in an imaginative fashion, pointing to her strengths and weaknesses in her relationship with God. As expected in a sermonizing treatise, the book turns biblical women and their stories into examples of women living faithfully in the presence of God. It is a privatizing and essentializing approach that changes only with the emergence of the second feminist movement.

"With a Feminist Hermeneutics": Women's Scholarship on the Hebrew Bible as Part of the Second Feminist Movement in Western Societies since the 1970s

When "life was turning upside down"[40] in the 1960s, when the civil rights movement in the United States, the growing opposition to the Vietnam War, and the global struggles against colonial and economic exploitation challenge

---

37. Ibid., 6, 7.

38. Clarence Edward Macartney, *Great Women of the Bible* (New York and Nashville: Abingdon Press, 1942), 5.

39. Ibid., 10.

40. For this expression, see Phyllis Trible, "Foreword," in *God and the Rhetoric of Sexuality* (Philadelphia: Fortress Press, 1978), xv.

the white, Eurocentric status quo, women rediscover their feminist voices after several decades of renewed compliance to patriarchal conditions. For sure, earlier twentieth-century women had spoken up. Virginia Woolf in her renowned book, *A Room of One's Own* (1929), and Simone de Beauvoir in her landmark publication, *The Second Sex* (1949), come most distinctly to mind. Yet their observations do not benefit from the energy of a large movement. It is only in the 1960s that Western women begin once more to question androcentric practices and traditions.

The roots of the second feminist movement's ruminations about and resistance to patriarchy are often connected with different feminist thinkers and their publications. Some mention *The Feminine Mystique* by the writer Betty Friedan, published in 1963. Others refer to the works of Susan Brownmiller, Angela Davis, Andrea Dworkin, Shulamith Firestone, Sheila Rowbotham, Alice Schwarzer, or Gloria Steinem. Still others, especially feminist theologians, cite Mary Daly whose *The Church and the Second Sex* (1968) and *Beyond God the Father: Toward a Philosophy of Women's Liberation* (1973) confront male-dominated church power and society with a theo-historical analysis that provokes traditional-minded readers even today. The driving force of the second feminist movement is "consciousness raising," and women's groups, bookstores, and teach-ins spring up all over Western societies.

For the first time in known history, women begin *methodically* examining the systems of patriarchy with theories grounded in liberal feminism, socialist, and Marxist feminism, black and postcolonial feminism, lesbian feminism, and radical feminism. And for the first time, too, women, especially those located in North America and working in religious organizations and in the academic disciplines of religious and theological studies, initiate systematic and comprehensive investigations about the impact of patriarchy in its intersectional manifestations on the religious life and consciousness of women throughout history. Their efforts have resulted in a rich and diverse variety of feminist, womanist, and *mujerista* theologies within the U.S.–American context, as well as feminist theologies of other regions, cultures and traditions.[41]

For the first time, too, women who earn graduate degrees in Hebrew Bible studies allow their works to be influenced by the socio-political movements of their time. They begin reading the Hebrew Bible with feminist questions in mind.

---

41. See, e.g. Letty M. Russell and Shannon J. Clarkson, *Dictionary of Feminist Theologies* (Louisville, KY: Westminster/John Knox Press, 1996); Anne M. Clifford, *Introducing Feminist Theology* (Maryknoll, NY: Orbis Books, 2001); Stephanie Y. Mitchem, *Introducing Womanist Theology* (Maryknoll, NY: Orbis Books, 2002); Ada Maria Isasi-Diaz, *Mujerista Theology: A Theology for the Twenty-First Century* (Maryknoll, NY: Orbis Books, 1996); Kwok Pui-lan, *Introducing Asian Feminist Theology* (Cleveland: Pilgrim, 2000); Mercy Amba Oduyoye, *Introducing African Women's Theology* (Cleveland: Pilgrim, 2001); Annette Esser and Luise Schottroff (eds), *Feminist Theology in a European Context* (Kampen: Kok Pharos, 1993); Elsa Tamez, *Through Her Eyes: Women's Theology from Latin America* (Maryknoll, NY: Orbis Books, 1989).

Among the pioneers of this group of women scholars is Phyllis Trible whose book *God and the Rhetoric of Sexuality* (1978) is the first feminist academic monography in Old Testament studies, employing a feminist hermeneutics "to recover old treasures and discover new ones in the house-hold of faith."[42] With her work, Trible responds to the challenge of radical feminist, theologian, and philosopher Mary Daly who rejects the Bible as utterly androcentric literature, as a detriment to women's rights that contributes little to the liberation of women from patriarchal oppression. Trible does not accept this generic judgment, finding it too simplistic. She and feminist Bible scholars following her path assert that a careful examination of the Hebrew Bible leads to a more complex and nuanced appreciation than conceded by the rejectionists. Their efforts have produced rich, wide-ranging, and multifaceted interpretations. Equipped with scholarly methods, tools, and investigative procedures, they develop a plethora of biblical readings from feminist perspectives. By now, a third generation of scholars is carrying on this important work in feminist biblical studies.[43] Let us look a little closer at some of the scholarly developments in feminist biblical studies, as they have taken place since the 1970s.

Discovering "Women" as a Category of Biblical Interpretation

Once women's voting right is established in Canada in 1919 and in the United States in 1920, the heyday of women's activism declines. Books on women and the Bible are still published, but they lack the political zeal and intellectual fervor of nineteenth-century suffragists. It does not help that very few women are admitted into the ranks of biblical scholarship from the 1920s to the 1950s. Those who become professors remain at the margins of the scholarly discourse, as a cursory look at the membership roster of the Society of Biblical Literature (SBL) illustrates.[44] This situation only changes with the emergence of the feminist movement in general and the early publications of Mary Daly in particular,[45] all of which radicalizes feminists of various religious traditions in North America.

42. Trible, *God and the Rhetoric of Sexuality*, xvi.

43. See, e.g. Caroline Vander Stichele and Todd Penner (eds), *Her Master's Tools? Feminist and Postcolonial Engagements of Historical-Critical Discourse* (Atlanta: Society of Biblical Literature, 2005); Harold C. Washington, Susan Lochrie and Pamela Thimmes (eds), *Escaping Eden: New Feminist Perspectives on the Bible* (New York: New York University Press, 1999).

44. See Dorothy C. Bass, "Women's Studies and Biblical Studies," *Journal for the Study of the Old Testament* 22 (February 1982): 6–12, esp. 9: "Similar growth between 1910 and 1920 brought women's membership to twenty-four in a total of 231, better than ten per cent … . After 1920, however, the figures began to slip. In 1930, women were at approximately eight per cent; in 1940, about six per cent; and in 1950, five per cent. Figures are missing for 1960, but by 1970 women were only three and one-half per cent of SBL members."

45. Mary Daly, *The Church and the Second Sex* (New York: Knopf, 1968); Daly, *Beyond God the Father: Toward a Philosophy of Women's Liberation* (Boston: Beacon, 1973).

Also important is a 1971 meeting in Atlanta during the gathering of two major professional societies, the American Academy of Religion (AAR) and the Society for Biblical Literature (SBL). The attendees decided to establish "a women's caucus in the field and to demand that program time be allotted to papers and panels on women and religion."[46] Rita Gross, a professor of comparative religion, remembers:

> That meeting, which occurred in November in Atlanta, was probably the single most generative event of the feminist transformation of religious studies. Before the meeting, isolated, relatively young and unestablished scholars struggled to define what it meant to study women and religion and to demonstrate why it was so important to do so. After the meeting, a strong network of like-minded individuals had been established, and we had begun to make our presence and our agenda known to the AAR and the SBL.[47]

At this meeting the AAR/SBL Women's Caucus is founded and two chairs are elected: Carol Christ, who becomes renowned for her work on goddess religions, and Elisabeth Schüssler Fiorenza, who serves as the first woman president of the Society of Biblical Literature in 1987.[48]

The creation of a feminist infrastructure at the scholarly level helps to gather momentum on the feminist hermeneutical level. In 1973, Phyllis Trible publishes a widely read article entitled "Depatriarchalizing in Biblical Interpretation."[49] Trible confronts a "terrible dilemma"[50] posed by the movement: to choose between "the God of the fathers or the God of sisterhood."[51] Yet she considers this choice to be a false dichotomy. To her, the Bible is not irredeemably patriarchal,[52] and so she asserts:

> The Women's Movement errs when *it* dismisses the Bible as inconsequential or condemns it as enslaving. In rejecting Scripture women ironically accept male

---

46. Rita Gross, *Feminism and Religion: An Introduction* (Boston: Beacon, 1996), 46.

47. Ibid., 47.

48. By 2016, only seven women scholars have served as SBL presidents: Phyllis Trible in 1994, Adele Berlin in 2000, Carolyn Osiek in 2005, Katherine Doob Sakenfeld in 2007, Carol Newsom in 2011, Carol Meyers in 2013, and Athalya Brenner in 2015. Patrick Gray calls the SBL "an exclusive fraternity" and finds this "not a wholly inappropriate term" despite the service of several women presidents since its founding in 1880; see Patrick Gray, "Presidential Addresses of the Society of Biblical Literature: A Quasquicentennial Review," *JBL* 125 (1) (2006): 167–77, esp. 167.

49. Phyllis Trible, "Depatriarchalizing in Biblical Interpretation," *JAAR* 41 (1) (March 1973): 30–48.

50. Ibid., 30.

51. Ibid., 31

52. Ibid.

chauvinistic interpretations and thereby capitulate to the very view they are protesting.[53]

Hence, Trible declares that "the Hebrew Scriptures and Women's Liberation do meet and ... their encounter need not be hostile."[54] She also warns that feminist Bible readers are "unfaithful readers" if they do not apply "the depatriarchalizing principle and recover it in those texts and themes where it is present, and ... accent it in our translation."[55] Otherwise they "neglect biblical passages which break with patriarchy"[56] and permit "interpretations to freeze in a patriarchal box of our own construction."[57]

Other feminist scholars also produce pioneering work. In 1974, Rosemary Radford Ruether, at the time professor at Garrett-Evangelical Seminary, edits a highly influential anthology entitled *Religion and Sexism: Images of Women in the Jewish and Christian Traditions.*[58] The volume includes one article on the Hebrew Bible by Phyllis Bird and another on the New Testament by Constance F. Parvey.[59] Bird presents a reading of Genesis 1–3 that assesses the biblical creation narratives from a feminist perspective grounded in historical criticism. According to Bird, the first story portrays humanity—female and male—with its biological functions as divinely created in the image of God. The second narrative stresses psychosocial rather than biological functions of women and men in ancient Israelite society. Bird's interpretation highlights gender with the aim of challenging essentialized meanings attributed to the biblical creation texts in Western society.

In the same book, Constance F. Parvey examines "how the early Church embodied theologically and socially different attitudes toward women as a consequence of Jesus" coming."[60] She explains that "[i]n contrast to Judaism, the Greco–Roman religions were more open to the participation of women."[61]

---

53. Ibid.

54. Ibid., 47.

55. Trible's proposal created important inner-feminist biblical critique; see, e.g. Nancy Fuchs-Kreimer, "Feminism and Scripture Interpretation: A Contemporary Jewish Critique," *Journal of Ecumenical Studies* 20 (1988): 539–41; Elisabeth Schüssler Fiorenza, *But She Said: Feminist Practices of Biblical Interpretation* (Boston: Beacon, 1992), 21–4.

56. Trible, "Depatriarchalizing," 48.

57. Ibid.

58. Rosemary Radford Ruether, *Religion and Sexism: Images of Women in the Jewish and Christian Traditions* (New York: Simon and Schuster, 1974).

59. Phyllis Bird, "Images of the Women in the Old Testament," in *Religion and Sexism*, 41–88; Constance F. Parvey, "The Theology and Leadership of Women in the New Testament," in *Religion and Sexism*, 117–49. For yet another influential early feminist interpretation, see Phyllis Trible, "Eve and Adam: Genesis 2–3 Reread," *Andover Newton Quarterly* (March 13, 1973): 251–8.

60. Parvey, "Theology and Leadership of Women in the New Testament," in *Religion and Sexism*, 117–18.

61. Ibid., 121.

Parvey also suggests that the Apostle Paul makes "a fundamental breakthrough in new images for women"[62] when he allows "a primary place for the participation of women."[63] She finds a similar attitude in the gospel of Luke which, in her view, prescribes a "dramatic new role for women."[64] Thus, to her, early Christian attitudes toward women stand in line with contemporary feminist sensibilities but contrast with Jewish practices at the time.

We should note that feminist New Testament scholars criticize this kind of historical analysis for its anti-Jewish stereotypes.[65] In 1983, Elisabeth Schüssler Fiorenza urges feminist Christian historians to identify egalitarian impulses within first-century Judaism to make the Jesus movement as "the discipleship of equals ... historically plausible."[66] Schüssler Fiorenza maintains that "[w]omen as the *ekklēsia* of God have a continuous history that can claim women in Judaism, as well as in the Jesus and the early Christian movements, as its roots and beginnings. This history of women as the people of God must be exposed as a history of oppression as well as a history of conversion and liberation."[67] The fact that scholars do not want to reconstruct women's lives in the first century with a competitive model—as if the emerging Christian movement stood above Judaism—speaks to the strength of Judaism. Instead, they show that an inclusive paradigm describes the complex interactions of first-century women in society and religion more adequately than a Christian supersessionist model.[68] At the end of the 1970s, then, the feminist study of biblical literature in North America bursts onto the scholarly scene.[69]

The Expansion of Sexual Politics and Gender in Feminist Biblical Perspectives during the 1980s

Feminist biblical scholars expand and deepen the study of the Bible in relation to women, gender, and sexuality in the 1980s. One publication, "The Effects of Women's Studies on Biblical Studies," illustrates the energies that began to manifest

---

62. Ibid., 128.

63. Ibid., 132.

64. Ibid., 137.

65. See, e.g. Judith Plaskow, "Christian Feminism and Anti-Judaism," *Cross Currents* 28 (1978): 306–9; Bernadette Brooten, "Jüdinnen zur Zeit Jesu: Ein Plädoyer für Differenzierung," *Theologische Quartalschrift* 161 (4) (1981): 280–5.

66. Elisabeth Schüssler Fiorenza, *In Memory of Her: A Feminist Theological Reconstruction of Christian Origins* (New York: Crossroad, 1983), 107.

67. Ibid., 350.

68. Supersessionism comes from the verb "supersede" and refers to the Christian theological notion that Christianity (the "Church") replaced Judaism ("Israel").

69. For additional details about this era, see Judith Plaskow, "Movement and Emerging Scholarship: Feminist Biblical Scholarship I the 1970s in the United States," in Elisabeth Schüssler Fiorenza (ed.), *Feminist Bible Studies in the Twentieth Century: Scholarship and Movement* (Bible and Women 9.1; Atlanta, GA: SBL Press, 2014), 21–34.

in the field. The volume contains the papers from a successful and inspiring panel discussion that took place during the 1980 SBL centennial celebration at the annual meeting of the Society of Biblical Literature. The papers are published in 1982 by the British *Journal for the Study of the Old Testament*,[70] not by the SBL's *Journal of Biblical Literature*. Pamela J. Milne points out that it must have been "surely an embarrassment to the SBL" when it became obvious that the SBL had missed the mark.[71] The editor of the volume, Phyllis Trible, hints at this dynamic when she explains:

> From the beginning, all of us involved in this session, speakers and listeners, knew that we were not celebrating a centennial. In the SBL, as in society at large, women have little, if anything, to celebrate.[72]

During this second phase, the nearly exclusive research focus is on women and gender. Already in 1982, Katherine Doob Sakenfeld acknowledges "the cultural and functional inseparability of racism, sexism, and classism"[73] and she sees these issues addressed "on the theological front" but not in biblical studies, where "the literature dealing with these three 'isms' remains on three separate tracks."[74] She recognizes that "we Bible specialists have more work to do in this area"[75] of analyzing the intersectionality of gender and other social categories.

One response comes from Toinette M. Eugene, an ethicist and womanist scholar, who articulates the parameters of a womanist biblical hermeneutics in 1987. She explains that, due to women of color's "doubly and triply oppressed" status in patriarchal society, it does not suffice to identify patriarchal oppression with androcentrism alone. Sexism must be understood as part of other oppressive ideologies, such as racism, militarism, or imperialism, because "the structures of oppression are all intrinsically linked."[76] She suggests that a feminist biblical

70. Phyllis Trible (ed.), "The Effects of Women's Studies on Biblical Studies," *JSOT* 22 (1982): 3–71.

71. Pamela J. Milne, "Toward Feminist Companionship: The Future of Feminist Biblical Studies and Feminism," in Athalya Brenner and Carole Fontaine (eds), *A Feminist Companion to Reading the Bible: Approaches, Methods, and Strategies* (Sheffield: Sheffield Academic Press, 1997), 42.

72. Trible, "The Effects of Women's Studies on Biblical Studies," 3.

73. Katharine Doob Sakenfeld, "Old Testament Perspectives: Methodological Issues," *JSOT* 22 (1982): 19.

74. Ibid.

75. Ibid.

76. Toinette M. Eugene, "A Hermeneutical Challenge for Womanists: The Interrelation between the Text and Our Experience," in Gayle G. Koontz and Willar Swartley (eds), *Perspectives on Feminist Henneneutic* (Elkhart, IN: Institute for Mennonite Studies, 1987), 20. For a general discussion of womanist theology, see, e.g. Delores S. Williams, "The Color of Feminism: Or, Speaking the Black Woman's Tongue," *JRT* 43 (1986): 42–58. See also Karen Baker-Fletcher, "Seeking Our Survival, Seeking Our Life, and Wisdom: Womanist

hermeneutics has "to articulate an alternative liberating vision and praxis for all oppressed people by utilizing the paradigm of women's experiences of survival and salvation in the struggle against patriarchal oppression and degradation."[77] Yet Eugene's general proposal *for* the inclusion of other forms of social analysis does not find full articulation in the 1980s. During this phase most feminist biblical scholars focus on gender and androcentrism only and despite some exceptions an intersectional analysis is not prominent in feminist biblical publications.[78]

The omission of race, class, and geopolitical dynamics as analytical categories is obvious today because many feminist interpreters embrace intersectional, postcolonial, and dialogical hermeneutics from around the world. Yet in the 1980s, North American feminist biblical scholars are mainly white women, located at departments of religious studies and schools of theology. They aim to establish themselves in academic institutions and in a discipline that defines exegetical work as objective, universal, and value neutral. At the time their exegetical focus on women and gender is in itself a challenge to the mostly white, male, and senior scholars who populate schools and departments, and usually they do not recognize feminist research as a legitimate area of scholarship. Yet even then some feminist biblical interpreters challenge modernist notions of objectivity, disinterestedness, and the possibility of extracting original meaning from the text. They understand their project as the critical analysis of multiaxial power relations in which gender, sexuality, race, ethnicity, nationality, age, physical abilities, and other ideological-theological stances play central roles.

In the 1980s, two feminist biblical publications stand out because they fuel the research agenda for years to come. These books, reframing epistemological, hermeneutical, and methodological priorities, lend scholarly legitimacy to women and gender research in biblical studies. Elisabeth Schüssler Fiorenza's *In Memory of Her* is one such book.[79] She explains in the introduction to the tenth anniversary edition that she "set out to explore the problem of women's historical agency in ancient Christianity in light of the theological and historical questions raised by the feminist movements in society and church and to do so in terms of critical biblical studies."[80] Schüssler Fiorenza shows that Christian women and men in the first century attempt to practice "the call to coequal discipleship" with various levels of success. At the time, she worries whether "feminists might label the book as male scholarship; whereas my colleagues in biblical studies might not

Approaches to the Hebrew Bible," in Susanne Scholz (ed.), *Feminist Interpretation of the Hebrew Bible in Retrospect* (Vol. 3: Methods; Sheffield: Sheffield Academic Press, 2016), 225–42.

77. Eugene, "A Hermeneutical Challenge," 25.

78. For a constructive critique of this situation, see, e.g. Nyasha Junior, "Womanist Biblical Interpretation," in Linda Day and Carolyn Pressler (eds), *Engaging the Bible in a Gendered World* (Louisville and London: Westminster John Knox Press, 2006), 44.

79. Elisabeth Schüssler Fiorenza, *In Memory of Her: A Feminist Theological Reconstruction of Christian Origins* (New York: Crossroad, 1994).

80. Ibid., xiv

take it seriously."[81] However, the book is immediately recognized as a milestone accomplishment; for instance, Beverly W. Harrison asserts, In Memory of Her is, I believe, the most fulsome proposal we yet possess for a feminist hermeneutics that addresses the full circle of human interpretation."[82]

The other work that galvanizes feminist biblical studies comes from Phyllis Trible. Her 1984 volume, Texts of Terror,[83] presents four biblical women: Hagar, Tamar, an unnamed woman, and the daughter of Jephthah. Informed by a feminist hermeneutic and rhetorical criticism, Trible selects these "ancient tales of terror" because, as she explains, they "speak all too frighteningly of the present."[84] She acknowledges that her study is possible only because of her earlier and more joyous work of 1978, God and the Rhetoric of Sexuality.[85] In it she exegetes several biblical texts, among them the Eve and Adam story in Genesis 2–3. Her literary reading displays a radically different view on the narrative than traditional androcentric commentaries, and Trible's reading challenges them on a profound level. It shows exegetically that initially the human of Genesis 2 is sexually undifferentiated and ought to be called "earth creature" because sexual identity appears only with the naming of the woman in Genesis 2:22-3. Trible also underscores the unusual qualities of Eve when Eve responds to the serpent's invitation to eat from the fruit. Trible states:

> The response of the woman to the serpent reveals her as intelligent, informed, and perceptive. Theologian, ethicist, hermeneut, rabbi, she speaks with clarity and authority …. The woman speaks; the man does not …. She acts independently, seeking neither his permission nor his advice. In the presence of the man she thinks and decides for herself …. Yet throughout this scene the man has remained silent; he does not speak for obedience. His presence is passive and bland. The contrast he offers to the woman is not strength or resolve but weakness …. He does not theologize; he does not contemplate; and he does not envision the full possibilities of the occasion. Instead, his one act is belly-oriented, and it is an act of acquiescence, not of initiative. If the woman is intelligent, sensitive, and ingenious, the man is passive, brutish, and inept.[86]

Trible offers a reading that identifies feminist qualities in the narrative and for Eve. At the time, in 1978, it is the first feminist interpretation produced by a properly accredited scholar and the first comprehensively articulated one. It is also the first reading that supports the second feminist movement by challenging the traditional sexist and androcentric understanding of this highly influential

---

81. Ibid.

82. Beverly W. Harrison, "Review of In Memory of Her, by Elisabeth Schüssler Fiorenza"; Horizons 11 (1984): 150.

83. Phyllis Trible, Texts of Terror: Literary-Feminist Readings of Biblical Narratives (Philadelphia: Fortress, 1984).

84. Ibid., xiii.

85. Phyllis Trible, God and the Rhetoric of Sexuality (Philadelphia: Fortress, 1978).

86. Phyllis Trible, "A Love Story Gone Awry," in God and the Rhetoric of Sexuality, 113.

tale. In short, it offers an alternative to the patriarchal meaning of this tale with its long and extensive history of interpretation. Trible's project jolts scholars and lay readers alike into a newfound awareness of these biblical texts and their tremendous significance for discussions on women and gender, with hints toward other forms of oppression, such as nationality and class.[87]

Many important studies appear in the 1980s that explore the complexities of female characters, topics, and references in biblical literature, history, and tradition. In Hebrew Bible studies they include the works of Phyllis Bird, Peggy L. Day, Tikva Frymer-Kensky, Esther Fuchs, Alice L. Laffey, Carol Meyers, Katharine Doob Sakenfeld, and Renita J. Weems.[88] In early Christian literature they include the studies by Bernadette Brooten, Mary Rose D'Angelo, Jane Schaberg, Sandra M. Schneiders, Luise Schottroff, Mary Ann Tolbert, and Antoinette Wire.[89] The publications of these and other scholars expand and deepen feminist research beyond anything ever written before. Yet it needs to be remembered that for institutional, hermeneutical, and socio-political reasons, feminist interpreters do not usually attend to other intersectional dynamics; in the 1980s, much of their scholarship practices, probably unconsciously, a politics of omission.

Beyond a Politics of Omission and Toward a Differentiation of Feminist-Womanist-Mujerista Exegesis in the 1990s

Things change in the 1990s, when voices of "otherness" become increasingly vocal in biblical studies. For the first time, voices of African American women scholars are joined by exegetes from South Africa and other African countries who criticize white feminist biblical discourse for neglecting race.[90] They prefer

87. See, e.g. ibid., 27.

88. Renita J. Weems, *Just A Sister Away* (New York: Grand Central Publishing, 1988); Carol Meyers, *Discovering Eve: Ancient Israelite Women in Context* (New York: Oxford University Press, 1988); Alice L. Laffey, *An Introduction to the Old Testament: A Feminist Perspective* (Philadelphia: Fortress, 1988); Peggy L. Day (ed.), *Gender and Difference in Ancient Israel* (Minneapolis, MN: Fortress, 1989).

89. Bernadette Brooten, *Women Leaders in the Ancient Synagogue* (Chico, CA: Scholars Press, 1982); and Mary Ann Tolbert, *The Bible and Feminist Hermeneutics* (Chico, CA: Scholars Press, 1983); Sandra M. Schneiders, *Women and the Word* (New York: Paulist, 1986); Jane Schaberg, *The Illegitimacy of Jesus: A Feminist Theological Interpretation of the Infancy Narratives* (San Francisco: Harper & Row, 1987).

90. See, e.g. Madipoane J. Masenya, "African Womanist Hermeneutics: A Suppressed Voice from South Africa Speaks," *JFSR* 11 (1995): 149–55; Maxine Howell, "Towards a Womanist Pneumatological Pedagogy and Re-reading the Bible from British Black Women's Perspectives," *Black Theology* 7 (2009): 86–99. For an example of a womanist interpretation on a specific biblical text, see, e.g. Ncumisa Manona, "The Presence of Women in Parables: An Afrocentric Womanist Perspective," *Scriptura* 81 (2002): 408–21; Raquel A. St. Clair, *Call and Consequences: A Womanist Reading of Mark* (Minneapolis, MN: Fortress, 2008).

the term "womanism" for Christian black women scholarship, from Alice Walker's definition of the term as coming "from womanish .... A black feminist or feminist of color. From the black expression of mothers to female children, 'You acting womanish,' like a woman. usually referring to outrageous, audacious, courageous or *willful* behavior."[91]

Womanist theologians state that racism is as urgent as sexism, and they demand that feminist biblical scholarship investigate both gender and race. They want biblical interpretations to focus "on *all* historically marginalized persons, women and men, who have been victimized by patriarchal dominance."[92] They advise white feminists to deal with their racist assumption[93] because "Black women *seek* to redeem life from patriarchal *and racist* death."[94] Womanists also criticize the binary distinction of female and male, urging feminist biblical scholars to transform not only socio-political and cultural-religious structures of oppression based on gender but also those based on racism, classism, sexuality[95] and geo-politics.[96] Otherwise, they caution that feminist scholarship would

91. See Alice Walker, *In Search of Our Mother's Gardens: Womanist Prose* (San Diego: Harcourt Brace Jovanovich, 1983), xi. See also the reference to Walker's definition in Delores S. Williams, "Womanist Theology: Black Women's Voices," in James H. Cone and Gayraud S. Wilmore (eds), *Black Theology: A Documentary History* (Vol. 2; Maryknoll, NY: Orbis, 1993), 265. William's essay was first published in 1987.

92. Clarice J. Martin, "Womanist Interpretation of the New Testament: The Quest for Holistic and Inclusive Translation and Interpretation," *JFSR* 6 (1990): 53. For a brief historical survey of biblical womanist scholarship, see also Michael Joseph Brown, "The Womanization of Blackness," in *Blackening of the Bible: The Aims of African American Biblical Scholarship* (Harrisburg, PA: Trinity, 2004).

93. See also the challenge by Asian feminist theologian Kwok Pui-lan, "Racism and Ethnocentrism in Feminist Biblical Interpretation," in Elisabeth Schüssler Fiorenza (ed.), *Searching the Scriptures: A Feminist Introduction* (New York: Crossroad, 1993), 101–16.

94. Mukti Barton, "The Skin of Miriam Became as White as Snow: The Bible, Western Feminism and Colour Politics," *Feminist Theology* 27 (May 2001): 80, emphasis added. See also Koala Jones-Warsaw, "Towards a Womanist Hermeneutic: A Reading of Judges 19–21," *JITC* 22 (1) (1994): 30. For a survey discussion, see Clarice J. Martin, "Womanist Biblical Interpretation," in John H. Hayes (ed.), *Dictionary of Biblical Interpretation* (Nashville, TN: Abingdon, 1999), 655–8. For the first book-length discussion on womanist biblical studies, see Nyaha Junior, *An Introduction to Womanist Biblical Interpretation* (Louisville, KY: Westminster John Knox Press, 2015).

95. See, e.g. Renee L. Hill, "Who Are We for Each Other? Sexism, Sexuality and Womanist Theology," in Cone and Wilmore (eds), *Black Theology* (Vol. 2), 345–51.

96. For early and influential publications, see Sheila Briggs, "Can an Enslaved God Liberate? Hermeneutical Reflections on Philippians 2:6-11," in Katie Geneva Cannon and Elisabeth Schüssler Fiorenza (eds), *Interpretation for Liberation* (Semeia 47; Atlanta, GA: Scholars Press, 1989), 137–53; Martin, "Womanist Interpretation of the New Testament," 4–61; Renita J. Weems, "The Hebrew Women Are Not Like the Egyptian Women: The Ideology of Race, Gender, and Sexual Reproduction in Exodus 1," in Tina Pippin and David

become "like patriarchal scholarship," "seeking its own perpetuation," and be "doomed."[97]

More recently, some black feminist/womanist biblical scholars acknowledge their ambivalence at being characterized as "womanist." Wilda C. M. Gafney explains that her "primary self-designation" is "a black feminist," a self-definition that reclaims the term *feminism* "from the pale hands of those who infected it with racism and classism."[98] She also acknowledges that in contexts dominated by racism and. classism she prefers the term *womanist* "to avoid being coopted by white feminists."[99] Sometimes she considers "a hybridized identifier, fem/womanist" most appropriate because it describes "the intersection of feminist and womanist practices."[100] New Testament scholar, Gay L. Byron, also recognizes the complexities of being classified as a "womanist Bible scholar." In a discussion on "my own brand of womanist biblical hermeneutics,"[101] she advises to take seriously the transnational context of black feminism in the U.S.A and to develop "a more sustained focus on the common themes that U.S.-Black feminists share with women of African descent throughout the world."[102] She urges feminist Bible scholars, particularly in the field of New Testament, "to listen to the voices of those who adhere to 'different' faiths, hail from 'other' cultures, and live in 'distant' lands as we reformulate the methodologies that might lead to a more representative form of global feminist biblical interpretation."[103]

We need to keep in mind that the number of womanist *biblical* scholars has been relatively small. In 2001, only forty-five African–American scholars held doctoral degrees in biblical studies. Eleven of them were women, eight of whom specialized in Hebrew Bible and three in New Testament. The 2015 SBL Report states: "Presently, 85% of members who claim to be United States citizens are

Jobling (eds), *Ideological Criticism of Biblical Texts* (Semeia 59; Atlanta, GA: Scholars Press, 1992), 25–34.

97. Renita J. Weems, "Womanist Reflections on Biblical Hermeneutics," in Cone and Wilmore (eds), *Black Theology* (vol. 2), 217. More recently, see Raquel St. Clair, "Womanist Biblical Interpretation," in Brian K. Blount (eds.), *True to Our Native Land: An African American New Testament Commentary* (Minneapolis, MN: Fortress, 2007), 54–62.

98. Wilda C. M. Gafney, "A Black Feminist Approach to Biblical Studies," *Encounter* 67 (Autumn 2006): 397.

99. Ibid.

100. Ibid.

101. Gay L. Byron, "The Challenge of 'Blackness' for Rearticulating the Meaning of Global Feminist New Testament Interpretation," in Kathleen O'Brien Wicker et al. (eds), *Feminist New Testament Studies: Global and Future Perspectives* (New York: Palgave Macmillan, 2005), 97.

102. Ibid.

103. Ibid., 95. For another call toward multimethodological, multireligious, and multi-perspectival hermeneutics, see, e.g. Cheryl B. Anderson, *Ancient Laws and Contemporary Controversies: The Need for Inclusive Biblical Interpretation* (New York: Oxford University Press, 2009).

of European descent, 3.8% are multiethnic, and 3.4% are of African descent. Members of Asian descent account for 2.3%, Latina/o descent totals 1.7%, and Native American, Alaska Native, or First Nation descent is 0.2%."[104] In light of these numbers in the field of biblical studies, many womanist *theologians* have published womanist Bible interpretations.[105] They have taken seriously Jacquelyn Grant's 1978 criticism that the black church and theologians "treat Black women as if they were invisible creatures" although "Black women represent more than 50% of the Black community and more than 70% of the Black Church."[106]

In the North American context, recognition of diversity among women's social locations is observed not only by womanist scholars but also by *mujerista* theologians. This term is derived from the Spanish word for woman, *mujer*. These theologians stress the distinctiveness of Hispanic women's contexts for the interpretation of the Bible. For instance, Ada Maria Isasi-Diaz, a trained Christian ethicist, proposes grounding biblical interpretations in the lives of Hispanic women so that the Bible serves as a direct support system to them. She also suggests that Hispanic women "analyze and test their lives against those sections of the Bible which are life-giving for them."[107] Yet, to date, a book on *mujerista* biblical interpretation published by a *mujerista* scholar with a doctoral degree in biblical studies does not exist.

104. See Society of Biblical Literature, "Society Report" (November 2015), 22; available online at https://www.sbl-site.org/assets/pdfs/SR2015_online.pdf (accessed December 12, 2016).

105. See, e.g. Kelly Brown Douglas, who acknowledged: "I am a theologian and not a biblical scholar … . It is important for me to approach this timely issue as a theologian and not a biblical scholar." See her article entitled "Marginalized People, Liberating Perspectives: A Womanist Approach to Biblical Interpretation," *ATR* 83 (Winter 2001): 41. For a historical survey on the significance of the Bible in African American communities, see Vincent L. Wimbush, "The Bible and African Americans: An Outline of an Interpretative History," in Cain Hope Felder (ed.), *Stony the Road We Trod: African American Biblical Interpretation* (Minneapolis, MN: Fortress, 1991), 81–97. For early womanist theological work, see Delores S. Williams, *Sisters in the Wilderness: The Challenge of Womanist God-Talk* (Maryknoll, NY: Orbis, 1993); Katie Geneva Cannon, *Katie's Canon: Womanism and the Soul of the Black Commumity* (New York: Continuum, 1995). See also Katie Geneva Cannon, "The Emergence of Black Feminist Consciousness," in Letty M. Russell (ed.), *Feminist Interpretation of the Bible* (Philadelphia: Westminster, 1985). For an introduction to womanist biblical interpretation, see Junior, *An Introduction to Womanist Biblical Interpretation.*

106. Jacquelyn Grant, "Black Theology and the Black Woman," in Cone and Wilmore (eds), *Black Theology* (Vol. 1), 334.

107. Ada Maria Isasi-Diaz, "The Bible and *Mujerista* Theology," in Susan Brooks Thistlethwaite and Mary Potter Engel (eds), *Lift Every Voice: Constructing Christian Theologies from the Underside* (Maryknoll, NY: Orbis, 1998), 274. See also, e.g. Ada Maria Isasi-Diaz, *En la lucha: In the Struggle: A Hispanic Women's Liberation Theology* (Minneapolis, MN: Fortress, 1993).

Despite the concerns articulated by womanist and *mujerista* theologians, feminist publications of the 1990s focus mostly on androcentrism.[108] The 1992 publication of the *Women's Bible Commentary,* edited by Carol A. Newsom and Sharon H. Ringe, contains interpretations on every biblical book of the Christian canon with a focus on women and gender, and the 1998 expanded edition includes the Apocrypha.[109] The editors explain that "women have read the Bible for countless generations," but "we have not always been self-conscious about reading as women."[110] They explain that the title of the commentary refers to women in the plural because the editors and contributors recognize the need for intersectional feminist readings even when individual interpretations do not always make such intersectional connections visible. The commentary is the first academically rigorous one-volume publication on all biblical books of the Christian canon that addresses women and gender. Its significance in the history of feminist biblical studies in North America cannot be overemphasized. Several one-volume commentaries have been published since then. One, edited by Catherine Clark Kroeger and Mary J. Evans, comes from feminist evangelical communities and appears in relative disjunction from feminist scholarly exegesis in 2002.[111] Another comes from Jewish feminist communities in the United States and, entitled *The Torah: A Women's Commentary* and edited by Tamara Cohn Eshkenazi and Andrea L. Weiss, features multiple Jewish feminist voices and approaches to the first five books of the Bible.[112] Another one-volume feminist

108. See, e.g. Sharon Pace Jeansonne, *The Women of Genesis: From Sarah to Potiphar's Wife* (Minneapolis, MN: Fortress, 1990); Tikva Frymer-Kensky, *In the Wake of the Goddesses: Women, Culture, and the Biblical Pagan Myth* (New York: Free Press, 1992); Danna Nolan Fewell and David M. Gunn, *Gender, Power and Promise: The Subject of the Bible's First Story* (Nashville, TN: Abingdon, 1993); Claudia V. Camp and Carole R. Fontaine (eds), "Women, War, and Metaphor: Language and Society in the Study of the Hebrew Bible," *Semeia* 61 (1993); Ilona N. Rashkow, *Taboo or Not Taboo: Sexuality and Family in the Hebrew Bible* (Minneapolis, MN: Fortress, 2000); Claudia V. Camp, *Wise, Strange, and Holy: The Strange Woman and the Making of the Bible* (Sheffield: Sheffield Academic Press, 2000); Joan L. Mitchell, *Beyond Fear and Silence: A Feminist-Literary Reading of Mark* (New York: Continuum, 2001); Dorothy Lee, *Flesh and Glory: Symbol, Gender, and Theology in the Gospel of John* (New York: Crossroad, 2002); Christina Grenholm and Daniel Patte (eds), *Gender, Tradition, and Romans: Shared Ground, Uncertain Borders* (New York: T&T Clark, 2005).

109. Carol A. Newsom and Sharon H. Ringe (eds), *Women's Bible Commentary* (Louisville, KY: Westminster John Knox, 1992; exp. 2nd edn; 1998). The volume appears in a significantly rev. 3rd edn in 2012.

110. Ibid., xix.

111. Catherine Clark Kroeger and Mary J. Evans (eds), *The IVP Women's Bible Commentary* (Downers Grove, IL: InterVarsity Press, 2002).

112. Tamara Cohn Eshkenazi and Andrea L. Weiss (eds), *The Torah: A Women's Commentary* (New York: WRJ/URJ Press, 2008).

commentary appears in the German language in 1998; it is edited by Luise Schottroff and Marie-Theres Wacker and was translated into English in 2012.[113]

The other highly influential publication of the 1990s is the nineteenvolume Feminist Companion series to the Hebrew Bible, edited by Athalya Brenner.[114] Although this series was neither edited nor published in North America, numerous contributors to the first series (1993–2001) and the second series (1998–2002) work and live in North America. Representing the diverse range of scholarship on women and gender, the articles explore biblical texts, characters and topics with historical, literary, and cultural methodologies. Some come from explicitly feminist perspectives, while others remain moderately neutral about their socio-political agenda. Although attention to intersectional hermeneutics is minimal, the nineteen volumes have made the extent of research on women and gender in biblical studies more accessible than any other anthology.[115]

113. Luise Schottroff and Marie-Theres Wacker (eds), *Feminist Biblical Interpretation: A Compendium of Critical Commentary on the Books of the Bible and Related Literature,* trans. Lisa E. Dahill, Everett R. Kalin, Nancy Lukens, Linda M. Maloney, Barbara Rumscheidt, Martin Rumscheidt, and Tina Steiner (Grand Rapids, MI and Cambridge: William B. Eerdmans, 2012). See also the original German publication: Luise Schottroff and Marie-Theres Wacker (eds), *Kompendium: Feministische Bibelauslegung* (Chr. Kaiser Gütersloher Verlagshaus, 1998). For a panel discussion on this translated commentary in the North American context, see Susanne Scholz (ed.), "A Commentary upon Feminist Commentary: A Report from the Feminist Biblical Trenches," *lectio difficilior: European Electronic Journal for Feminist Exegesis* 1 (2014): http://www/lectio.unibe.ch/14_1/scholz_susanne_feminist_commentary_upon_feminist_commentary.html (accessed December 12, 2016).

114. The first series was edited by Athalya Brenner from 1993 to 2001 (with the exception of one co-edited volume) and published by Sheffield Academic Press: *A Feminist Companion to Genesis* (1993); *A Feminist Companion to Judges* (1993); *A Feminist Companion to the Song of Songs* (1993); *A Feminist Companion to Ruth* (1993); *A Feminist Companion to Samuel and Kings* (1994); *A Feminist Companion to Wisdom Literature* (1995); *A Feminist Companion to Esther, Judith, and Susannah* (1995); *A Feminist Companion to the Latter Prophets* (1995); *A Feminist Companion to the Hebrew Bible in the New Testament* (1996); Brenner and Carole Fontaine (eds), *A Feminist Companion to Reading of the Bible* (2001). The second series was also edited by Athalya Brenner from 1998 to 2002 (with the exception of one co-edited volume) and published with Sheffield Academic Press: *Genesis: A Feminist Companion to the Bible (Second Series)* (1998); *Judges: A Feminist Companion to the Bible (Second Series)* (1999); *Ruth and Esther: A Feminist Companion to the Bible (Second Series)* (1999): *Samuel and Kings: A Feminist Companion to the Bible (Second Series)* (2000); *Exodus and Deuteronomy: A Feminist Companion to the Bible (Second Series)* (1998); *The Song of Songs: A Feminist Companion to the Bible (Second Series)* (2000); *Prophets and Daniel: A Feminist Companion to the Bible (Second Series)* (2002); Brenner and Fontaine (eds), *Wisdom and Psalms: A Feminist Companion to the Bible (Second Series)* (1998). The editor of the New Testament series is Amy-Jill Levine, who has published a growing series with Bloomsbury Publishing since 2000.

115. For other anthologies, see, e.g. Linda Day and Carolyn Pressler (eds), *Engaging the*

In short, the third phase in feminist biblical studies embraces the clarion call toward the inclusion of minoritized voices in history, society, and religion. Yet in practice feminist biblical studies often focus on women and gender at every conceivable level of scholarly discourse and activity—from teaching courses at undergraduate and graduate schools of religious and theological studies to doctoral research projects and scholarly publications. Methodologically, the field has also moved toward the development of cultural studies.[116] However, after twenty years of feminist scholarly activities, the institutionalization of a feminist infrastructure in biblical studies still depends largely on individual efforts and hiring practices. Thus the hope that a biblical feminist hermeneutics "empowers women to forge strategic bonds with other women—not just with women who share their same demographic profile, but women of differing religious, ethnic, political, class, and geographical identities and locations"[117] represents an ongoing challenge to Bible scholars of all persuasions—feminist, womanist, *mujerista,* and others. By the 1990s, it is clear that biblical literature needs to be interpreted together with social categories such as gender, race, class, sexual orientation, disability, and geopolitical concerns, so that feminist biblical scholarship contributes to the dismantling of the "rhetoric of empire"[118] prevalent in the world today. Yet at the same time, the academic infrastructure for feminist biblical studies is far from securely established, and most feminist biblical scholars continue to function on the margins of the scholarly and institutional establishment.

Bible in a Gendered World (Louisville and London: Westminster John Knox Press, 2006); Alice Bach (ed.), *Women in the Hebrew Bible: A Reader* (New York: Routledge, 1999); Harold C. Washington et al. (eds), *Escaping Eden: New Feminist Perspectives on the Bible* (New York: New York University Press, 1999); Victor H. Matthews et al. (eds), *Gender and Law in the Hebrew Bible and the Ancient Near East* (Sheffield: Sheffield Academic Press, 1998).

116. See, e.g. J. Cheryl Exum, *Plotted, Shot, and Painted: Cultural Representations of Biblical Women* (Sheffield: Sheffield Academic Press, 1996); Cheryl Exum (ed.), *Beyond the Biblical Horizon: The Bible and the Arts* (Leiden: Brill, 1999); Kristen E. Kvam and Linda S. Schearing (eds), *Eve and Adam: Jewish, Christian, and Muslim Readings on Genesis and Gender* (Bloomington: Indiana University Press. 1999); Susanne Scholz, *Rape Plots: A FeministCultural Study of Genesis 34* (New York: Lang, 2000); Yvonne Sherwood, *A Biblical Text and Its Afterlives: The Survival of Jonah in Western Culture* (Cambridge: Cambridge University 2000). See also *The Bible and the Women: An Encyclopædia of Exegesis and Cultural History*, a twenty-two-volume project with an international publishing team with a focus on the European contexts and published in English, German, and Spanish. For further information, http://www.bibleandwomen.org/EN/ (accessed December 12, 2016).

117. Byron, "The Challenge of 'Blackness,'" 96.

118. For this terminology, see Elisabeth Schüssler Fiorenza, *The Power of the Word: Scripture and the Rhetoric of Empire* (Minneapolis, MN: Fortress, 2007).

Fostering Global Intersectionality and Dialogical Relationships in the Early Twenty-first Century

In the early years of the second millennium CE, North American feminist biblical research is dealing with several new challenges. One challenge relates to the function of feminist biblical scholarship within the institutional boundaries of higher education. Another challenge—probably the most intellectually productive—pushes feminist studies toward investigations of "otherness" of all sorts, such as queer, ethnicity, race, and postcolonial studies; Chapter 5 and Chapter 6 respectively explore these challenges in feminist biblical studies. Yet another challenge comes from evangelical-conservative Christian and the Christian right's approaches on "women" and gender that appear in a plethora of publications widely distributed to lay audiences; Chapter 7 of this book goes into further details on this challenge.

Here I want to outline only the first challenge as it relates to the function and status of feminist biblical scholarship within the institutional boundaries of higher education. North American feminist biblical scholarship has unquestionably developed primarily within institutions of higher education and is found in numerous undergraduate and graduate departments of religious and theological studies and seminaries. This development means that feminist biblical scholars are required not only to earn the usual academic credentials and to comply with established standards of tenure and promotion, but they also need to adapt to the dominant academic discourse and scholarly norms in teaching and research projects.[119]

Publications, grants, and the development of feminist knowledge are judged by hegemonic scholars. The feminist call to action—one of the initial drives of feminist scholarship in the 1970s—has all too often become secondary and, consequently, the impetus toward socio-political, economic, and cultural transformation has been neglected. Perhaps unsurprisingly, then, feminist biblical research has turned into increasingly specialized, depoliticized, and co-opted projects that comply with dominant standards, norms, and expectations. As Caroline Vander Stichele and Todd Penner observe, the guild of biblical studies "maintains a strong line of male identified scholarly assessment and production"[120] and "the difference that is tolerated does not challenge the phallocentric and colonial structures of the guild" but rather contributes to "solidify its hold."[121] Feminist biblical scholarship, like other marginalized discourses by the "excluded

---

119. For a critique of the institutional situation, see especially Esther Fuchs, "Points of Resonance," in Jane Schaberg et al. (eds), *On the Cutting Edge: The Study of Women in Biblical Worlds* (New York: Continuum, 2004), esp. 12. See also her work entitled *Sexual Politics in the Biblical Narrative: Reading the Hebrew Bible as a Woman* (Sheffield: Sheffield Academic Press, 2000).

120. Caroline Vander Stichele and Todd Penner, *Contextualizing Gender in Early Christian Discourse: Thinking Beyond Thecla* (London: T&T Clark, 2009), 169.

121. Ibid., 170.

other," functions as a "fetish" and "is granted access to the formal structure as a beneficent gesture."[122]

Consequently, in North American institutions of higher education, feminist biblical research often serves as an add-on to the existing academic content management and distribution systems. Feminist biblical scholars must adapt to dominant academic expectations, the evaluation procedures of publishers, and the waning feminist sensibilities of their students. Moreover, as Pamela J. Milne notes, the emergence of feminist biblical studies and the inclusion of "others" into the field of biblical studies have concurrently led to "the devaluing of the field that we can now observe at many institutions." She insists that this development "may well be linked to the fact that what was once a virtually all-male discipline is no longer so."[123] Hector Avalos goes even further. He states that "the SBL is the agent of a dying profession" because it lacks teaching positions at credible academic institutions.[124] In this situation of gradually disappearing teaching positions, the "long-term viability" of feminist biblical scholarship is at stake because innovation is "endangered or at least impeded."[125]

Because of the survival mode in the humanities, the impetus toward maintaining the status quo discourages bold proposals for epistemological and hermeneutical change, including those from feminist biblical scholars.[126] At their best, then, feminist biblical scholars contribute to developing, promoting, and cultivating textual interpretations as "site[s] of struggle";[127] Bible readings ought to be focused on issues that are "our own in this present world."[128] In other words, the ongoing marginalization of feminist biblical work in institutions of higher education has dampened the powerful energies that were set free in the 1970s. It certainly does not help that neoliberal hegemonies in the global economies of the world have also infected universities, colleges, and seminaries everywhere. That these developments have created considerable intellectual and economic difficulties for progressive scholars in academia is widely known. Its impact on contemporary

---

122. Ibid., 169.

123. Milne, "Toward Feminist Companionship," 38–60.

124. Hector Avalos, *The End of Biblical Studies* (Amherst, NY: Prometheus, 2007), 316.

125. Milne, "Toward Feminist Companionship," 43.

126. See, e.g. Marc Bousquet, *How the University Works: Higher Education and the Low-Wage Nation* (New York: New York University Press, 2008).

127. Schüssler Fiorenza, *Power of the Word*, 254.

128. Vander Stichele and Penner, *Contextualizing Gender*, 173. For books that take seriously contemporary issues of the world today, see, e.g. Anne F. Elvey, *An Ecological Feminist Reading of the Gospel of Luke: A Gestational Paradigm* (Lewiston: Edwin Mellen, 2005); Deryn Guest, *When Deborah Met Jael: Lesbian Biblical Hermeneutics* (London: SCM, 2005); Carole R. Fontaine, *With Eyes of Flesh: The Bible, Gender, and Human Rights* (Sheffield: Sheffield Phoenix, 2008); Susanne Scholz, *Sacred Witness: Rape in the Hebrew Bible* (Minneapolis, MN: Fortress, 2010).

feminist biblical exegesis should thus not surprise anyone who realizes the grave implications of neoliberalism on people's welfare everywhere.[129]

Her Master's Tool or a Source of Liberation? A Conclusion

Without question, then, women have read and re-read the Hebrew Bible for centuries, and thanks to the second feminist movement there is now a rich and varied canon of feminist studies on virtually every female character and feminine metaphor in the Bible. From feminist commentaries to feminist biblical anthologies and monographs and countless articles in scholarly journals, women have interpreted and continue to interpret the many verses, chapters and books of the Hebrew Bible.[130] Whether their activities serve feminist goals is not always clear. Especially in the increasingly specialized field of feminist biblical studies, the pressures of professional and institutional hierarchies and prestige should not be underestimated.

Elizabeth Cady Stanton felt the consequences of women wanting to make it in patriarchal society when she had difficulties finding contributors to her volume at the end of the nineteenth century. Nowadays, professional women interpreters make a living as biblical scholars in the academy, but in our socio-politically conservative climate they face daily decisions on whether to challenge students with feminist readings, publish in feminist journals, or submit feminist research to mainstream publishing houses or feminist outlets. Tenure decisions are still based on androcentric-heteronormative standards such as peer-reviewed

---

129. For an extensive discussion on these developments, see, e.g. Henry A. Giroux, *Neoliberalism's War on Higher Education* (Haymarket Books, 2014). For a discussion about the impact of neoliberalism on feminist, queer, and gendered biblical studies, see Theresa Hornsby, "Capitalism, Masochism and Biblical Interpretation," in Teresa J. Hornsby and Ken Stone (eds), *Bible Trouble: Queer Reading at the Boundaries of Biblical Scholarship* (Atlanta, GA: Society of Biblical Literature Atlanta, 2011), 137–56.

130. See, e.g. Carol A. Newsom and Sharon H. Ringe (eds), *Women's Bible Commentary with Apocrypha* (Louisville, KY: Westminster/John Knox Press, 1992, 1998, 2012); Luise Schottroff and Marie-Theres Wacker (eds), *Kompendium Feministische Bibelauslegung* (2nd edn; Gütersloh: Chr. Kaiser/Gütersloher Verlagshaus, 1998); Carol Meyers, Toni Craven and Ross S. Kraemer, *Women in Scripture* (Grand Rapids, MI: Eerdmans, 2000); Athalya Brenner (ed.), *A Feminist Companion to Genesis* (Sheffield: Sheffield Academic Press, 1993); Athalya Brenner (ed.), *Genesis: A Feminist Companion to the Bible (Second Series)* (Sheffield: Sheffield Academic Press, 1998); Alice Bach (ed.), *Women in the Hebrew Bible: A Reader* (New York: Routledge, 1998). For an electronic journal, see, e.g. *lectio difficilor: European Electronic Journal for Feminist Exegesis*, http://www.lectio.unibe.ch/index.html. See also Susanne Scholz (ed.), *Feminist Interpretation of the Hebrew Bible in Retrospect* (vols. 1–3; Sheffield: Sheffield Phoenix Press, 2016 [2014, 2013]); Elisabeth Schüssler Fiorenza (ed.), *Feminist Biblical Studies in the 20th Century* (The Bible and Women: An Encyclopaedia of Exegesis and Cultural History, 9.1; Atlanta, GA: SBL Press, 2014).

journals, and the adjective "feminist" can still determine who gets which job. The backlash against feminism is real,[131] and many women scholars do not dare to engage in intellectual conflict or to build an academic life on the professional margins. Sometimes they reach for professional power and prestige among their peers and in academic institutions. The price, of course, is a loss of feminist conviction, not an entirely new phenomenon, as this chapter on the history of feminist biblical interpretation indicates.

So it is not the fault of the Hebrew Bible that its readers have used biblical texts to support hegemonic practices and to argue for women's secondary status in patriarchal, racializing, and colonizing Western societies. Readers shape and, indeed, have always shaped the meanings of biblical texts. This is a central lesson of the history of interpretation. And when women with a feminist consciousness interpret the Hebrew Bible, sometimes they reject the interpretations of the masters and fight for biblical meanings saturated by liberatory and emancipatory power. With this in mind, it is now high time to turn our attention to several influential feminist interpreters and to discover why they decided to spend their working lives on the feminist study of the Hebrew Bible.

---

131. For a review of backlash literature in the area of feminist biblical studies, see, e.g. Susanne Scholz, "The Christian Right's Discourse on Gender and the Bible," *Journal of Feminist Studies in Religion* 21 (1) (Spring 2005): 83–104. See also Karen Strand Winslow, "Recovering Redemption for Women: Feminist Exegesis in North American Evangelicalism," in Susanne Scholz (ed.), *Feminist Interpretation of the Hebrew Bible in Retrospect: Social Locations* (vol. 2; Sheffield: Sheffield Academic Press, 2014), 269–89.

Chapter 2

A CAREER AS A FEMINIST BIBLICAL SCHOLAR: FOUR STORIES

Feminist biblical interpretation is not only history, as the previous chapter explained. It is alive and well, and so we turn our attention now to four contemporary feminist scholars of the Hebrew Bible: Phyllis Trible, Athalya Brenner, Elsa Tamez and, Marie-Theres Wacker. They come from a range of generational, religious, national, and scholarly backgrounds, and they all expressly identify their work as feminist. All four of them represent the pioneering and second generation of feminist biblical studies. In addition, they work in various geopolitical settings, as in the United States, Israel and The Netherlands, Costa Rica and Columbia, and, Germany. Finally, they read the Hebrew Bible with a variety of historical, literary, and cultural methods, as they have been developed and are employed in the field of biblical studies. This chapter describes their distinguished careers, the difficulties they encountered in a male-dominated profession, and their scholarly contributions to the field as they have uniquely shaped contemporary feminist biblical discourse. These profiles are based on personal conversations and illustrate that "real" women—with lives marked by hopes, vulnerabilities, frustrations, and successes—are behind their groundbreaking feminist work of interpreting biblical literature.

A key caveat: admittedly, the selection of only four feminist Bible scholars is small, especially in light of the growing number of female professors in the field. In the United States their number has, despite the persistent dominance of male scholars, increased exponentially, as any national meeting of the Society of Biblical Literature (SBL), a renowned scholarly association in the United States, illustrates. In German-speaking countries there are currently more than twenty female doctoral students and professors of the Hebrew Bible. In South Korea, women scholars are also making headway, and on the African continent several women scholars are established professors. The field is burgeoning despite consistent and widespread conditions of scarce academic resources and few employment opportunities at colleges, seminaries, and universities. Still, even with these continued institutional challenges, biblical studies have been immeasurably enriched by the contributions of women, and many feminist researchers contribute actively to the field. The focus on the four selected scholars introduces some of the issues and personalities involved in this intellectual endeavor which increasingly impacts the academic study of the Hebrew Bible.

A personal note as we begin: I know all of these scholars to varying degrees, but one more than others. Phyllis Trible was my doctoral adviser at Union Theological Seminary in New York City. I met her for the first time in person when I became a student there in the Fall of 1990 and enrolled in one of her courses, "Literary Criticism and the Hebrew Bible," which turned out to be of singularly significance not only for my professional future but also for my life in general. At the end of that Fall semester I applied to Union's PhD programme in Old Testament with Trible as my advisor. She shared stories about her life and work mentioned below in the classroom, her office, and over dinners in the past few decades. In acknowledging my professional and personal debt, I want to be clear: feminist biblical scholarship is not merely a point of intellectual discovery for me. It is something of a calling in my life, and the friendship of fellow scholars has been a foundation and source of help, encouragement, and affirmation as I continue my work.

"I Have Been a Feminist since Birth": The Story of Phyllis Trible (1932)

Feminist biblical studies did not exist in the academy when Phyllis Trible was born a child of the segregated south in Richmond, Virginia, but she has always been aware of the difficulties women faced in U.S.–American patriarchal society. "I have been a feminist since birth," she firmly asserts. Trible's parents were Southern Baptists and Trible recalls her religious education as a child in Sunday school. During those days, Sunday school classes were segregated not only by race but also by gender. Trible remembers that one day her Sunday school teacher told the story of Genesis 2, the creation of woman. The teacher stated that God's creation became better and better, and then she asked the class, "Little girls, what did God create last?" The girls chirped in unions, "Man!" But the teacher replied: "No, woman was created last." Whenever Trible recounts how, in rather subtle ways, her Sunday school teacher subverted Christian teachings of this biblical tale, she smiles with fond memory and affection. Early religious education nurtured in Trible a deep love for the Bible and contributed to her steadfast conviction that Scripture is more than androcentric literature. It contains moments of joy, subversion, and liberation, also for women.

Trible attended Meredith College, a private independent women's college in Raleigh, North Carolina, where many women professors with outstanding qualifications taught. At that time, two decades prior to the rise of the second feminist movement in the United States, many renowned universities and colleges did not hire female faculty and did not admit female students. Like other small colleges, Meredith College provided educational and professional opportunities for female students and faculty. Trible thrived at Meredith College and upon graduation she began her graduate work, soon with the goal of a PhD in Old Testament in the joint programme of Union Theological Seminary and Columbia University in New York City. When she finished her PhD in 1963, women students were regularly enrolled at Union, but female faculty were not yet hired.[1] Trible completed her PhD with a thesis on the book of Jonah, guided by her mentor, James Muilenburg, for whom she holds the greatest reverence.[2] Trible went on to her first teaching assignment at Wake Forest University, where she taught from 1963 to 1971. Then she moved to a position at Andover-Newton Theological Seminary until 1980, and from 1980 to 1998 she returned to her alma mater, Union Theological Seminary, as a professor of Old Testament and later as the Baldwin Professor of Sacred Literature. She retired from Union in May 1998 but continued her academic career at the newly established Divinity School at Wake Forest University, teaching courses on Old Testament and feminist biblical studies until 2013. From 2003 to 2013, the school offered the Trible Lecture Series, an annual lectureship in her honour, offering program related to feminist theological studies.[3]

Trible is a pioneer, the first properly credentialed woman scholar in Hebrew Bible studies whose work engages directly questions, concerns, and issues raised by the feminist movement of the 1970s. She set out "to examine interactions between the Hebrew Scriptures and the Women's Liberation Movement" despite opposing voices that did not recognize a correlation between the two phenomena or rejected religion as thoroughly patriarchal.[4] Yet Trible was not deterred by such opponents. Steadily she examines biblical texts with a feminist perspective and asserts that "the Hebrew Scriptures and Women's Liberation do meet and that their encounter need not be hostile."[5] Because of her pioneering accomplishments, her work is considered seminal although some contemporary scholars believe that "she is no longer by any means the paramount figure within it."[6]

While scholars can debate such points, no one can deny the power and significance of Trible's work: Her first book, *God and the Rhetoric of Sexuality: Literary-Feminist Readings of Biblical Narrative*,[7] was published during the heyday

---

1. Sophia Lyon Fahs (1876–1977) and Mary Ely Layman (1887–1975) were among the first women faculty members at Union in the 1920s, hired as Instructors in Religious Education. See Archives of Women Theological Scholarship (AWTS), The Burke Library at Union Theological Seminary; available online: http://library.columbia.edu/locations/burke/archives/awts/exhibit.html.

2. Phyllis Trible, "Studies in the Book of Jonah" [microform] (unpublished PhD thesis: New York, 1963).

3. For more information on the lecture series, see http://divinity.wfu.edu/2012/03/trible-lectures-tenth-anniversary/ (accessed December 12, 2016). For a publication that resulted from the lecture series, see Letty M. Russell and Phyllis Trible (eds), *Hagar, Sarah, and Their Children: Jewish, Christian, and Muslim Perspectives* (Minneapolis, MN: Fortress, 2006).

4. Phyllis Trible, "Depatriarchalizing in Biblical Interpretation," *Journal of the American Academy of Religion* 41 (March 1973): 30.

5. Ibid., 47.

6. J'Annine Jobling, *Feminist Biblical Interpretation in Theological Context* (Hampshire: Ashgate, 2002), 60.

7. Phyllis Trible, *God and the Rhetoric of Sexuality: Literary-Feminist Readings of Biblical*

of the second feminist movement and it interprets selected biblical studies from a feminist perspective. Her readings seek to recover and reclaim the Hebrew Bible from patriarchal domination which she accepts as a major characteristic of biblical literature. As early as 1973, she states unambiguously, "It is superfluous to document patriarchy in Scripture."[8] Biblical literature is androcentric but Trible aims to "translate biblical faith without sexism."[9]

Trible began formally interpreting the Hebrew Bible from a feminist perspective when she lived in Boston in the 1970s. At the time, the Boston academic and religious community was ablaze from the work of radical feminist philosopher Mary Daly: Intrigued, Trible attended lectures by Daly and read her books, *The Church and the Second Sex,* and *Beyond God the Father.*[10] These books investigate the patriarchal history and tradition of Christianity and, to Daly, both Christianity and the Bible are thoroughly patriarchal and oppressive to women. Daly thus advised women to leave patriarchal religions behind and to take seriously women-centered spirituality and space. Trible recalls that Daly referred to Genesis 2–3 as an important narrative for women's oppression in Western societies. To Daly, the story blames women for the evil in the world because Eve was tempted by the serpent and human nature has been corrupted ever since. Writing in 2000, Trible recalls those days when feminists challenged the authority of the Bible:

> I had left the South to live in the Northeast where I found a theological world in ferment. Feminists were faulting the Bible for patriarchy, faulting it for promoting the pernicious paradigm of male dominance and female subordination. I did not have to be convinced. I knew that even before God formed me [in] the womb, feminism was bone of my bones and flesh of my flesh. At the same time, I also knew—decidedly at variance with many feminists—that the Bible fed my life in rich and beneficial ways; that the book I had grown up with in Sunday School where sword drills were routine and memory verses mandatory, continued to make a positive claim upon me, despite its well-documented and oppressive patriarchy. To be sure, I had learned at Meredith College and later in graduate school that the Bible was rather different from what Sunday School teachers and some preachers said. But not even critical and sophisticated ways of studying it diminished or supplanted my love for it. There is a power in the document, and need not work adversely for women or for men. This I knew and this I know, no matter how much others rush to say it isn't so.[11]

Narrative (Minneapolis, MN: Fortress, 1978). See also her anthology, co-edited with B. Diane Lipsett, *Faith and Feminism: Ecumenical Essays* (Louisville, KY: Westminster John Knox, 2014).

8. Trible, "Depatriarchalizing in Biblical Interpretation," 30.

9. Ibid., 31.

10. Mary Daly, *The Church and the Second Sex* (New York: Harper & Row, 1968); *Beyond God the Father: Toward a Philosophy of Women's Liberation* (Boston: Beacon, 1973).

11. Phyllis Trible, "Take Back the Bible," *Review and Expositor* 97 (Fall 2000): 428. See also her "If the Bible's so Patriarchal, How Come I Love It," *Bible Review* 8 (October 1992): 44–7, 55;

Trible did not let go of the Hebrew Bible despite Daly's condemning assessment of its androcentric bias. She went home to her desk and started re-reading Genesis 2–3 and other biblical narratives with exegetical methods, especially rhetorical criticism—the method of her revered teacher Muilenburg.[12] She investigates the literary structure of the Hebrew syntax, compares vocabulary, and reads the commentaries, as she was trained. She asks herself if perhaps she overlooked the Bible's oppressive qualities for women and if it is possible that her love for the Bible makes her excuse patriarchal bias. She also remembers her Sunday school teacher, and so she turns her attention to the story of Eve and Adam in Genesis 2–3. It results into one of the most innovative and controversial interpretations during the past few decades.[13]

Trible's pioneering contribution to feminist biblical studies is not limited to Genesis 2–3. Her second book, published in 1984 and entitled *Texts of Terror*,[14] is perhaps even more well-known and respected than her first one. Conceptualized as a companion to her earlier book, this volume is not an invitation "to laugh and dance" but it brings "a time to weep and mourn."[15] The book contains sad stories about women in the Hebrew Bible. More precisely, Trible presents four narratives about horrendous violations of women: Hagar who, alone with her baby boy, was left to die in the desert (Gen. 16; 21), Tamar who was raped by her own brother (2 Sam. 13), the unnamed woman who was gang-raped, murdered, and cut into twelve pieces (Judg. 19), and Jephthah's daughter whose father killed her to keep his vow (Judg. 11). Trible examines these stories of terror "to recover a neglected history; to remember a past that the present embodies, and to pray that these terrors shall not come to pass again."[16] Her interpretations are filled with literary analyses, and her dictum that "proper articulation of form-content yields proper articulation of meaning"[17] shines throughout. She also "wrestle(s) with the silence,

"Treasures Old and New: Biblical Theology and the Challenge of Feminism," in Francis Watson (ed.), *Open Text: New Directions for Biblical Studies?* (London: SCM Press, 1993): 32–56.

12. James Muilenburg, "Form Criticism and Beyond," *Journal of Biblical Literature* 88 (1969): 1–18.

13. See Chapter 1 in this volume for more details on this interpretation. See also Phyllis Trible, "Eve and Adam: Genesis 2–3 Reread," *Andover Newton Quarterly* 13 (March 1973): 251–8; "Not a Jot, Not a Tittle: Genesis 2–3 after Twenty Years," in Kristen E. Kvam, Linda S. Schearing, and Valarie H. Ziegler (eds), *Eve and Adam: Jewish, Christian, and Muslim Readings on Genesis and Gender* (Bloomington: Indiana University Press, 1999) 439–44. Both articles are also printed in Susanne Scholz, *Biblical Studies Alternatively: An Introductory Reader* (Upper Saddle River, NJ: Prentice Hall, 2003), 94–106.

14. Phyllis Trible, *Texts of Terror: Literary-Feminist Readings of Biblical Narrative* (Philadelphia: Fortress, 1984).

15. Ibid., xiii.

16. Ibid., 3.

17. Phyllis Trible, *Rhetorical Criticism: Context, Method, and the Book of Jonah* (Minneapolis, MN: Fortress, 1994), 91.

absence, and opposition of God."[18] After all, these stories appear in the sacred text of Christianity and Judaism. Why are they included, what is their lesson? To Trible, they are like mirrors imitating life. Then and now audiences shiver when they hear them because they are filled with terror. Even Trible acknowledges that "without the joy of the first book, I should have found unbearable the sorrow of the second."[19]

After this book on women's terror, she works on more hopeful biblical stories, not all of them focused on women's characters. Her third book completes what she began as a doctoral student. A comprehensive book on method, this publication explains the art of rhetorical criticism, articulated first by her teacher and mentor, James Muilenburg, and it also includes a detailed application of this method to the book of Jonah. To Trible, rhetorical criticism is a most useful approach to the biblical text, preventing the anarchy of subjectivity and honoring the poetic quality of biblical literature. Yet while this volume teaches the art of rhetorical analysis, it culminates in theology. As is generally known, the book of Jonah begins with God demanding repentance from the Ninevites but, according to Trible's rhetorical analysis, the book's theology of repentance does not have the last word. She identifies a "theology of pity" in the final verses of the book of Jonah (4:10-11) and the rhetorical analysis makes visible the shift from repentance to pity. The verses in Jonah 4:6-9 describe that a plant grows and gives shade to the prophet when suddenly the plant dies because of a worm. At this moment Jonah wishes to die rather than to continue sitting in the sweltering sun. Here is the significant rhetorical discovery: the text does not mention that Jonah felt pity when the plant dies. This characterization of Jonah's reaction appears only when God speaks to Jonah in 4:10-11, drawing a parallel between Jonah feeling pity for the death of the plant and God feeling pity for the Ninevites. Trible explains that only when a reader sees "the strategy of delayed information," it becomes clear that "Jonah's showing of pity becomes a valid premise from which to argue for Yhwh's showing of pity."[20] In other words, the prophet's behavior toward the plant serves as a model for God in which repentance is not required for God to have pity on the Ninevites. Trible's literary analysis of the book of Jonah, then, identifies two theologies: a theology of repentance and a theology of pity.[21]

The three books have cemented Trible's reputation as a respected biblical scholar. In 1994, she became the president of the Society of Biblical Literature—the first woman of the Hebrew Bible to receive this honour. Her presidential speech during the annual meeting of the Society presented a rhetorical analysis of the Elijah and Jezebel stories. True to form, Trible sticks to the biblical text, bringing new meaning to the polarity of the two characters under consideration.

18. Trible, *Texts of Terror*, 2.
19. Ibid., xiii.
20. Trible, *Rhetorical Criticism*, 222.
21. Ibid., 223.

Her speech combines her passion for the subtle recovery of women's stories with the method of rhetorical criticism.[22] She writes about Elijah and Jezebel:

> Entrapped by hostile editors and male lords, Jezebel appears as evil object, neither speaking nor acting. Free of editorial restraints, Elijah appears as good subject, exalting himself in word and deed. She is female and foreign; he, male and native. She comes from the coastlands; he, from the highlands. She thrives in a sea climate; he, in a desert climate. She belongs to husband and father; he, neither to wife nor father. She embodies royalty; he, prophecy. Both bear theophoric names that united them in opposition: Jezebel the Baal worshiper and Elijah the YHWH worshiper.[23]

Despite, or rather because of, the rhetorical emphasis on the couple's polarity, Trible suggests that in the end "opposites converge." The prophet of God and the queen of idols have more in common than the Deuteronomistic writers admit because "[d]issimilarities produce similarities to unite the incompatible." Trible explains:

> In behavior and mode of being Elijah and Jezebel become mirror images that haunt the ages. To have one is to have the other. Wherever he appears, she is there. She haunts not only him but all that he represents in the saga of faith .... To understand their inseparability is to perceive the limits of polarized thinking and so alter the strictures of theological discourse. Though we may find the convergence repugnant, we can be sure that we are heirs to it, indeed that we participate in it.[24]

In this sense, then, Trible reads the Elijah and Jezebel stories as an indirect critique of a self-assured and overconfident insistence on knowing or owning theological truth, the right exegetical method, or the exclusive privilege or participation. Her essay affirms the value of ambiguity and diversity of meaning. It is part of Trible's appreciation for biblical "remnant traditions" that "provide more than enough sustenance for life."[25] She writes about the Bible:

> To love this book is not to claim that it is without faults, imperfections, violence, and evil. To the contrary, to love this book is to understand that it sets before us life and death, blessing and curse. To love this book is to understand that a single text may yield life in one setting and death in another. And to love this book is to understand that it places upon us, readers and listeners alike, the

22. Phyllis Trible, "Exegesis For Storytellers and Other Strangers," *Journal of Biblical Literature* 111 (1) (1995): 3–19.

23. Ibid., 4–5.

24. Ibid., 18.

25. Phyllis Trible, "Five Loaves and Two Fishes: Feminist Hermeneutics and Biblical Theology," *Theological Studies* 50 (2) (1989): 295.

responsibility to choose rightly. That choice is not made for us; rather it is made by us, at the boundary of text and reader.[26]

Trible champions ambiguity of biblical meaning. The reading of the Bible cannot be reduced to an "either/or" approach unless we commit the sin of Elijah and Jezebel. Consequently, she urges her readers to follow her life-long wrestling with the biblical text when she commands:

> Do not abandon the Bible to the bashers and thumpers. Take back the text. Do not let go until it blesses you. Indeed, make it work for blessing, not for curse, so that you and your descendants, indeed so that all the families of the earth, may live.[27]

It's Not All Suffering—So Enjoy! The Story of Athalya Brenner (1943)

When I saw Athalya Brenner, Professor of Hebrew Bible at the University of Amsterdam in The Netherlands, for the first time, we stood at the departure gate for our plane at the airport in Cleveland, Ohio, waiting to attend the annual conference of the Society of Biblical Literature (SBL). She did not look like a stereotypical Bible scholar. I remember her spiky blond hair style, her funky outfit with orange sneakers and a bright green jacket, and her raspy voice while she fumbled with her cigarette container, unable to light up in an American airport building. "It's not all suffering when you read the Bible—so enjoy," she advises, and her advice comes from an outspoken feminist Bible scholar who edited one of the most comprehensive and inclusive commentary series in biblical studies, the nineteen volumes of the Feminist Companion series on the Hebrew Bible.[28]

---

26. Phyllis Trible, "Take Back the Bible," *Review and Expositor* 97 (4) (Fall 2000): 431.

27. Ibid. Among her other recent articles are: "Genesis 22: The Sacrifice of Sarah," in J. P. Rosenblatt and J. C. Sitterson (eds), *Not In Heaven: Coherence and Complexity in the Biblical Narrative* (Indianapolis: Indiana Press, 1991), 170–91; "Bible in the Round," in Margaret A. Farley and Serene Jones (eds), *Liberating Eschatology: Essays in Honor of Letty M. Russell* (Louisville, KY: Westminster John Knox, 1999), 47–54; "Eve and Miriam: From the Margins to the Center," in Hershel Shanks (ed.), *Feminist Approaches to the Bible: Symposium at the Smithsonian Institution* (Washington, DC: Biblical Archaeology Society, 1995), 5–24; "The Pilgrim Bible," in Sarah Cunningham (ed.), *We Belong Together: Churches in Solidarity with Women* (New York: Friendship, 1992), 15–17; "Subversive Justice: Tracing the Miriamic Traditions," in Walter J. Harrelson, Douglas A. Knight, and Peter J. Paris (eds), *Justice and the Holy* (Atlanta: Scholars, 1989), 99–109.

28. Among her monographs are: *Intercourse of Knowledge: On Gendering Desire and "Sexuality" in the Hebrew Bible* (Leiden and New York: Brill, 1997); *On Gendering Texts: Female and Male Voices in the Hebrew Bible* (with Fokkelien van Dijk-Hemmes) (Leiden and New York: Brill, 1993); *Song of Songs* (Sheffield: JSOT Press, 1989); *Ahavat Rut* (Tel Aviv: HaKibbutz HaMeu'chad Press, 1988 [Hebrew]). Among her edited volumes are: *Are*

Despite such acclaimed work, Brenner did not have it easy in the male-dominated and traditional field of Hebrew Bible scholarship. An Israeli, she earned degrees of BA in Bible and English language at the University of Haifa and MA in Biblical Studies at the Hebrew University in Jerusalem. She was ready for doctoral work when she met Old Testament scholar, James Barr, who at the time taught at the University of Manchester in England. Brenner decided that she wanted to study with him and enrolled in the PhD program of the Department of Near Eastern Studies (now Middle Eastern Studies) at Manchester from where she was awarded the degree in 1979. Brenner enjoyed her work with Barr tremendously and recalls her years as a doctoral student as a "period of illumination." She characterizes herself as a-religious and a non-believer. Luckily, her doctoral advisor, an ordained minister, did not interfere with her convictions and enabled her to grow into her own scholarly voice. She has "nothing but praise" for him, appreciating his scholarly and pedagogical openness as a mentor. During her years as a doctoral student, she taught at the University of Haifa where she continued teaching after she completed her PhD work.[29]

In 1986, she applied for promotion and tenure at the University of Haifa, but the faculty rejected her application. Brenner had been a feminist since the early 1970s due to the feminist social environment in Haifa where she had been living and her second book reflected this perspective. Published in 1985 and entitled *Israelite Woman: Social Role and Literary Type in Biblical Narrative*,[30] the book is a scholarly treatise on biblical women in metaphoric speech and in the social positions of queens, wise women, poets and authors, prophets, magicians, sorcerers, witches, prostitutes, mothers, temptresses, and foreign women. However, the tenure committee at Haifa found the work too journalistic and an insignificant contribution to the field. They dismissed her efforts to

We Amused? Humour about Women in the Biblical Worlds (London: T&T Clark, 2003); *Bible Translation on the Threshold of the Twenty-First Century: Authority, Reception, Culture and Religion* (with Jan Wilken van Henten) (London: Sheffield Academic Press, 2002); *Recycling Biblical Figures: Papers Read at a NOSTER Colloquium in Amsterdam, 12–13, 1997* (with Jan Willem van Henten) (Leiden: DEO Publishing, 1999); *Reflections on Theology and Gender* (with Fokkelien van Dijk-Hemmes) (Kampen, The Netherlands: Kok Pharos Publishing House, 1994); *On Humour and the Comic in the Hebrew Bible* (with Yehuda T. Radday) (Sheffield: Sheffield Academic Press, 1990); The series Feminist Companion consists of nineteen volumes, which Brenner edited from 1998 (beginning with a volume on *A Feminist Companion to Genesis*) until 2001. She co-edited three additional volumes with Carole Fontaine, including *A Feminist Companion to Reading the Bible: Approaches, Methods and Strategies* (Sheffield: Sheffield Academic Press, 1997).

29. Her thesis resulted in a book entitled *Colour Terms in the Old Testament* (Sheffield: JSOT Press, 1982).

30. Athalya Brenner, *Israelite Woman: Social Role and Literary Type in Biblical Narrative* (Sheffield: JSOT Press, 1985). The book has been republished and includes two important additions; see Athalya Brenner-Idan; *The Israelite Woman: Social Role and Literary Type in Biblical Narrative*; (Cornerstone Series; London: Bloomsbury, 2015).

integrate feminist perspectives with biblical research and even suggested that Brenner had gone "mad." Despite the rejection, she was invited to come back as an adjunct teacher, a temporary and semester-based teaching assignment, which Brenner declined.

It took her more than a decade to recover from this academic setback, suffering from physical and psychological injuries. During these years, Brenner taught as an adjunct professor at various schools in Israel such as the Oranim College of Education, Tel Aviv University, and the Technion-Israel Institute of Technology in Haifa. She also became a "special professor of Feminism, Christianity and Judaism" at the Catholic University, of Nijmegen in The Netherlands from 1993 to 1998. Finally, in 1997, she was offered a professorship in Hebrew Bible at the University of Amsterdam in The Netherlands, a prestigious and well-funded position which she accepted. Her journey traverses the path from tenure rejection to the status of an internationally recognized scholar in feminist biblical studies; it includes substantial contributions on feminist interpretation of the Hebrew Bible. Currently, she is Professor Emerita of Hebrew Bible/Old Testament at the University of Amsterdam and Professor in Biblical Studies at Tel Aviv University. In 2015, she served as the President of the Society of Biblical Literature.[31] For sure, her multi-volume series stands out among her many important scholarly accomplishments because the series contains the full range of feminist research over the entire decade of the 1990s. What Brenner admired so much about her doctoral advisor, James Barr, his openness and ability to negotiate difference of perspective, Brenner cultivated in her own work. She has opened up the field and created dialogue and opportunity for feminist biblical scholars of all persuasions.

This point has to be emphasized because sometimes Brenner wonders whether her personal sacrifices and her stubborn persistence to pursue her scholarly career despite the considerable obstacles she encountered were worth it. For instance, she acknowledges her doubts when she writes in 2015: "In view of the price I personally paid, and also the rewards that came later and should neither be denied nor underestimated, I am not sure and I do not know the answer that is suitable for anybody, perhaps not even for myself."[32] Is sticking to one's convictions worth the price paid in the form of geographical relocation, the energies set free by tremendous anger and outrage over the experienced academic injustice, and the books published that have given space to so many feminist exegetes, such as Brenner's nineteen volumes of *A Feminist Companion Series*, published between 1993 and 2001? The answer seems obvious for those of us who follow in the footsteps of Brenner and other feminist Bible scholars. Where would we be without their scholarly contributions made despite serious hurdles encountered along the way? Luckily, Brenner did not give up on her path of forging a feminist scholarly career.

For Brenner, "Jewish, a native Israeli, a woman, a mother, divorced, fifty-three years old [in 1997] ... born in the-then 'Palestine' under the British UN

---

31. Athalya Brenner-Idan, "On Scholarship and Related Animals: A Personal View from and for the Here and Now," *Journal of Biblical Literature* 135 (1) (Spring 2016): 6–17.

32. Brenner-Idan; *The Israelite Woman*, xv.

mandate, in 1943,"[33] the Bible has been in her "bones," it has been part of her "cultural identity" and in her "veins." She grew up in a home in which Hebrew was the privileged language because her parents wanted her to be among the first generation of fully integrated Israelis. Her parents preferred the Hebrew Bible to post-biblical Jewish literature, valuing it as a source for spiritual life and human existence. Hence, Brenner acknowledges that "[t]he HB for me is intimate. We learnt it at school, great portions of it, from second grade onwards, until we were fed up with it. It was treated as a secular sacred text. I know the language of the HB first hand: it is similar to mine, albeit different too .... The Bible is home in the same way that a mild version of Marxist theory and praxis is."[34]

Born Jewish but describing herself as "a-religious" and as a "non-believer," Brenner cannot imagine life without the Hebrew Bible, a book essential to the West and to her life. Her goals for studying this text are shaped by her a-religious perspective. She examines the Bible simultaneously from two viewpoints: etic, since she looks at religion, including Judaism, from without; and emic, since her ever-unfolding identity is bound up with it by birth and since childhood. Thus to her, the Hebrew Bible is a "cultural commodity"[35] available to everyone. Its study should be encouraged because nobody owns it and our various cultures have been deeply shaped by it. Consequently, Brenner wants the biblical field to make it easy to raise all kinds of questions and to be ready to entertain all kinds of answers. She looks for candid, open, and controversial debate among people whom she invites to study the Hebrew Bible from many perspectives and social locations because each has something different to contribute to biblical meaning. Since everybody comes from a particular context and with particular interpretative interests, Brenner wants the field to be more explicitly concerned with these hermeneutical matters than it currently is. The same applies to feminist biblical studies, which, to her, should be viewed as an integral part of the larger field.

Brenner's conviction that the Hebrew Bible is central does not make her defensive or apologetic as a feminist. She clearly articulates its androcentric nature when she explains that "gender issues in the Hebrew Bible can hardly be redeemed" even though "[s]mall consolations can indeed be gleaned from one specific text or another," as for instance from the Song of Songs which she regards as consoling poetry. Brenner recognizes the Hebrew Bible as "a predominantly M [male] document which reflects a deeply rooted conviction in regard to woman's otherness and social inferiority." Thus Brenner claims the Hebrew Bible as her "heritage" with a "bitter taste in [her] mouth" and confesses, "I am stuck with it. I cannot shake it off. And it hurts."[36]

---

33. Brenner, "'My' Song of Songs," in *A Feminist Companion to Reading the Bible*, 568.

34. Ibid., 569.

35. In a private interview, December 20, 2005.

36. All quotes are taken from Athalya Brenner, "The Hebrew God and His Female Complements," in Timothy K. Beal and David M. Gunn (eds), *Reading Bibles, Writing Bodies; Identity and The Book* (London and New York: Routledge, 1997), 70.

Her recognition of the androcentric nature of biblical literature makes Brenner an uncompromising critic of biblical literature that seems to condone, if not advance, violence against women, particularly in the so-called marriage metaphor in Jeremiah 2–5, Ezekiel 16 and 23, Isaiah 47, Nahum 3, and Malachi 2. Brenner questions the very terminology of the "marriage" metaphor when she writes, "What, precisely or approximately, is the meaning of 'marriage' here? Marriage is a social contract, time- and place-bound, to be sure. What kind of social contract is constructed/reflected in such passages, and how is it gendered?"[37] She then answers her question:

> Do we know enough about marriage in 'biblical' times to justify speaking about marriage in the passages listed above? The texts allude to taking a 'wife,' 'divorcing' her, or taking her back. We try to step back and look at the texts from afar, as if we could suspend subjectivity for a while in favor of temporary objectivity, to read the metaphor against its implied original setting[s]. But in spite of our honorable intentions, and because we know so very little about social practices in the biblical worlds – what we have are prescriptive and fictive texts, whose mirroring quality can be pondered again and again – we falter, we have no choice, and ultimately we return to rely, perhaps unconsciously, on our own marriage praxis. The result is an inevitable seesaw movement between vehicle and tenor (in the metaphor), past and present, in which some items are privileged and others are lost from view.[38]

Here Brenner acknowledges the difficulties in establishing unambiguous biblical meaning, especially since ancient Israelite social life remains largely unknown. We do not know enough about marriage practices in biblical times to understand adequately the ancient historical meaning of the prophetic marriage metaphors, and we tend to project our contemporary notions onto the biblical text. Yet feminist readers assert that these texts contain "marriage metaphors" as if the ancient biblical meaning of marriage is clear. Readers assume that God is the husband and Jerusalem the wife according to generally accepted norms, and they minimize the possibility that marriage in ancient Israel was different from today's notions about married life. But, for instance, we know that marriage in ancient Israel was often polygamous. Thus the question is what it would mean to imagine God as a polygamous husband. How would this notion challenge our understanding of the biblical marriage metaphor, our language for God, and the violence implied in the metaphor? After all, the metaphor describes God as

---

37. Athalya Brenner, "Some Reflections on Violence against Women and the Image of the Hebrew Bible," in Jane Schaberg, Alice Bach and Esther Fuchs (eds), *On the Cutting Edge: The Study of Women in Biblical Worlds: Essays in Honor of Elisabeth Schüssler Fiorenza* (New York and London: Continuum, 2004), 70. See also "On Prophetic Propaganda and the Politics of Love," in Fokkelien van Dijk-Hemmes and Athalya Brenner (eds), *Reflections on Theology and Gender* (Kampen: Kok Pharos Publishing House, 1994), 87–105.

38. Ibid., 71.

a sexually abusive husband of his wife. Most importantly, Brenner rejects the idea promoted by some feminist interpreters who excuse these prophetic texts of gender violence because they are only metaphors. To Brenner, metaphoric violence is problematic as the text describes literal violence. She asks, "Can violence of any kind ever be considered only metaphorical? Predominantly metaphorical?"[39] To Brenner, violent descriptions are always violent whether or not they are part of metaphoric speech.

Brenner is critical of feminist scholarship that does not seriously question the viability of biblical discourse. She demands an uncompromising attitude. In the case of the marriage metaphor, Brenner urges contemporary readers to translate sexual violence in the Hebrew Bible into contemporary language. If this is done, the marriage metaphor describes foremost a sadomasochistic relationship, and it is thus not enough to emphasize the defunct and violent relationship between God and Israel. Worse, according to Brenner, these texts accept the norms of "the s/m vision,"[40] based not on mutual consent but initiated by the male partner who tortures the female. Brenner explains:

> Let me emphasize the obvious once more. I regard the violent description of YHWH as a professional soldier and dissatisfied husband who tortures his 'wife' as unacceptable, on general humanistic-ethical as well as theological and social-gendered grounds. I regard the relevant passages as pornographic and beyond salvation not only for feminists but also for any objector to violence, be that violence divine or religious or otherwise .... Ultimately, no reconsideration of the 'original circumstances,' whether grounded in reconstructed history or anthropology or religious studies or psychology or developmental theory or positivism, can change that or serve as an excuse of 'understanding' .... Focus on the consequences rather than on excuses for the biblical prophets. Look, for instance, at women's fate in war—as in Isaiah 3 or 47, and Lamentations, and beyond.[41]

To Brenner, these passages are unredeemable, serve androcentric purposes and enforce, stereotypical gender roles. Historical or socio-cultural statements that explain or even justify this kind of divine behavior are apologetic and must be rejected. Interpreters have to identify the male-oriented outlook of these passages and refrain from rationalizing or dodging sexual violence as metaphoric or poetic language. Brenner always stresses that contemporary readers create textual meanings and are responsible for them. To her, readers are in the center of the interpretative process. She states:

> The Bible, contrary to popular and even scholarly beliefs, does *not* speak or *say*. Its readers do. Because this is our heritage, because this is what we read and

39. Ibid., 73.
40. Ibid.
41. Ibid., 79.

have been contemplating for millennia, it is up to us to choose to disown this description. We can also choose to use it as the mirror it is, a negative teacher so to speak, and draw our conclusions about our own nature. If, by doing that, we step back from fourth-wave feminist thinking to second-wave anger, so be it. But whatever our choice, merely condemning past practices is clearly not enough. Speaking in metaphors should be understood for what it represents, for readers perhaps more than for the authors of the 'original' biblical texts – whoever they were, whenever and wherever they lived, if they did, and whatever they intended.[42]

Brenner's perspective is refreshing because it encourages a non-apologetic stance toward the Hebrew Bible and invites readers to be honest about the origins of biblical meanings. Ultimately, biblical meanings are created by readers who have the responsibility to evaluate them according to the ethical and moral standards of their time. As a firm believer in negotiated meaning, Brenner is a feminist non-believer who does not abandon her religious tradition. She stays with the biblical "s/m texts," but in struggle. The result is a rich and innovative approach of reading that demands contemporary attention.

"Dreaming of Justice and Living Ecumenically": The Story of Elsa Tamez (1950)

Elsa Tamez demands changing the world toward justice and peace for women and also for men, for disempowered people stricken with poverty and suffering from discrimination and oppression. As a Latin American liberation theologian, Elsa Tamez never loses sight of these issues when she reads the Bible. They are primary in her interpretations because, to Tamez, the study of the Bible is not a privatized, personalized, or historicized exercise. It is an academic practice with far-reaching socio-political, economic, and ecclesiological ramifications, and therefore her readings are always connected to people's lived experiences.

A retired professor of Biblical Studies at the Latin American Biblical University in San Josè in Costa Rica, a translation consultant at the United Biblical Societies, and a theological advisor for the Latin American Council of Churches, Tamez insists on contextualizing biblical interpretations. Grounded in liberation theological theory and practice, Tamez's hermeneutics makes strong connections between biblical text and the contemporary world. This approach does not enjoy mainstream academic recognition because it challenges the scholarly, socio-political, economic, and religious status quo. For instance, it is impossible for Tamez to discuss the prophetic poem in Isaiah 65, written during the Babylonian exile, without explicit references to Latin American poverty and gender violence. Read in the context of Latin America, Isaiah 65 emerges as a vision that refers directly to contemporary people's hopes and "encapsulates the life we desire, not

42. Ibid., 79–80.

the life we live."[43] To Tamez, Isaiah 65 is thus not only a poem from and about ancient Israelite times. As a feminist Protestant and Latin American theologian, she develops the meaning of Isaiah 65 in light of "being the church today" that consists mostly of women.[44] When the poem proclaims that the unhappy past is overcome, Tamez disagrees. In the lives of today's Latin American women and girls, oppression and exploitation is a daily experience. They suffer from poverty and violence, and Tamez urges us to read the poem in the context of their socio-political and economic conditions.

This hermeneutical move, characterizing Tamez's approach to biblical texts, has made her well known beyond the narrow confines of the biblical guild. Tamez publishes in non-biblical journals and magazines, and so the reach of her writing is uncommonly broad. Her primary allegiance is with impoverished people on her continent, making her interpretative work highly politicized. She always addresses the suffering of women, men, and children in Latin America and relates it to biblical meaning.

Born into a Protestant family in 1950, Tamez grew up in Mexico, a deeply Catholic country. She remembers that during her childhood she was discriminated against for being Protestant. Encouraged by their parents, children bullied her in school, and when she was a teenager living in Mexico City, Catholic "fanatics" threw stones at her church. She "had to learn to be an evangelical in a mainly Catholic country,"[45] but she does not feel bitter about her experiences of religious discrimination. Later she studied Protestant Theology at the Latin American Bible Seminary in Costa Rica, the institution where she taught prior to her retirement.

In the early years, Catholic students or faculty members were not part of the Seminary community, and the school distributed anti-Catholic manuals and anti-Catholic courses were part of the Protestant theological curriculum. In 1969, when Tamez began her theological studies, the Seminary was a conservative Protestant institution. Four years later, she earned a Bachelor's degree in Theology and, in 1979, she received a Licentiate of Theology. In 1990, she was awarded a doctorate in Theology from the University of Lausanne, Switzerland.[46] Today, the Latin American Bible Seminary nurtures ecumenical dialogue among students and faculty who represent the full spectrum of Christian denominations. Lay

43. Elsa Tamez, "An Ecclesial Community: Women's Visions and Voices," *Ecumenical Review* 53 (1) (January 2001): 57.

44. Ibid., 58.

45. Elsa Tamez, "Living Ecumenically: An Absolute Necessity: Reflections from Academic Experience," *Ecumenical Review* 75 (7) (January 2005): 15.

46. In addition, she hold a Bachelor degree in Literature and Linguistics (1983, *Bachillerator en Literatura y Lingüística*) and Licentiate in Literature and Linguistics (1985, *Licenciatura en Literatura y Lingüística*) from the National University in Heredía, Costa Rica. See her dissertation, *Amnesty by Grace: Justification by Faith from a Latin American Perspective* (Nashville: Abingdon Press, 1993). See also her *The Scandalous Message of James: Faith Without Works is Dead* (New York: Crossroad, 1990).

Catholics as well as nuns and priests, Protestants, including Pentecostals, and students and teachers with indigenous spiritualities are part of the seminary community. Indigenous and traditional African religions have become increasingly visible, challenging faculty and students towards inclusive ecumenical positions.

These combined experiences—her childhood and a career as a biblical scholar—have all contributed to turning Tamez into a committed and outspoken proponent of ecumenism who articulates the relationship between anti-ecumenical attitudes and social injustice. Tamez is a strong supporter of educating people about the "vital importance of ecumenism today"[47] because she is convinced that "the more ecumenical living that there is amongst Christians from different churches as well as with the Jewish, African, and indigenous religions that are represented here [in Latin America], the less violence there will be, and the more prepared, available and understanding people will be towards other religions ..."[48] She is also convinced that ecumenical living leads to less gender violence and the elimination of poverty among Latin American peoples and elsewhere. Yet the development of ecumenical living presupposes a re-reading of the Bible which, to Tamez, is essential for a social transformation toward justice and peace. Such a re-reading of the Bible requires a hermeneutics that counters and disqualifies interpretations which "justify positions of inequality."[49] Her hermeneutics is therefore closely aligned with political commitments in support of social change and improvements in the lives of poor and disadvantaged people. Clearly, Tamez's approach is different from the often reclusive ideals of biblical studies and academia in general. Hers is grounded in the theological-feminist commitment toward ecumenical dialogue and practice.

Tamez's concern for feminist biblical studies is, then, not purely academic, and she views herself as standing within the tradition of Latin American liberation theologies more so than in the tradition of Western feminist Bible readings. That is not to say that Tamez rejects the latter. Yet her theological commitment to "the preferential option of the poor"—the classic principle of Latin American liberation theology—makes her prioritize social and economic justice and peace for oppressed people, female and male. Tamez is a feminist theologian because, as she explains, the goal to eradicate poverty in Latin America and elsewhere is a feminist goal. After all, 70 percent of the world's poor are women.[50] The "feminization of poverty" makes it necessary to combine feminist with economical analyses, and much of Tamez's work has done just that.

For instance, in her book *The Bible of the Oppressed* she examines the terminology of poverty in biblical literature.[51] She shows that the biblical God is on the side of poor people and their plight is central to ancient Israelite writers who

47. Ibid.
48. Ibid., 17.
49. Tamez, "Ecclesial Community," 62.
50. Ibid., 59.
51. Elsa Tamez, *Bible of the Oppressed* (Maryknoll, NY: Orbis Books, 1982).

detest economic exploitation and seek financial security for women, men, and children. Tamez's support of an egalitarian economy that permeates biblical prose and poetry parallels her commitment to reading the Bible with the eyes of Latin American poor people. God sides with poor people in Israelite times, and so God sides with Latin American people living in poverty today. Since in our time most poor people are women, gender issues cannot be separated from economic analysis. Accordingly, to Tamez, God is on the side of poor women.

Sometimes, Tamez writes explicitly about female biblical characters, but even then economic issues are always integral to her interpretations. For instance, Tamez writes about Hagar as "the woman who complicated the history of salvation." The enslaved woman who bears a child to Sarah and Abraham (Gen. 16; 21) emerges as a poor single mother like many Latin American poor and single mothers who lack adequate emotional and financial support and are forced to raise their children alone. The biblical story of Hagar shows that God acts on their behalf and, as a result, Christians, too, need to be on their side.[52] In short, Tamez's approach is a contextualized approach to the Bible; hers is a Latin American hermeneutic intertwined with feminist, indigenous, and African Latin perspectives.

Tamez's feminist biblical work goes hand in hand with the ethical needs of Latin American societies in which poverty prevails, and the Bible is an aid to "illuminate a miserable present" in which "objectivity is impossible."[53] Tamez always deals with the patriarchal, imperialist, and racist traditions in the Bible, the world, and in the churches. She recognizes that her hermeneutics is partial, context-specific, and a contribution to a society "where there is room for all men and women."[54] Its starting point is "real life, corporeal and sensual, lived in different concrete contexts," and it searches for "a word of encouragement, dignity, solidarity, and strength" for the poor, marginalized, and excluded.[55] Her goal is to

---

52. Elsa Tamez, "The Woman Who Complicated the History of Salvation," in John S. Pobee and Bärbel von Wartenberg-Potter (eds), *New Eyes For Reading: Biblical and Theological Reflections By Women From the Third World* (Geneva: World Council of Churches, 1966), 5–17. Among her publications are also edited volumes and articles such as: *Against Machismo: Interviews with Male Latin American Liberation Theologians* (Yorktown Heights, NY: Meyer-Stone Books, 1987); "Women's Rereading of the Bible," in Virginia Fabella and Mercy Amba Oduyoye (eds), *With Passion & Compassion* (Maryknoll, NY: Orbis Books, 1988); *Through Her Eyes: Women's Theology from Latin America* (Maryknoll, NY: Orbis Books, 1989).

53. Ibid., 9. Her book, *When the Horizons Close; Rereading Ecclesiastes* (Maryknoll, NY: Orbis Books, 2000), stresses the globalized economics of the twenty-first century as the crucial context for reading Qoheleth but it does not contain explicit feminist references. She sees both women and men affected by "the inversion of values" (7) that imperialist economic success enforced on Qoheleth's and Tamez's contemporaries.

54. Elsa Tamez, "Rereading the Bible Under a Sky Without Stars," in Walter Dietrich and Ulrich Luz (eds), *The Bible in a World Context: An Experiment in Contextual Hermeneutics* (Grand Rapids, MI: Eerdmans, 2002), 10.

55. Ibid., 9, 7.

create connections between gender and class and to contribute to economic and gender justice in our world, both now and in the future.

From Math to Feminist Theology: The Story of Marie-Theres Wacker (1952)

Neither an academic career nor feminist theology were clearly defined goals when Marie-Theres Wacker began her university studies as a young woman after the obligatory thirteen years of schooling in West Germany. Her high school teacher introduced her to the possibility of theology as an academic discipline and impressed her tremendously when he wrote Akkadian words on the chalkboard. The young student knew immediately that she wanted to know more about this ancient language and the world from which it had derived. Wacker loved learning ancient and modern languages and was eager to learn more about her Catholic faith, its history, and dogmatic teachings. Yet as the first family member to go to college, she received only skepticism from her parents when she told them of her desire to study Catholic theology. "This is nothing for a girl and you cannot become a priest either," they explained.

To appease their concerns for her future, Wacker decided to train as a high school teacher in both mathematics and Catholic theology. In Germany, the academic training for teachers is quite comprehensive and requires aspiring teachers to obtain a master's degree. Wacker began her studies at the University of Bonn, majoring in mathematics and classical Greek from 1971 to 1974. As customary for many students at German universities, she changed the university after a preliminary degree (*Vordiplom*), and from 1974 to 1977 she attended the University of Tübingen. There she completed her degree in Catholic Theology (*Diplom*) in 1977. Her original desire to study theology had outrun parental advice, and she had dropped the goal of becoming a school teacher and instead had begun pursuing an academic career in Catholic theology.

Looking for more theology, she went on to study at the École Biblique in Jerusalem, Israel, from 1977 to 1978, and began focusing on the Hebrew Bible, the field in which a year later she began her doctoral studies at the University of Tübingen. In 1981, she completed her doctorate with a thesis on a Jewish apocalyptic book, the Ethiopian book of Enoch.[56] Typical for the German academic system at the time, she began working as an academic assistant to Old Testament professor, Peter Eicher, at the University of Paderborn and taught as an adjunct professor at other theology departments at several German universities. In May 1995, she completed a second doctoral thesis, a unique German academic requirement called *Habilitation*, which made her eligible to work as a full-time professor in Germany. Since 1998, Wacker has been professor of Hebrew Bible and Women's Research in Theology at the University of Münster. During this

---

56. Her thesis was published as *Weltordnung und Gericht: Studien zu 1 Henoch 22* (Forschung zur Bibel, 45; Würzburg: Echter Verlag, 1982).

fairly traditional regimen of German university training, Wacker morphed from a student of mathematics, trying to please her parents, to an accomplished feminist Hebrew Bible scholar.

Yet even today Wacker has the air of a mathematician about her. Her work is systematically numbered—certainly also a characteristic of German academic prose, she evaluates minutely the various exegetical arguments, and she always carefully tests the inherent logic of other positions. Wacker acknowledges freely that her female students pushed her towards feminist theology in the early 1980s, but once she stared reading feminist scholarship, she was hooked. Ever since, she has embraced questions and concerns of the feminist movement and its impact on theology. In Germany during the 1980s, feminist writers had just discovered the matriarchal era of pre-biblical goddess religions and Wacker began examining the historical, literary, and cultural issues involved in ancient goddess research and its significance for biblical monotheism and feminist biblical interpretations.[57]

Writers on ancient goddess religions, such as Heide Göttner-Abendroth, Elga Sorge, Eliszabeth Gould David, and Gerda Weiler, reached large audiences in the late 1970s and early 1980s as they reconstructed goddess worship and women-centered societies in pre-biblical times.[58] In their historical reconstructions, the biblical God emerges as a victorious symbol of patriarchy that erased matriarchal and goddess traditions from cultural, political, and religious memory. Wacker has been one of the first feminist Hebrew Bible scholars who explains why such a historical description is problematic from a Christian feminist-theological perspective. These reconstructions advance patriarchal and anti-Jewish values, especially as promoted by Gerda Weiler, when they depict a time in which women led empowered and self-defined lives. During this time period, nature was supposedly not exploited because people considered it as holy and an access

---

57. See, e.g. her edited books: *Der Gott der Männer und die Frauen* (Düsseldorf: Patmos, 1987); *Theologie feministisch: Disziplinen, Schwerpunkt, Richtungen* (Düsseldorf: Patmos, 1988); *Der eine Gott und die Göttin: Gottesvorstellungen des biblischen Israel im Horizont feministischer Theologie* (with Erich Zenger) (Freiburg: Herder, 1991). See also her articles in journals and anthologies, such as: "Kosmisches Sakrament oder Verpfändung des Körpers? 'Kultprostitution' im biblischen Israel und im hinduistischen Indien," *Biblische Notizen* 61 (1992): 51–75; "Gottes Groll, Gottes Güte und Gottes Gerechtigkeit im Joel-Buch," in Ruth Scoralick (ed.), *Das Drama der Barmherzigkeit Gottes* (Stuttgart: Katholisches Bibelwerk, 2000), 107–24; "God as Mother? On the Meaning of a Biblical God-Symbol for Feminist Theology," in Anne E. Carr and Elisabeth Schüssler Fiorenza (eds), *Motherhood: Experience, Institution, Theology* (Edinburgh: T&T Clark, 1989), 103–11.

58. See the detailed analyses by Marie-Theres Wacker, especially "Matriarchale Bibelkritik—ein antijudaistisches Konzept?," in Leonore Siegele-Wenschkewitz (ed.), *Verdrängte Vergangenheit, die uns bedrängt: Feministische Theologie in der Verantwortung für die Geschichte* (München: Kaiser, 1988), 181–242. See also Tikva Frymer-Kensky, *In the Wake of the Goddess: Women, Culture, and the Biblical Transformation of Pagan Myth* (New York: Macmillan, 1993); Tikva Frymer-Kensky, "Goddesses: Biblical Echoes," in *Studies in Bible and Feminist Criticism* (Philadelphia: The Jewish Publication Society, 2006), 69–83.

point to the divine. This spirituality celebrated archetypal images and streams of consciousness about the Great Goddess whereas the Hebrew Bible supposedly created patriarchal domination over women and goddess. Wacker rejects this negative assessment of the Hebrew Bible and characterizes it as anti-Jewish because it blames Judaism for patriarchy. To her, goddess historians stand in the long anti-Jewish tradition of Western Christianity which culminated in the Holocaust in Nazi Germany.

Wacker also maintains that Western history gives ample evidence of how anti-Jewish attitudes and misogyny often joins forces to enhance patriarchal domination. A historical reconstruction that considers early Jewish life as the main cause for the demise of matriarchy reproduces only patriarchal structures and has to be dismantled and unilaterally rejected. Moreover, this kind of historiography is not new, Wacker observes,[59] but repeats patterns of patriarchal historiography.

In her systematic deconstruction of matriarchal historiography, Wacker turns her attention to research on biblical monotheism.[60] She wants to understand how biblical traditions articulate faith in the one God and relate to ancient Near Eastern traditions of the goddess. Thus, in the 1990s, Wacker writes and co-edits several books and many articles on biblical monotheism. She also completes her *Habilitation*, a study on the prophetic book of Hosea, which combines her various research interests: reading the Hebrew Bible from a woman-focused perspective, engaging the historical quest for the goddess, and examining androcentric interpretations.[61] A dense scholarly analysis and a detailed reinterpretation of many Hosea texts, the study examines Hosea from the perspective of "a woman." Wacker emphasizes the literary presentation of feminine metaphors and language, and she conceptualizes her feminist re-reading in contrast to past and present androcentric interpretations. The *Habilitation* is a learned contribution to both androcentric and feminist scholarship that does not only re-read important

59. See her argumentation, e.g. in "Matriarchale Bibelkritik—ein antijudaistisches Konzept," in *Verdrängte Vergangenheit*. See also her article "Feminist Theology and Anti-Judaism: The Status of the Discussion and the Concept of the Problem in the Federal Republic of Germany," *Journal of Feminist Studies in Religion* 61 (1992): 51–7; Luise Schottroff and Marie-Theres Wacker (eds), *Von der Wurzel getragen: Christlich-feministische Exegese in Auseinandersetzung mit Antijudaismus* (New York: Brill, 1996).

60. See, e.g. Wacker, "Feministisch-theologische Blicke auf die neuere Monotheismus-Diskussion: Anstösse und Fragen," in Wacker and Zenger (eds), *Der eine Gott und die Göttin* (Freiburg: Herder, 1991), 17–48; Wacker, "God as Mother," in Carr and Schüssler Fiorenza (eds), *Motherhood: Experience, Institution, Theology* (Edinburgh: T&T Clark, 1989), 103–11.

61. Marie-Theres Wacker, *Figurationen des Weiblichen im Hosea-Buch* (Freiburg: Herder, 1995). See also her articles on the topic: "Spuren der Göttin im Hoseabuch," in Bob Becking and Meindert Dijkstra (eds), *On Reading Prophetic Texts: Gender-Specific and Related Studies in Memory of Fokkelien van Dijk-Hemmes* (Leiden and New York: Brill, 1996), 265–82.

passages such as Hosea 1–3 but it also includes Hosea 4–14, biblical texts particularly relevant for ancient goddess research. Wacker refers consistently to historical critical concerns, source criticism and ancient Near Eastern references, and so the arguments are complex and detail-oriented—certainly a typical characteristic of any *Habilitation*. Yet despite the academic agenda, Wacker wants her work to be understood within the contexts of both a church-oriented and particularly Catholic tradition that relies on the second women's movement in Germany and biblical research for discussions on ecclesiological practice.[62]

During her emerging scholarly career, Wacker marries her husband, Bernd, also a theologian with a doctorate, and they raise two children. He has supported her fully in her academic career and performed the main responsibility of child care so that she had the necessary research time. This is a rare arrangement even today, and Wacker feels lucky to have met her supportive partner. She also remembers that during the heyday of feminism in Germany during the 1980s it was not always easy for her as a married woman to find acceptance in feminist groups. Does she not live the patriarchal norms of heterosexual marriage, which many feminists characterize as oppressive to women? Wacker has developed a nuanced understanding about what it means to be a feminist based on a saying credited to Jesus: "Anyone who is not against us is for us" (Mk 9:40). To her, a person is a feminist when s/he is committed to work against gender discrimination and the elimination of gender stereotypes and role expectations for women. With this definition in mind, she reads the Hebrew Bible as a historical and literary document of ongoing relevance to women today and tomorrow. She defines the current feminist-theological challenge as transmitting her generation's accomplishments to the next generation of women scholars, pastors, and teachers. Her many articles, books, and co-edited volumes assist in this knowledge transfer.[63]

62. Wacker's conclusion articulates these issues, see *Figurationen des Weiblichen*, 327–30.

63. Luise Schottroff and Marie-Theres Wacker (eds), *Kompendium Feministische Bibelauslegung* (2nd edn; Gütersloh: Chr. Kaiser/Gütersloher Verlagshaus, 1999). The commentary is translated into English in 2012; see *Feminist Biblical Interpretation: A Compendium of Critical Commentary on the Books of the Bible and Related Literature*, trans. Martin Rumscheidt et al. (Grand Rapids, MI: Eerdmans, 2012). See also Luise Schottroff, Silvia Schroer, and Marie-Theres Wacker, *Feminist Interpretation: The Bible in Women's Perspective* (Minneapolis, MN: Fortress, 1998); Marie-Theres Wacker, "Rizpa oder: Durch Trauer-Arbeit zur Versöhnung (Anmerkungen zu 2 Sam 21, 1–14)," in Kalus Kiesow und Thomas Meurer (eds), *Textarbeit: Studien zu Texten und ihrer Rezeption aus dem Alten Testament und der Umwelt Israels* (Festschrift für Peter Weimar) (Münster: Ugarit Verlag, 2000), 545–67.

And the Next Generation: A Conclusion

The third generation of feminist interpreters is currently emerging worldwide emphasizing the need to bring gendered readings into conversation with questions about race, ethnicity, class, postcolonialism, cultural studies, queer studies, and post-postmodernity.[64] In this sense, then, the future of feminist biblical studies looks bright. Yet there should also be some concern at a time when Western societies in Europe, North America, and Australia are increasingly torn between a post-biblical culture and Christian fundamentalism with its emphasis on a literal, historicizing, and narrowly defined faith-based approach to the Bible.[65] Conservative Christian readings appear to become increasingly popular in African, Asian, and Latin American churches.

This situation puts the next generation of feminist Bible scholars in a difficult position. On the one hand, their interpretations presuppose a theologically sophisticated audience of readers, which is increasingly difficult to obtain in post-biblical societies. On the other hand, secularized people lack the educational basis that, for instance, Phyllis Trible found so valuable in her own religious upbringing. Her love of the Bible was in no uncertain ways inspired by Sunday school classes "where sword drills were routine and memory verses mandatory."[66] Recall, too, Athalya Brenner's admission that she feels "stuck" with the Bible, and that she "cannot shake it off."[67]

This emotional connection to the Hebrew Bible has certainly changed in the minds of many feminist interpreters of the third generation. We are far removed from a time when people considered the Bible as the main cause for

64. See, e.g. the following publications: Caroline Vander Stichele and Todd Penner (eds), *Her Master's Tools? Feminist and Postcolonial Historical-Critical Discourse* (Atlanta, GA: Society of Biblical Literature, 2005); Yeong-Mee Lee, *Isaiah's Theology of Salvation with Special Attention to the Female Imagery of Zion* (Seoul: Malgunulim, 2004 [Korean]); Kwok, Pui-lan, *Discovering the Bible in the Non-Biblical World* (Eugene, OR: Wipf and Stock, 2003); Hedwig-Jahnow-Forschungsprojekt (ed.), *Körperkonzepte im Ersten Testament: Aspekte einer feministischen Anthropologie* (Stuttgart: W. Kohlhammer, 2003); Musa W. Dube (ed.), *Other Ways of Reading: African Women and the Bible* (Atlanta and Geneva: Society of Biblical Literature/WCC Publications, 2001); Musa W. Dube, *Postcolonial Feminist Interpretation of the Bible* (St. Louis: Chalice, 2000); Walter Dietrich and Ulrich Luz (eds), *The Bible in a World Context: An Experiment in Contextual Hermeneutics* (Grand Rapids, MI: Eerdmans, 2002); Phyllis Bird (ed.), *Reading the Bible as Women: Perspectives from Africa, Asia, and Latin America* (Atlanta: Scholars Press, 1997). For a comprehensive listing of recent publications in this research area, see my "Feminist Scholarship of the Old Testament," *Oxford Bibliographies Online Research Guides* (2012), http://www.oxfordbib-liographies.com/view/document/obo-9780195393361/obo-9780195393361-0020.xml (last accessed and updated June 18, 2015).

65. See Chapter 7 of this book for details and the scholarly feminist literature.

66. Trible, "Take Back the Biblem," 428.

67. Brenner, "The Hebrew God and His Female Complements," 70.

androcentrism or when they believed that a critical analysis of sexist passages would dismantle sexist forces in society, as Elisabeth Cady Canton once asserted forcefully. Children growing up in Christian fundamentalist churches might still share some of the feelings expressed by earlier generations of feminist Bible readers, but even they are confronted with the phenomenon of people distancing themselves from religiously defined worldviews. Christian fundamentalists are therefore often more apologetic and defensive towards the Bible than earlier faith-based hermeneutics ever were.

The third generation of feminist scholars of the Hebrew Bible, then, needs to address this increasingly post-biblical context tainted by religious conservatism and even fundamentalism. Today, we might feel compelled to devise marketing strategies to explain why it still makes sense to spend considerable resources on the study of the Bible. The dominant economic ideology of free-market capitalism does not like to support intellectual endeavors that do not promise immediate profit and power. Biblical studies, feminist or not, do not speak to mainstream audiences that favor a celebrity culture, shallow diversion from everyday concerns, and spiritual fast-foods.

The challenge therefore is to analyse biblical literatures constructively without repeating old-seated patterns of oppression and discrimination. It seems high time to develop ways of reading biblical texts that foster intellectual-religious maturity, historical-cultural understanding, and literary-ethical engagement. Athalya Brenner puts it succinctly, as already partially quoted in the Introduction chapter of this volume:

> *Quo vadis*, feminist biblical scholarship? *Quo vadis*, postcolonial scholarship? What is beckoning? Where do you want to go? Is the Master's House still the house you long to possess, only that you would like to become its legitimate(d) masters and mistresses instead of marginal(ized) lodgers? ... Should we not simply demolish the house instead of merely deconstructing it and its inhabitants, in order to build a completely new one instead? ... Indeed, whose Bible is it anyway? The contenders are many and the audiences are dwindling, as we are becoming more and more radicalized. Whose scholarship will matter, say, twenty-five years hence?[68]

So where will the field be in twenty-five years? Have we accomplished everything that needs to be done? Wherever we stand on this matter, it seems clear that feminist biblical studies have accomplished much in the past forty years. The sampled stories of Phyllis Trible, Athalya Brenner, Elsa Tamez, and Marie-Theres Wacker encourage us to develop further bold, creative, and innovative exegetical studies and to examine fully the historico-cultural impact of the Hebrew Bible on women's and gendered lives in the past and present.

---

68. Brenner, "Epilogue: Babies and Bathwater on the Road," in Vander Stichele and Penner (eds), *Her Master's Tools*, 338.

Chapter 3

GENDERING THE HEBREW BIBLE: METHODOLOGICAL CONSIDERATIONS

The previous two chapters described the history of women reading the Hebrew Bible and introduced representative contemporary women scholars and their work. It is now time to discuss the main methods with which feminist scholars have interpreted the Hebrew Bible during the past few decades. The discussion follows the order of the so-called "Hermeneutical Triangle" that organizes the main methodological approaches around a triangle's three corners. The methods are historical, literary, and cultural criticism. They have shaped the scholarly study of biblical literature since the beginning of the modern era. The following describes first the purpose and goals of each method and then selectively presents each method's contributions to feminist biblical scholarship.

Historical Criticism

Although all three methods have enjoyed prominence at various times and all of them continue to inform feminist biblical work, the development of historical criticism marks the beginning of modern biblical research and scholars rely on this development whether they are historical, literary, or cultural critics. Since the emergence of historical criticism went hand-in-hand with the modern scientific world view, the method has been singularly important for biblical studies and continues to enjoy special status in the field. Some contemporary Bible scholars still do not accept any other method as academically legitimate.[1] Because of its chronological primacy and ongoing significance, then, historical criticism appears on the top corner of the hermeneutical triangle. Historical criticism provides the tools to learn more about biblical authorship and the settings from which biblical texts emerged. Due to discoveries made under the aegis of historical criticism, scholars question divine authorship and the historicity of biblical claims about the origins of the universe and many events described in the Bible. Initially, the

---

1. For a discussion of recent methodological trends from the perspective of a historical critic, see John Collins, *The Bible after Babel: Historical Criticism in a Postmodern Age* (Grand Rapids, MI: Eerdmans, 2005).

quest for the world "behind" the text challenged religious authorities who, in turn, perceived the method as a threat to church hierarchy and doctrine. Only since the end of the nineteenth century have historical critics gained scholarly recognition in Western academia and even today the method often disturbs fundamentalist-literalist readers.[2]

Historical criticism has proven to be popular because it has inscribed itself on the modern Western mind. It seems like a "natural" approach for people raised within a modern-scientific world view, and so most people find historical questions central for understanding biblical literature. They assume that the determination of historical accuracy is the primary purpose for studying the Bible. Why else would one need to read biblical literature outside of the synagogue or church? The method, though not cutting-edge anymore, has lost little intellectual power for people taking for granted the modern scientific world view.

Women readers have also taken advantage of historical criticism, especially after earning PhDs in biblical studies and working as biblical scholars in universities, colleges and seminaries. This, of course, was not always the case. Prior to the nineteenth century when women were not allowed to receive a formal academic education except perhaps when they came from wealthy families, women readers were oblivious to the early historical-critical debates. Yet the public conflict over the historical-critical study of the Bible, especially during the latter half of the nineteenth century, brought great attention to this scholarly approach—the result being, for instance, that Elizabeth Cady Stanton referred to historical-critical issues in her commentary, *The Woman's Bible*, and even today historical criticism is a method popular among feminist scholars of the Hebrew Bible.

Literary Criticism

In the 1950s, literary criticism gained prominence in literature departments of the English-speaking academic world. Literary critics were not interested in the quest for authorial meaning because it provided only information about the history *behind* the text. Reading *within* the text, literary critics examine literature with literary methods. The interest in the literary dimensions of the Hebrew Bible emerged in biblical studies during the late 1960s and 1970s when critics started to appreciate structural patterns, verbal sequences, and stylistic devices of biblical texts. In 1969, James Muilenburg, who at the time served as the president of the Society of Biblical Literature, made an influential proposal. He suggested employing literary methodologies in biblical studies and advocated the use of

2. For more information on the development of historical criticism, see, e.g. Roy A. Harrisville and Walter Sundberg, *The Bible in Modern Culture: Baruch Spinoza to Brevard Childs* (2nd edn; Grand Rapids: Eerdmans, 2002); John Sandys-Wunsch, *What Have They Done To the Bible: A History of Modern Biblical Interpretation* (Collegeville, MN: Liturgical Press, 2005).

what came to be called rhetorical criticism.[3] Not wanting to break with the goals and standards of his field, Muilenburg proposed to study both "the texture and fabric of the writer's thought" and the careful literary structure of a literary unit's form.[4] In the late 1960s, this idea was quite radical, but slowly some biblical scholars followed his call, among them his student, Phyllis Trible.[5]

During the 1970s and 1980s, other literary approaches, such as poetics, structuralism, reader-response criticism, and deconstruction, found their way into biblical studies.[6] The growing acceptance of literary methodology has produced influential and innovative interpretations. They have increased the importance of rabbinic commentaries in a field that has long been shaped by Protestant research interests. Jewish scholars in particular have unearthed countless literary observations prevalent in rabbinic literature, making literary readings fashionable, productive and, ecumenically significant.[7] Literary methods, thus, enjoy considerable prominence in contemporary biblical studies, and also among feminist readers.[8]

Cultural Criticism

Cultural criticism concentrates on the significance of readers in the meaning-making process. It expressly investigates the interplay between text and reader. The approach has emerged quietly and on the margins since the 1970s with at

3. James Muilenburg, "Form Criticism and Beyond," *Journal of Biblical Literature* 88 (1969): 1–18.

4. Ibid., 7.

5. As mentioned in Chapter 2, she also wrote a volume on rhetorical criticism; see Phyllis Trible, *Rhetorical Criticism: Context, Method, and the Book of Jonah* (Minneapolis, MN: Fortress Press, 1994).

6. For more extensive discussions of literary methods, see The Bible and Culture Collective, *The Postmodern Bible* (New Haven: Yale University Press, 1995). See also Gale A. Yee (ed.), *Judges & Method: New Approaches in Biblical Studies* (Minneapolis, MN: Fortress Press, 1995); J. Cheryl Exum and David J. A. Clines (eds), *The New Literary Criticism and the Hebrew Bible* (Valley Forge, PA: Trinity Press International, 1993).

7. For an example of literary readings of the Bible done by Jewish and Christian scholars, see, e.g. Robert Alter and Frank Kermode (eds), *The Literary Guide to the Bible* (Cambridge, MA: Harvard University Press, 1987).

8. For feminist literary work on the Hebrew Bible, see, e.g. Alice Bach, *Women, Seduction, and Betrayal in Biblical Narrative* (Cambridge: Cambridge University Press, 1997); Katheryn Pfisterer Darr, *Far More Precious than Jewels: Perspectives on Biblical Women* (Louisville, KY: Westminster/John Knox Press, 1991); Cheryl Exum, *Fragmented Woman: Feminist (Sub)Versions of Biblical Narratives* (Valley Forge, PA: Trinity Press International, 1993; 2nd edn; London and New York: Bloomsbury T&T Clark, 2016); Yvonne M. Sherwood, *The Prostitute and the Prophet: Hosea's Marriage in Literary-Theoretical Perspective* (Sheffield: Sheffield Academic Press, 1996).

least two concurrent developments: challenges raised by liberation theologians to the social, political, and theo-religious status quo, and questions posed by politically progressive literary critics about the modern-scientific doctrines of epistemological objectivity, ethical, and, moral value-neutrality and singularity of truth.[9] The emergence of postmodern epistemologies, as most notably articulated by Jacques Derrida and Michel Foucault, also strengthened the development of cultural analysis in biblical studies.

The origins of cultural criticism are usually traced back to the British scholars Richard Hoggart and Raymond Williams, prominent figures and founders of the Centre for Contemporary Cultural Studies at the University of Birmingham in the 1950s and 1960s. Steeped in Marxist thought, Hoggart and Williams researched the ethnography of English working-class culture based on three premises:

> [T]he first is that cultural processes are intimately connected with social relations, especially with class relations and class formations; the second is that culture involves power and helps to produce asymmetries in the abilities of individuals and social groups to define and realize their needs; and the third, which follows from the other two, is that culture is neither an autonomous nor an externally determined field, but a site of social differences and struggles.[10]

According to these ideas, cultural criticism is concerned with class analysis, the investigation of various social groups, especially those that are socially marginalized, and the recognition of the inherent power struggles in the formation of culture. This delineation of the task of cultural criticism is broad, and critics recognize its apparent limitlessness and general scope. For instance, the editorial team of an anthology on cultural criticism explains that cultural studies are "committed to the study of the entire range of a society's arts, beliefs, institutions, and communicative practices."[11] To the editorial team, the approach "has no distinct methodology, no unique statistical, ethnomethodological, or textual analysis to call its own."[12] Consequently, the kind of questions asked, methods

---

9. See, e.g. Itumelung J. Mosala, *Biblical Hermeneutics and Black Theology in South Africa* (Grand Rapids, MI: Eerdmans, 1989); Gerald O. West and Musa W. Dube Shomana (eds), *The Bible in Africa: Transactions, Trajectories, and Trends* (Leiden: Brill, 2000); Bible and Culture Collective, *The Postmodern Bible* (New Haven: Yale University Press, 1995).

10. J. Cheryl Exum and Stephen D. Moore, "Biblical Studies/Cultural Studies," in *Biblical Studies/Cultural Studies* (Sheffield: Sheffield Academic Press, 1998), 22.

11. Cary Nelson, Paula A. Treichler and Lawrence Grossberg, "Cultural Studies: An Introduction," in Lawrence Grossberg, Cary Nelson and Paula Trichler (eds), *Cultural Studies* (New York: Routledge, 1992), 4. See also Kenneth Surin, "Culture/Cultural Studies," in A. K. M. Adam (ed.), *Handbook of Postmodern Biblical Interpretation* (St Louis, MI: Chalice Press, 2000), 49–54.

12. Ibid., 2.

used and, research strategies applied vary greatly depending on the goals of researchers and their disciplines.

US–American cultural critics in particular face the challenge of accountability—"how and why such work is done, not just its content"[13]—because of the acquiescing pressures of living in the most prominent and powerful capitalist society in the world. Sometimes, therefore, cultural critics propose that cultural investigations should examine connections between apparently separate cultural areas, such as science and religion, to identify common language patterns and socio-political conventions. Investigations need to focus on "the everyday terrain of people"[14] and challenge hierarchical notions of cultural practices, languages, and, conventions. By making connections between apparently separate cultural areas and by questioning established orders of hierarchy, cultural critics commit themselves to those who are disempowered, marginalized, and underrepresented in the political and economic sphere. They want to challenge the status quo because cultural criticism "requires us to identify the operation of specific practices, of how they continuously re-inscribe the line between legitimate and popular culture, and of what they accomplish in specific contexts. At the same time, cultural studies must constantly interrogate its own connection to contemporary relations of power, its own stakes."[15]

When this understanding of cultural studies is brought to the field of biblical studies, artifacts of all forms and shapes become potential research areas traditionally left unexplored by the field. Films, games, paintings, comic books, newspapers, magazines, oral traditions, music, theatre plays, online blogs, and internet websites emerge as rich resources for the understanding of biblical texts and discourse. Such work does not only demonstrate the cultural influence of the Bible throughout the centuries, but it also uncovers the centuries-old cycle of biblical meaning as re-inscribed by cultural appropriation. The Bible has undoubtedly shaped culture but culture, too, has shaped biblical meaning, which itself is shifting, turning, and open rather than historically fixed, static, and closed. In the last few years, feminist scholars have begun reading the Hebrew Bible with this methodological set of questions in mind.

The following sections describe how feminist readers apply the various methods to the reading of the Hebrew Bible. The exploration begins with historical reconstructions of women and their roles in ancient Israel. The description continues with feminist-literary approaches that highlight female characters in biblical literature. It concludes with the work of feminist scholars who examine biblical representations of gender in culture. The point of the discussion is not to be comprehensive but to provide concrete examples, texts, and scholarly

13. Ibid., 11.

14. Ibid.

15. Ibid., 13. See also the excellent discussion on the difference between "cultural analysis" and "cultural studies" by Jonathan Culler, "What Is Cultural Studies?" in Mieke Bal (ed.), *The Practice of Cultural Analysis: Exposing Interdisciplinary Interpretation* (Stanford: Stanford University Press, 1999), 335–47.

contributions and to illustrate the development of feminist biblical work as it has moved from historical to literary and cultural methodologies.[16]

Women in Ancient Israelite Society

Scholars of all ideological stripes generally agree that ancient Israelite society was patriarchal and men dominated private, and public life. But an attendant, and still unanswered, question is how precisely biblical texts reflect this reality. Since biblical writers and editors were mostly men coming from the elite strata of Israelite society, feminist scholars have tried to determine the reliability of biblical prose and poetry for the historical reconstruction of women's life in ancient Israelite society. Since there is a difference between what people say they do and what they actually do, this incongruence should also be assumed for the Hebrew Bible. Biblical texts, then, do not necessarily serve as evidence for what ancient Israelites actually did. Exterior evidence is needed, such as archaeological data and ancient Near Eastern documents, as well as anthropological and sociological theories, to create a historically reliable picture about women's lives in ancient Israel.

A comprehensive historical portrayal of Israelite women has been developed by Carol L. Meyers, Professor of Hebrew Bible at Duke University. She has presented a differentiated perspective on women in ancient Israel that challenges deeply ingrained ideas about patriarchy in biblical times.[17] Based on historical, archaeological and, anthropological analysis, Meyers argues for a model that recognizes how women's lives changed during Israelite history. She maintains that the biblical record deliberately distorts how Israelite women and men lived because the Hebrew Bible was created by elite men with distinct religious, political, and social interests who tried to advance their vision about life, customs, and order in ancient Israel. Consequently, their writings are not reliable depictions of ancient Israelite life, especially not in Israel's early time.

According to Meyers, Israelite society moved from an egalitarian to an increasingly patriarchal social order, a development that occurred during several centuries. In the earliest strata of the Iron Age, the Israelites lived in rural, small, and decentralized communities in the highlands of central Palestine. They were organized in family households in which women and men held equal status, responsibilities, and economic rights. Meyers explains that this situation is still visible in some biblical texts. For instance, the incest taboos in Leviticus 18 and 20 stem from this earliest period when people lived in complex and large family households that required strict sexual laws for a life in extended families.

---

16. For an extensive analysis of the various exegetical methods, see Susanne Scholz (ed.), *Feminist Interpretation of the Hebrew Bible in Retrospect* (Vol. 3: Methods; Sheffield: Sheffield Phoenix Press, 2016).

17. Carol Meyers, *Discovering Eve: Ancient Israelite Women in Context* (New York: Oxford University Press, 1988).

Similarly, the narratives in Genesis 12–50 reflect the early period during which Israelites were organized in large family households and each family member's work contributed equally to the group.[18] Only later ancient Israelite society began to implement patriarchal structures in which women were valued less than men. Meyers suggests that this dramatic shift occurred during the monarchic period in the tenth century BCE when much of what we now call the Hebrew Bible was composed. The writers expressed their socio-political and economic views in stories that were transmitted to them from previous generations, and they modified the tales to fit their agenda: promoting a vision of society in which women are subordinate to men.

In short, Meyers proposes that historical reconstructions on women's lives in ancient Israel take into account the influence of this literate and male power elite during the monarchic era. These men were central players in the decline of gender equality, and once their vision became reality, they controlled Israelite society. From that time onward, Israelite women enjoyed few civil, legal, and public rights. It was only then that biblical descriptions merged with the lives of actual people for it was then that the androcentrically transformed texts began to legitimize women's secondary status. This development must be remembered in historical-critical reconstructions, Meyers contends, because the monarchic and post-monarchic literature in particular does not adequately depict women's lives during the early Israelite era, a golden age for women.

Other historians do not share Meyer's optimistic assessment of women's egalitarian status in early Israelite history. One of them is Silvia Schroer, professor of Old Testament at the University of Bern in Switzerland. She sees "fluctuation of liberation and oppression, power and powerlessness" in women's lives throughout the centuries-long history of ancient Israel.[19] The world behind the Hebrew Bible was always patriarchal, Schroer asserts, and there was never an egalitarian moment neither during the early nor the later strata of Israelite society. Consequently, all biblical texts have to be examined with a hermeneutics of suspicion. The task is to avoid perpetuating the inherent androcentric bias and to question selective biblical reports, distortions, and omissions of women's lives as accurate historical depictions.

Schroer's diachronic survey presents four main stages in Israelite history. The first stage covers the pre-historical era to the end of the late Bronze Age

---

18. Ibid., 122–38.

19. Silvia Schroer, "Diachronic Sections," in Luise Schottroff, Silvia Schroer, and Marie-Theres Wacker (eds), *Feminist Interpretation: The Bible in Women's Perspective* (Minneapolis, MN: Fortress Press, 1998), 104. See also her other publications, e.g. Silvia Schroer and Thomas Staubli, *Die Körpersymbolik der Bibel* (Gütersloh: Gütersloher Verlagshaus, 2005); Othmar Keel and Silvia Schroer, *Schöpfung: Biblische Theologien im Kontext altorientalischer Religionen* (Göttingen: Vandenhoeck & Ruprecht, 2002); Othmar Keel and Silvia Schroer, *EVA—Mutter alles Lebendigen. Frauen- und Göttinnenidole aus dem Alten Orient* (Fribourg 2004); Silvia Schroer, *Die Weisheit hat ihr Haus gebaut. Studien zur Gestalt der Sophia in den biblischen Schriften* (Mainz: Matthias Grünewald Verlag, 1996).

(c. 12000–1250 BCE), the second stage the Iron Age (1100–1000 BCE), the third stage the time of the monarchy (1000–587 BCE), and the fourth stage the exilic and post-exilic period to the end of the Persian Rule (600/587–333 BCE). Schroer describes Israelite women's history as complex and varied during each time period. Archaeological findings feature prominently in her historical descriptions, and the various literary and archaeological sources enrich understanding about the lives of Israelite women. For instance, she depicts women's lives in the exilic and post-exilic era in the fifth and sixth centuries BCE in this way:

> From the time of the Exile onwards, we need to keep in view several groups of peoples as well as diverse carriers of the religious tradition, all of which lived in highly different political, social, and cultural contexts. All of this diversity had an impact on the religious imagination. That within three generations developments diverged noticeably can be seen in the social and religious tensions that emerged when the Babylonian exiles (at most forty thousand people) were allowed to return home in approximately 520 BCE, after the Persians had conquered the ancient Near East. In all these controversies, a central role is played by women, the image of women, and the question of goddess worship. Generally speaking, the collapse of the monarchy and the destruction of the temple in Jerusalem shook profoundly the well-fortified orders of patriarchy, giving new chances to women, since the traditional role models or faith structures were no longer automatically valid. Suddenly, Israel's religious identity was once again solidly tied to family or clan, as it had been before Israel became a state .... The world of women after the Exile is made visible in an extraordinary manner in Ruth and partly in Esther.[20]

To Schroer, the exilic and post-exilic books of the Hebrew Bible provide crucial insight into the historical struggles between the androcentric biblical writers and women's religious practices and actual lives. When the Hebrew Bible is read with this conflict in mind, it provides information about women who otherwise remain in the shadows of history. For instance, prophet Jeremiah condemns women for worshipping the goddess (Jer. 44), but the same text also gives evidence of women's religious leadership in goddess worship and women's independence from the Yahweh cult.

Similarly, the book of Leviticus (e.g. Lev. 12; 15:19-33; 21; also Ezek. 44:22) testifies to androcentric efforts of controlling women's bodies and thereby reducing women's autonomy and freedom. It also contains one of the most blatantly androcentric and offensive passages, Leviticus 27, which describes men's and women's monetary value. It states: "Your valuation of a male from twenty years old up to sixty years old shall be fifty shekels of silver .... If the person is a female, your valuation shall be thirty shekels" (Lev. 27:3-4). Yet, according to Schroer, this text must be understood as an attempt of the priestly writers to cement women's secondary status during the post-exilic period, and it indicates that women and

20. Schroer, "Diachronic Sections," 132–3.

men did not necessarily conform to these androcentric views about women, sexuality, and religious practice. Otherwise the priestly elite would not have needed to describe the difference between women and men so strongly.

Moreover, during the same period other biblical texts attest to gender-egalitarian views. For instance, Deutero-Isaiah and Trito-Isaiah use inclusive language and motherly terminology for God (e.g. Isa. 43:6; 49:22; 42:14; 49:15; 51:2). To Schroer, historical feminist critics have to investigate with great care the many archaeological artifacts and biblical texts and to identify the complexities, contradictions, and alternatives present in biblical texts and in the world behind the texts. Only then, Schroer believes, will feminist historians be able to reconstruct the roles, responsibilities, and freedoms of women during the biblical era, without falling prey to the androcentric bias of the biblical authors.[21]

Literary Representations of Biblical Mothers

When feminist scholars use literary approaches, they turn their attention to the inner-textual dynamics of biblical literature. They investigate how biblical narrators characterize female characters, what they say to each other and what is omitted, how female characters act in contrast to male characters, when they are absent in the storyline and when they dominate. Feminist literary critics also examine how biblical narrators describe action, how the writers create dialogue and for whom, and whose perspective is advanced. Like other literary critics, feminist biblical scholars search for textual gaps, ambiguities, type-scenes, word repetitions, and the sequencing of stories and poems. In short, feminist critics use standard literary strategies for gaining a comprehensive understanding about the literary representations of biblical women and feminine metaphors.

Many literary interpretations—even contradictory ones—are available and this section focuses on the topic of motherhood, a central theme for feminist theory in general and biblical narrative in particular. After all, there are many women in the Hebrew Bible who are mothers, want to be mothers, or are denied motherhood, and so it is unsurprising that feminist literary critics pay attention to these mothers, among them Eve, Sarah, Hagar, Lot's daughters, Rebekah, Leah and Rachel, Bilhah and Zilpah, Ms. Manoah, Hannah, Peninnah, the Shunammite woman, and Ruth and Naomi.

The question for feminist critics is what to do with the abundance of mothers in biblical literature. Does it indicate that the Hebrew Bible contains a "depatriarchalized" strain in which women are prominent, autonomous and strong, as for instance in the story of Rebekah? Rebekah herself agrees to marriage (Gen. 24:58) and takes the initiative when she supports her favored son Jacob (Gen. 27). Is

---

21. Sometimes such studies include searching for traces of female authorship. The work of Fokkelien van Dijk-Hemmes is particularly renowned; see, e.g. Athalya Brenner and Fokkelien van Dijk-Hemmes, *On Gendering Texts: Female & Male Voices in the Hebrew Bible* (Leiden: Brill, 1996), esp. 17–109.

she not a "decisive matriarch" who "is forthright in expressing her desires and feelings"?[22] After all,

> [s]he gives a resounding affirmation of her willingness to risk going to Canaan with the servant to meet a stranger. She expresses her pain and anxiety over her difficult pregnancy and openly laments Esau's marriages to foreign women. She inquires of God without hesitation, and God speaks to her. She risks her husband's curse in obtaining the blessing for Jacob and continues to protect him when he is threatened by Esau. All of these actions are given without a polemical context, and the narrator does nothing to indicate that these were unusual activities for a woman to take.[23]

The characterization of Rebekah demonstrates that she and other Israelite mothers are of central importance in biblical literature and seemingly these women do not suffer from androcentric bias.

Literary feminist critic J. Cheryl Exum agrees at least initially with this view. She maintains that the positive characterization of mothers indicates a pro-women and anti-patriarchal tendency in biblical literature. Other narratives affirm this tendency, such as the story of Shiphra and Puah, the midwives in Exodus 1.15-21. There, too, mothers receive a positive assessment that "undermine[s] patriarchal assumptions and temper[s] patriarchal biases, often challenging the very patriarchal structures that dominate the narrative landscape."[24] Yet later in a study on biblical matriarchs, Exum questions her initial positive assessment of biblical motherhood. She asks: "And, since Genesis is the product of a patriarchal world view, in what ways do these stories of Israel's mothers serve male interests?"[25] Exum notices that in Genesis 12–25 the matriarchs are mostly absent and when they are present, they are usually secondary characters. Even when they play a prominent role, they do so only to advance the future of their sons, "the future patriarchs: either to ensure that the 'right' son becomes the bearer of the promise … or to increase Israel … but never as characters in their own right."[26] Exum thus concludes that biblical narrators are not interested in mothers for themselves. Rather mothers serve androcentric purposes that center on male characters, and most, if not all, narratives are silent on questions such as these:

---

22. Sharon Pace Jeansonne, "Rebekah: The Decisive Matriarch," in *The Women of Genesis: From Sarah to Potiphar's Wife* (Minneapolis, MN: Fortress Press, 1990), 69.

23. Ibid.

24. J. Cheryl Exum, "'Mother in Israel': A Familiar Figure Reconsidered," in Letty Russell (ed.), *Feminist Interpretation of the Bible* (Philadelphia: Westminster Press, 1985), 74.

25. J. Cheryl Exum, "The (M)other's Place," in *Fragmented Women: Feminist (Sub)versions of Biblical Narratives* (Valley Forge, PA: Trinity Press International, 1993), 96. See also the republished version with a new preface, published by Bloomsbury in 2015.

26. Ibid., 103–4

How does Sarah react to Abraham's telling foreigners she is his sister, and to being taken into a foreigner's harem? What is the suspense like for Rebekah while Jacob executes her plan for stealing the blessing? Does Leah meekly accept being used by her father to deceive Jacob, and have no reservations about the fact that Jacob, who prefers her sister, is tricked into marrying her? And how do Bilhah and Zilpah, whose point of view is never shown, react to being given to Jacob by their mistresses?[27]

In other words, Exum changes her mind, now explaining that the stories do not promote mothers and are silent on their perspectives. Although the narratives include many positive descriptions of biblical mothers, they are not free of androcentric tendencies. Exum writes: "The androcentric narrative conveys an ambivalent message about mothers."[28] The literary situation is thus complicated. On the one hand, biblical narratives acknowledge the importance of mothers for Israel's future as they are essential for the continuation of male Israel's lineage. On the other hand, biblical narratives characterize mothers as women who are "mean-spirited, deceptive, and untrustworthy" and ultimately "dangerous."[29] Biblical narratives limit women to traditionally accepted roles in patriarchal societies—motherhood—and warn women to conform to this role.

Exum's ambiguous assessment is pushed even further by Esther Fuchs.[30] This literary critic is clear why there are so many biblical narratives about mothers. To Fuchs, the stories promote motherhood as the superior female role because it reinforces androcentric convictions and strengthens patriarchal power. Fuchs states:

> The patrilineal interest in the services of the institution of motherhood explains why mother-figures are the most common and affirmed gynotypes in the biblical narrative.[31]

Because mothers conform to androcentric interests, they are popular in biblical stories. For instance, the courage and strength of Tamar helps Judah, her hesitant father-in-law and then husband, to increase his family (Gen. 38). The resourcefulness and boldness of Ruth builds up the lineage of Boaz (Ruth 4) and the

27. Ibid., 103.

28. Ibid., 135.

29. Ibid., 135–6.

30. Esther Fuchs, "The Biblical Mother: The Annunciation and Temptation Type-Scenes," in *Sexual Politics in the Biblical Narrative: Reading the Hebrew Bible as a Woman* (Sheffield: Sheffield Academic Press, 2000). See also Esther Fuchs, "The Literary Characterization of Mothers and Sexual Politics in the Hebrew Bible," in Adela Yarbro Collins (ed.), *Feminist Perspectives on Biblical Scholarship* (Atlanta: Scholars Press, 1985), 117–36. See also Esther Fuchs, *Feminist Theory and the Bible: Interrogating the Sources* (Feminist Studies and Sacred Texts; Lanham, MD: Lexington Books, 2016).

31. Ibid., 45.

humility of the Shunammite woman gives her a son (2 Kgs 4:1-16). Since biblical mothers support the males in their lives, biblical androcentrism has much to gain from uplifting the image of motherhood. It reinforces patriarchal goals, even in narratives about barren women. Their stories, too, serve patriarchy because they portray barren women as lacking control over their own fertility. Barrenness signifies that women are not agents of their own lives but depend on external forces such as God. For instance, Sarah receives a promise about her pregnancy from mysterious visitors (Gen. 18:13-14) and Rachel's request for a son depends entirely on God's memory: "Then God remembered Rachel, heard her and opened her womb" (Gen. 30:22). Fuchs explains candidly:

> By questioning the natural ability of mother-figures to give birth, and by questioning the moral stature of naturally fertile mothers, the text is questioning the rights and privileges that accrue to maternity .... Mothers are clearly essential for the survival of patriarchy, but their essential role must not be given too much credit.[32]

According to biblical ideology, then, children are from God and mothers are divine instruments perpetuating the status quo. In other words, biblical sexual politics validate motherhood because motherhood functions to validate patriarchal hierarchy, and so, according to Fuchs's literary analysis, biblical narratives provide only a superficially positive view on motherhood.

The problem is aggravated in biblical stories in which mothers are absent. This is the case in Genesis 22, known as the binding (*Akedah*) of Isaac in Judaism and the testing of Abraham in Christianity. Phyllis Trible exposes the patriarchal bias in this narrative in which Sarah, the mother of Isaac, is never mentioned. Sarah's absence is the result of androcentric bias, Trible maintains, although Sarah is attached to her only son, Isaac, and she needs to let him go and learn to attach herself to God only. The story addresses her problem and not Abraham's but androcentrism distorts this relationship between the mother and her son. Trible comments:

> Attachment is Sarah's problem. Nevertheless, Genesis 22 drops Sarah to insert Abraham. The switch defies the internal logic of the larger story. In view of the unique status of Sarah and her exclusive relationship to Isaac, she, not Abraham, ought to have been tested. The dynamic of the entire saga, from its genealogical preface on, requires that Sarah be featured in the climactic scene, that she learn the meaning of obedience to God, that she find liberation from possessiveness, that she free Isaac from maternal ties, and that she emerge a solitary individual, nonattached, the model of faithfulness. In making Abraham the object of the divine test, the story violates its own rhythm and movement .... Patriarchy has denied Sarah her story, the opportunity for freedom and blessing.[33]

---

32. Ibid., 64–5.
33. Phyllis Trible, "Genesis 22: The Sacrifice of Sarah," in Jason P. Rosenblatt and

Absent in the androcentric story, Sarah has to be reinserted into Genesis 22 for the drama to make sense. It is Sarah who has to learn to put God above her son and not Abraham. Abraham already obeys God whenever he is asked to. When God wants Abraham to leave his country, he does (Gen. 12:1-4). Abraham has also no trouble passing off his wife to other men (Gen. 12:10-20; 20:1-18). He is even at ease giving away his possessions to another king (Gen. 14:1-24), and he relinquishes power over Hagar to his wife and God (Gen. 16:1-16; 21:1-21). Abraham does not suffer from too much attachment to Isaac. According to Trible, "[n]owhere else in the entire narrative sequence does he appear as a man of attachment."[34] It is Sarah's problem that requires a divine test. Yet androcentric bias does not grant Sarah such a central literary position. The narrative replaces her with Abraham even though the story does not fit him. Trible mourns the absent mother, the missing character, and in her view only a literary focus on Sarah provides healing.

Examples like these are proof that literary analyses of biblical motherhood have produced a wide range of interpretations. They celebrate the role of mothers, dismantle the characterization of biblical motherhood as androcentric propaganda, and re-imagine the motherly presence or rather absence in the narrative. In short, feminist explorations have produced innovative and insightful literary readings on mothers in the Hebrew Bible that both conform and challenge the androcentric bias of the literary composition.

Renderings of Biblical Gender in Culture

As stated previously, cultural studies focus on the interplay of texts, histories of interpretation, and the social locations of readers. Accordingly, biblical-cultural critic, Fernando F. Segovia, defines cultural criticism as "a joint critical study of texts and readers, perspectives and ideologies" with a focus on "the flesh-and-blood reader: always positioned and interested; socially and historically conditioned and unable to transcend such conditions ...".[35] No longer is an investigation directed to go *behind* the biblical text—the task of historical criticism—or intent on discovering the literary structures *within* the text—the task of literary

Joseph C. Sitterson (eds), "*Not in Heaven*": *Coherence and Complexity in Biblical Narrative* (Bloomington: Indiana University Press, 1991), 188–9.

34. Ibid, 188.

35. See his article, "'And They Began to Speak in Other Tongues': Competing Modes of Discourse in Contemporary Biblical Criticism," in Fernando F. Segovia and Mary Ann Tolbert (eds), *Reading from this Place: Social Location and Biblical Interpretation in the United States (Vol. 1)* (Minneapolis, MN: Fortress Press, 1995), 28–9. See also his follow-up article "Cultural Studies and Contemporary Biblical Criticism: Ideological Criticism as Mode of Discourse," in Fernando F. Segovia and Mary Ann Tolbert (eds), *Reading from this Place: Social Location and Biblical Interpretation in Global Perspective (Vol. 2)* (Minneapolis, MN: Fortress Press, 1995), 1–17.

criticism. Rather, cultural critics analyse *in front of* the biblical text. They explore the geo-political, economic, social, and religious settings in which readers create their readings. The approach is based on the epistemological conviction that biblical meaning is intrinsically connected with readers and their contexts, and every interpretation is always situated, interested, and ideologically grounded "somewhere."[36]

Feminist cultural critics have joined the ardent process of investigating biblical-cultural productions. The exegetical horizon targets resources from potentially any time period and many countries, whenever and wherever gendered biblical discourse has made an impact on local history, media, and creative outlet. Yet in contrast to the numerous examples of feminist scholarship applying historical and literary methodologies, investigations on cultural renderings about women and gender are still relatively rare—though that is slowly changing. The following discussion presents examples. Studies focus mainly on biblical appropriations in Western art, film, or music but they have also come to embrace the postcolonial move and include readings of and about women from the East and the South.

The extensive history of reading biblical literature in Western culture is a vast research opportunity, and when gender is the center of attention, scholars turn to biblical women figures of great renown such as Bathsheba, Delilah, and Ruth and Naomi. It is fascinating to understand how painters, film-makers, or musicians shape women's characters from the ambiguities and gaps of biblical texts. For instance, the notion of Bathsheba as David's seducer is deeply ingrained in the Western imagination, and paintings by major Western artists significantly contributed to this view on 2 Samuel 11. As J. Cheryl Exum demonstrates in a cultural analysis on biblical women, twentieth-century Hollywood movies further inscribe this androcentric notion into cultural memory.

There are two famous cinematic versions of this story, one is called *David and Bathsheba* produced in 1951 and the other is *King David* from 1985. The 1951 film plays with the idea that Bathsheba had to obey the order from the king. In the film she says: "You are the king. What other answer can I give, sire? You have sent for me and made known to me your will, what else is there for me to say?"[37] The film entertains the possibility that Bathsheba had no choice but to obey the king, but

---

36. For biblical-cultural studies in general, see, e.g. George Aichele (ed.), *Culture, Entertainment and the Bible* (Sheffield: Sheffield Academic Press, 2000); Michael J. Gilmour, *Tangled Up in the Bible: Bob Dylan & Scripture* (New York: Continuum, 2004); J. Cheryl Exum (ed.), *Beyond the Biblical Horizon: The Bible and the Arts* (Leiden: Brill, 1999); Exum and Moore, *Biblical Studies/Cultural Studies*; Stephen D. Moore (ed.), *In Search of the Present: The Bible Through Cultural Studies* (Semeia 82; Atlanta: Society of Biblical Literature, 1998).

37. J. Cheryl Exum, "Bathsheba Plotted, Shot, and Painted," in *Plotted, Shot, and Painted: Cultural Representations of Biblical Women* (Sheffield: Sheffield Academic Press, 1996), 23. See also David M. Gunn, "Bathsheba Goes Bathing in Hollywood: Words, Images, and Social Locations," *Semeia* 74 (1996): 75–102.

in the end this view is rejected. The king replies to Bathsheba: "So I said nothing to you until you told me that there is no love in your marriage. Yes, you told me that, and so did Uriah ...".[38] David's response indicates that she is responsible for his interest in her because she told him about her unhappy marriage and places the seed in his mind. The film thus suggests that she knows what she is doing. She seduces him by bathing outside on the roof top and eventually gets what she wants. David is characterized as innocent, and so in the 1951 cinematic inter-pretation Bathsheba is held responsible for the seduction of David.

The film of 1985 pursues a slightly different path. There David does not call Bathsheba to the palace when he sees her on the roof. He has sex with her only after they are married and Uriah is dead. Yet even in this film, Bathsheba is not characterized as a hapless victim but is aware of David watching her on the roof. In this movie, too, Bathsheba is David's seducer. The film makes this clear during their first meeting. When David tells her he had seen her before, she replies, "I know."[39]

Both films advance a reading in which the woman is at least as guilty as the king, a message that is also promoted in other cultural appropriations. For instance, Rembrandt painted a famous scene of Bathsheba in which she has just come out from the bath and is naked in full view. Exum describes the painting thus:

> The imagery is essentially frontal because the sexual protagonist is the spectator/owner who is looking at it. Bathsheba's body, however, is slightly twisted, as if she were in the act of turning away, and her crossed legs are a modest gesture in relation to the spectator. The pose is ambivalent, making it difficult to decide: is she or is she not an exhibitionist? .... Whereas Bathsheba's body is turned toward us, offering itself to our view, her head is turned away, indicating her reluctance to be seen .... [The painter] has managed to reveal an inwardness and an inaccessibility in the expression of her body and face. This humanizing of the female nude tells the spectator that she is not simply naked for him.[40]

The painter leaves it to viewers to imagine the story and to fantasize about the future encounter between the couple. In androcentric culture a woman's nakedness symbolizes her willingness to participate in the scheme. Viewers turn into voyeurs and sympathize with the man, David, who understandably cannot resist the temptation. In a discussion of another but similar portrayal of Bathsheba, Exum explains: "We—and, again, I mean specifically the male spectator—are invited to identify with David's perspective by means of the woman's body, which signifies his sexual arousal. What we see is female nakedness as the cause of male desire

---

38. Ibid.
39. Ibid., 24.
40. Ibid., 32–3.

...".[41] In short, Western culture imagines Bathsheba as a willing participant in the plot, as the cause for the troubles between David and Uriah.

This pervasive cultural view of woman as trouble for man is probably most dramatically and famously set into musical score with the story of Samson and Delilah (Judg. 13–16). It should not surprise that this biblical narrative and female character has inspired many Western artists, among them musicians.[42] As the biblical archetype of a woman who overpowers a man, Delilah is the nightmare of the androcentric imagination. She is the personified seductress who kills men with her power over them and has to be avoided at all costs. Musical interpretations emphasize this lesson.

The well-known opera *Samson et Delilah* by Camille Saint-Saëns, performed to this day at major opera houses such as the Metropolitan Opera in New York, presents the woman, Delilah, as irresistible. In the opera, Delilah betrays Samson cold-bloodedly despite the sensual duet they sing just prior to the betrayal. The music makes listeners sympathize with Samson while Delilah seems deceptive, cruel, and calculating. She deserves to die and Saint-Saëns ends the opera exactly that way. Just before Samson pulls down the temple, Delilah comes back to mock him and both are buried in the ruins of the building. She, Samson, and everybody else are dead at the conclusion of the opera, an ending that differs from the biblical tale. Other operas end differently still. For instance, sometimes Delilah does not come back, seeks his forgiveness, or is portrayed as a representative for women in general whom men cannot trust because their seductiveness is dangerous to them.[43] Helen Leneman sums up the dilemma of cultural appropriations of biblical women like Delilah: "The arts have done a great deal to popularize biblical stories, but this popularization has not resolved the ambiguities of the original stories in a favorable way for the female characters."[44] After all, Western culture has long been steeped in androcentrism.

That Western culture is deeply troubled about gender issues, specifically as they relate to queer sexualities and the Bible, is also obvious. The gender trouble is also visible if one goes online and explores the Internet, that great depository of cultural cross-referencing. The story of Sodom and Gomorrah (Gen. 19) is often mentioned in debates on homosexuality and the Bible. Born-again Christians explain that sodomy is the reason for the destruction of the cities because God had to remove "this awful sin." In contrast, progressive Christians read the story as a critique of inhospitality and pride.[45] Websites present archaeological data trying to prove the historical location of the cities; commercial sites sell

41. Ibid., 33.

42. For a comprehensive survey on cultural artifacts related to this narrative, see David Gunn, *Judges* (Oxford: Blackwell, 2005), 172–230.

43. Ibid., 213–17.

44. Helen Leneman, "Portrayals of Power in the Stories of Delilah and Bathsheba: Seduction in Song," in Leonard Jay Greenspoon and Bryan F. Le Beau (eds), *Sacred Text, Secular Times: The Hebrew Bible in the Modern World* (Omaha, NE: Creighton University Press, 2000), 239.

45. For a full discussion, see Susanne Scholz, "Sodom and Gomorrah (Genesis 19:1-29)

collectibles on Sodom and Gomorrah; pornographic references make heavy use of the controversial storyline; and science fiction pages elaborate on the cities" relationship to the history of planet Earth. The Internet is replete with biblical gender terminology and so contributes to the contemporary struggle over sexuality, biblical authority, and religious fervor. Biblical terms, characters, and stories continue to be appropriated by today's culture that is dominated by androcentric and heteronormative views about women, gender, and sexuality. In short, cultural appropriations of the Hebrew Bible present overwhelming evidence for the hegemony of patriarchal bias toward women and gender, which feminist cultural critics collect, examine, and interrogate as part of the larger societal bias about women, gender, and sexuality.

Methodological Considerations: In Conclusion

This survey on the methodological appropriations by feminist biblical scholars demonstrates the wide variety of methods that have enriched and shaped feminist interpretations of the Hebrew Bible. All major methods, ranging from historical to literary and cultural criticisms, contribute to manifold examinations on women, gender, and sexuality in biblical texts. Clearly, different approaches yield different interpretative results, and the entire discussion has moved away from a simplistic model that merely rejects or accepts the Bible. Whether the studies are historical, literary, or culturally oriented, they offer nuanced and complex reasoning on gender behind, within, and in front of the biblical text. Interpretations are diverse, manifold, and complex, sometimes even opposing each other. Feminist historical critics disagree on the status of women in early Israel, and literary critics challenge each other's characterizations of biblical motherhood. Gone are the days when one single feminist voice determines the characterization of biblical literature. Nowadays, diversity, disagreement, and plurality of methodology define the field of feminist biblical studies. Some feminist scholars thus consider the ongoing marginalization of feminist biblical work as a grave problem and demand full recognition for the benefit of the entire field of biblical studies. Indeed, compared with early efforts such as Elizabeth Cady Stanton's *The Woman's Bible Commentary*, the current methodological plurality and range of feminist biblical views are nothing but impressive.

As in the field of biblical studies at large, feminist work that takes advantage of the developments in cultural criticism holds the greatest potential for innovation and significance. Cultural approaches allow researchers to investigate biblical meanings in any time period and place in which the Bible is read, argued with, and used as an authoritative text for social, political, economic, and religious policies and practices. Most recently, postcolonial feminist readers have begun examining the Bible as a significant force of colonial power. Since cultural criticism invites a

on the Internet," *Journal of Religion and Society* 1 (1999), www.creighton.edu/JRS (accessed December 12, 2016).

focus on flesh-and-blood readers, postcolonial feminist readers are in the midst of extensively researching the connections between the Bible and the implementation of all kinds of policies related to (post)colonial experiences of Third-World countries in Africa, Asia, and Latin America. Cultural criticism has thus attracted biblical interpreters far beyond the traditionally narrow boundaries of white, Western, and male-dominated scholarship. In short, many different methods have been welcomed and successfully employed and developed by feminist scholars of diverse backgrounds and social locations. Some function in more traditional academic ways; others invite seemingly limitless horizons and participation. In the process, exegetical methods support feminist interpretations developed in intellectually structured and rationally defendable ways.

Finally, the full integration of critical methods into the feminist study of the Hebrew Bible demonstrates that different methods lead to different feminist meanings. Sometimes, the same method leads to different interpretative results. Biblical meaning thus does not only depend on a particular method used by a feminist scholar, but also how she uses the chosen method in the interpretative process. Methods are only the tools that enable feminist readers to further their interpretative goals of describing the various historical phases of Israelite society, discovering new literary patterns, or identifying cultural appropriations of biblical characters, stories, and events. Exegetical methods have made it possible to create feminist readings that are complex, diverse, and vibrant whether they are grounded in historical reconstruction, literary analysis, or cultural appropriation. The choice of method is always with the readers, and their interpretative goals and social locations shape their biblical meanings. After several decades of feminist biblical work, a multiplicity of voices and interpretations enriches the discussion. For sure, future work will further contribute feminist understandings of biblical literature to history, literature, culture, politics, and religion.

Chapter 4

RAPE, ENSLAVEMENT, AND MARRIAGE: SEXUAL VIOLENCE IN THE HEBREW BIBLE

After historical, biographical, and methodological examinations, this chapter discusses how feminist scholars have dealt with the theme of sexual violence in biblical literature. Sexual violence, of course, has a much longer history than publication dates indicate, whether in the field of feminist, women's, and gender studies, or biblical studies. For centuries, sexual violence has plagued gender relations although differences in time and space have sometimes created differences in experience and reaction. Androcentric perspective usually blames the mostly female victim-survivors for rape, molestation, sexual abuse, incest, or murder. Legislation, lax or strong, has rarely deterred mostly male perpetrators from committing these crimes.

Religion, too, has contributed little to the elimination of sexual violence although the sacred texts of Christianity and Judaism contain many narratives and poems on the topic. Steeped in patriarchal ideology, interpreters have ignored these "texts of terror"[1] for centuries and when they have read them, they have found love, desire, and even mutually consensual acts in them. Condemnation of sexual violence and sympathy for victim-survivors seldom make it into commentaries and textbooks written for students of theology who train for the ministry, teaching positions, or counseling responsibilities. Only during the past few decades have feminist exegetes identified crude, aggressive, and one-sided forms of sexual relations in biblical literature.

Feminist biblical scholars began examining sexual violence in the 1970s when the feminist movement became conscious of the relentless violence against women in past and present societies. Even today, women are sexually abused, molested, raped, and murdered at astonishing rates—and to an extent that remains unabated in many countries, cultures, and traditions. Feminists have tried to explain the disproportionate violence women suffer by men, and they have connected it to bigoted institutions, policies, and customs of patriarchal societies. They have also examined histories and cultures to identify differences and similarities in the prevalence of sexual violence, and they insist on connecting

---

1. For this phrase, see Phyllis Trible, *Texts of Terror: Literary-Feminist Readings of Biblical Narratives* (Philadelphia: Fortress Press, 1984).

gender violence with other forms of discrimination such as racism, classism, the caste system, or colonialism.

The academic interest in understanding sexual violence has led to many different explanations. Early feminist theories universalize women's experiences as if the phenomenon is the same whether it occurs among the ancient Sumerians, in the Middle Ages, or in the United States today. More recently, theorists have begun challenging explanations that essentialize sexual violence, and designed historically and culturally specific studies. They show that sexual violence occurs almost anywhere and at any time although reactions and experiences vary greatly. As a result, whether sexual violence is explained on the basis of biological differences between women and men or viewed as a historically specific strategy that tyrannizes mostly women, the scholarly output has made it impossible to ignore sexual violence as a crucial research topic. Biblical scholars, too, have joined this important area of investigation and focus much attention on the contributions of the Hebrew Bible to the ongoing existence of sexual violence.

This chapter introduces the breadth and depth of biblical literature as it relates to sexual violence, particularly rape. Primary and secondary sources are abundantly available and the chapter illuminates biblical prose and poetry as well as scholarly approaches.[2] The discussion illustrates the spectrum of exegetical positions taken and biblical meanings created by feminist scholars who refuse to comply with sexual violence in the Hebrew Bible and in today's world.

Raped and Enslaved: Sexual Violence in Biblical Narrative

Many biblical narratives contain stories about sexual violence although these tales have not been at the forefront of Jewish and Christian communities for centuries.

2. For biblical and ancient Near Eastern rape legislation, see Cheryl B. Anderson, *Women, Ideology, and Violence: Critical Theory and the Construction of Gender in the Book of the Covenant and the Deuteronomic Law* (London and New York: T&T Clark International, 2004); Susanne Scholz, "Back Then It Was Legal: The Epistemological Imbalance in Readings of Biblical and Ancient Near Eastern Rape Legislation," *Journal of Religion and Abuse* 7 (3) (December 2005): 5–35; also published in *The Bible and Critical Theory* 1 (4) (December 2005), http://novaojs.newcastle.edu.au/ojsbct/index.php/bct/issue/view/4 (accessed December 12, 2016). See also the following book-length studies on rape and sexual violence in the Hebrew Bible: Susanne Scholz, *Rape Plots: A Feminist Cultural Study of Genesis 34* (New York: Lang, 2000); Cheryl A. Kirk-Duggan, *Pregnant Passion: Gender, Sex, and Violence* (Atlanta, GA: SBL Press, 2003); Mary Anna Bader, *Sexual Violation in the Hebrew Bible: A Multi-Methodological Study of Genesis 34 and 2 Samuel 13* (New York: Lang 2006); Frank M. Yamada, *Configurations of Rape in the Hebrew Bible* (New York: Lang, 2008); Caroline Blyth, *The Narrative of Rape in Genesis 34: Interpreting Dinah's Silence* (New York: Oxford University Press, 2010); Susanne Scholz, *Sacred Witness: Rape in the Hebrew Bible* (Minneapolis, MN: Fortress Press, 2010); Julia M. O'Brien, *The Aesthetics of Violence in the Prophets* (New York: T&T Clark, 2010).

They did not and still do not appear in Christian lectionaries and are rarely identified as rape stories in synagogue readings. It was only when feminist scholars began systematically studying the Hebrew Bible that they stumbled over the many narratives of rape, sexual abuse, molestation, incest, and murder. Among them are the stories of Hagar, Sarah, Rebekkah, Bilhah and Zilpah, Dinah, Lot's daughters, the anonymous woman in Gibeah, the daughters of the tribe of Benjamin, Abishag, Tamar—the daughter of King David, this king's so-called concubine, and Rizpah. In the narratives women endure sexual violence in the forms of threatened or executed rape, incest, murder, and sexual abuse. The following discussion focuses on a particular area of sexual violence—rape, which is here defined as sexual intercourse by force, fear, or threat of retaliation, and against the will of a person.

Some scholars maintain that Israelite society considered women as property of men and women never had the right to consent to sexual intercourse, especially when they were married or when marriage was promised. To these interpreters, the classification of biblical stories as rape narratives is anachronistic because the Israelites themselves did not recognize what is nowadays defined as forced sexual intercourse. They claim that women's consent did not matter in Israelite society and contemporary interpreters, too, should not impose current vocabulary onto biblical texts.[3]

This position is, however, not convincing because interpretation always involves contemporary language and perspective. Even if it were true that the Israelites did not recognize rape as a sexual violation, contemporary readers always bring contemporary vocabulary and sensitivity to the interpretative process, and in today's world the biblical texts under consideration describe specific instances of rape. Of course, androcentric readers might still not define some or most of these narratives as rape stories. But to argue that such a view is objective and historically accurate is epistemologically problematic, even deceptive, when androcentric convictions are the premise of the argumentation.[4] If readers make claims of objectivity and historical accuracy, their hermeneutical assumptions have to be carefully evaluated, especially when the topic is rape. Are they perhaps part of an androcentric strategy, unconsciously or consciously held, that tries to ignore sexual violence in the past and present? Or is the interpretation perhaps part of an effort to make the Hebrew Bible seem "rape-free" because religious texts, including the sacred texts of Christianity and Judaism, should not be involved in discussions on sexual violence? These are some of the questions that have to be addressed when rape terminology is viewed as anachronistic in biblical interpretation.

Furthermore, biblical literature has a tendency to be ambiguous, and so readers create biblical meanings. Most, if not all, narratives are inherently open for inter-pretation and do not offer easy answers. Readers decide whether they emphasize compliance with or outrage for stories that report great horror in a terse, dense,

---

3. Ellen J. Wolde, "Does 'innâ Denote Rape? A Semantic Analysis of a Controversial Word," *VT* 52 (4) (2002): 528–44.

4. For an opposing viewpoint, see Alice Ogden Bellis, "Objective Biblical Truth versus the Value of Various Viewpoints: A False Dichotomy," *Horizons in Biblical Theology* (June 17, 1995): 25–36.

and factual style. Even narratives that are one-sided and negligent of a woman's viewpoint can still be interpreted against the grain of androcentric and rape-prone meaning, if readers decide to do so. Yet if readers do not question the androcentric status quo, the ambiguity of biblical literature allows readers to turn rape into love or consensual sex, as the history of interpretation demonstrates abundantly.

In addition, the argument that in biblical times women were the "property" of men—and therefore rape did not exist in the ancient Israelite "mind"—is flawed because the historicity of biblical texts, including biblical rape stories, is far from certain. To assume a generic acceptance of rape-prone belief and behavior among ancient Israelites for many centuries reveals a stereotypical characterization of a past which remains difficult to reconstruct. Research of the last decades has demonstrated the inherent problems in establishing historical accounts of ancient Israel, and the same difficulties apply to assumptions about gender expectations, roles, and rights.[5] In short, then, the Hebrew Bible contains many rape stories that cannot be explained away with references to androcentric structures in Israelite society, politics, and economics. What is needed—and this is a central argument of this chapter—is an unapologetic look at rape in biblical literature.

As we proceed, the following pages examine the stories of two enslaved women (Gen. 29:31–30:24; 35:22) to illustrate the preponderance of rape in biblical narratives.[6] The stories of Zilpah and Bilhah are particularly important because they relate rape to the societal force of classism which leads to considerable differences among women in androcentric society. Here women of a higher class, Leah and Rachel, are co-opted into their androcentric class privilege, using strategies of sexual violation to gain societal prestige.[7]

---

5. For the current scholarly dispute on ancient Israelite historiography, see, e.g. "*Minimalists* on Parade: An Academic Conference in Rome Highlighted the Positions of Scholars Who Think the Bible Has Little or No Reliable History," *Biblical Archaeology Review* 31 (1) (January–February 2005): 16–17; Thomas L. Thompson, "The Role of Faith in Historical Research," *Scandinavian Journal of the Old Testament* 19 (1) (2005): 111–34; Hershel Shanks (ed.), "The Search for History in the Bible," *Biblical Archaeology Review* 26 (2) (March–April 2000): 22–51; Ben C. Ollenburger, "The History of Israel Contested and Revised," *Modern Theology* 16 (4) (October 2000): 529–40; Iain Provan V. Philips Long and Tremper Longman III (eds), *Biblical History of Israel* (Louisville, KY: Westminster/John Knox Press, 2003); Philips V. Long (ed.), *Israel's Past in Present Research: Essays on Ancient Israelite Historiography* (Winona Lake, IN: Eisenbrauns, 1999).

6. Another woman who is enslaved and raped during her enslavement is Hagar whose story appears in Gen. 16:1-16; 21:9-21. For a discussion on Hagar's story, see Jessica Grimes, "Reinterpreting Hagar's Story," *lectio difficilior: European Electronic Journal of Feminist Exegesis* 1 (2004), http://www.lectio.unibe.ch/04_1/inhalt_e.htm.

7. For an extensive analysis of these and related rape stories of enslaved women, see Susanne Scholz, "Gender, Class, and Androcentric Compliance in the Rapes of Enslaved Women in the Hebrew Bible," *lectio difficilior: European Electronic Journal of Feminist Exegesis* 1 (2004), http://www.lectio.unibe.ch/04_1/Scholz.Enslaved.htm (accessed December 12, 2016).

The Story of Bilhah and Zilpah

Women play a central role in Genesis 29:31–30:24, in which the prominent characters are Leah and Rachel. They compete with each other for children and husbandly love. In the process, they force their slaves, Bilhah and Zilpah, to become pregnant by Jacob (Gen. 29:31–30:24). The story is painful: One of the sisters, Leah, is "hated" by the husband, but gives birth to six sons and one daughter. When her fertility ceases, she gains two more sons from her slave, Zilpah. The other sister, Rachel, loved by her husband, is infertile. She competes with her sister's fertility by forcing her slave, Bilhah, to become pregnant by Jacob. Consequently, Bilhah gives birth to two sons. Only toward the end of the story does Rachel herself give birth to a son. In a later chapter she has another son and then she dies in child birth (cf. Gen. 35:16-20). In Genesis 29–30 two women are the main actors, and two women are their slaves. Husband Jacob appears on the margins, speaking once (Gen. 30:2), while his wives do not stop talking. The story is troubling because the sisters, Leah and Rachel, use enslaved women to secure their progeny.[8]

Yet despite the story's central placement in the book of Genesis and its significance in explaining the origins of the twelve tribes of Israel, the narrative has not gained much attention in the scholarly literature. Whether readers subscribe to traditional, feminist, or womanist perspectives, the tale of two free and two enslaved women does not figure prominently in the Jewish or Christian imagination. It is not only a story about the sisters, Leah and Rachel—both married to Jacob, but it is also one about two women, Bilhah and Zilpah, enslaved by other women who encourage their husband to rape their slaves. Perhaps Bilhah's and Zilpah's silence made them invisible to interpreters. Bilhah and Zilpah do not protest their treatment and they do not run away. They also do not encounter God unlike another enslaved woman, Hagar, who also endures sexual violence (Gen. 16:1-16; 21:1-21) and is renowned among feminist and womanist interpreters. Yet Bilhah's and Zilpah's sons become central and equal members of the twelve tribes of Israel. It seems that their oppression turns into liberation in the next generation, and God supports at least their sons.

On Whose Side Is God?

Here then lies the theological crux of the story: On whose side is God? The beginning of the narrative suggests that God supports Leah. "When Yahweh saw that Leah was unloved, God opened her womb" (Gen. 29:31). Later God also "remembers Rachel" (30:22), which leads to her long-awaited first pregnancy and the birth of Joseph. Yet no reference is made to Bilhah and Zilpah. For the enslaved women, raped and silenced, God seems absent. Womanist theologian,

---

8. Sometimes scholars suggest that this custom was common in the ancient Near East, as if to normalize a horrendous practice; see, e.g. Raymond Westbrook, "The Female Slave," in Victor H. Matthews et al. (eds), *Gender and Law in the Hebrew Bible and the Ancient Near East* (Sheffield: Sheffield Academic Press, 1998), 214–38, esp. 224–9.

Delores S. Williams, observes that biblical narratives depict God as choosing when to side with the oppressed and when to side with the oppressor.[9] In Genesis 29–30, God sides with the slave-owners, first with Leah and later with Rachel (Gen. 29:31; 30:22). This is not an attractive power dynamic for feminist and womanist readers. Is it thus surprising that Genesis 29–30 has received little exegetical attention from them?

An exception is the feminist reading of Esther Fuchs.[10] She examines the story carefully in a study on androcentrism in biblical narrative. To Fuchs, the literary characteristics of Genesis 29–30 belong to a genre that justifies polygamy with references to a wife's infertility. The genre is found both in Genesis 16 and 29–30, Fuchs argues, where it exhibits androcentric bias that always centers on men and male concerns. The husbands, Abraham and Jacob, have sex with Hagar and Leah because these women are "naturally" fertile and share "a rather dubious array of characteristics, like foreignness, pridefulness, unattractiveness."[11] The concern for the men's need for progeny justifies their polygamous behavior; it also illustrates the inherent androcentric nature of biblical narratives.

While Fuchs's interpretation should be commended for dealing with Genesis 29–30, its lack of class analysis is problematic. According to Fuchs, Leah is a victim of patriarchy despite the fact that in the world of the narrative Leah actively participates and benefits from her social status as a slave-owning woman. Fuchs ignores the differences in the social positions of Hagar and Leah, as if the women's shared fertility were the only characteristics for their fate in society. Yet Hagar is an enslaved woman and Leah a married woman of considerable social status. Unlike Hagar, Leah is not a slave who is raped by the husband of her owner. She complies with androcentric standards when she demands sexual intercourse with her husband. Leah also holds power as a slave-owning woman who forces her slave, Zilpah, to have sex with her husband. It would thus be more appropriate to compare the fate of Hagar with the enslaved women, Zilpah and Bilhah, and not with Leah.[12]

---

9. Delores S. Williams, *Sisters in the Wilderness: The Challenge of Womanist God-Talk* (Maryknoll, NY: Orbis Books, 1993), 199.

10. For other feminist interpretations, see, e.g. Irmtraud Fischer, "Genesis 12–50: Die Ursprungsgeschichte Israels als Frauengeschichte," in Luise Schottroff und Marie-Theres Wacker (eds), *Kompendium Feministische Bibelauslegung* (2nd edn; Gütersloh: Gütersloher Verlagshaus, 1998), 19.

11. Esther Fuchs, *Sexual Politics in the Biblical Narrative: Reading the Hebrew Bible as a Woman* (Sheffield: Sheffield Academic Press, 2000), 63.

12. Ibid., 63, 154–5, 158. For a parallelism of Hagar and the two enslaved women, see, e.g. Cynthia Gordon, "Hagar: A Throw-Away Character Among the Matriarchs?," in Kent H. Richards (ed.), *Society of Biblical Literature 1985 Seminar Papers* (Cambridge, MA: Society of Biblical Literature, 1985), 273; Renita J. Weems, "Do You See What I See? Diversity in Interpretation," *Church & Society* 82 (September–October 1991): 35; Ina J. Petermann, "'Schick die Fremde in die Wüste!' Oder: Sind die Sara-Hagar-Erzählungen aus Genesis 16 und 21 ein Beispiel (anti-)rassistischer Irritation aus dem Alten Israel?" in Silvia

Fuchs is not the only interpreter ignoring the class distinctions in Genesis 29–30. Other interpreters, too, neglect this aspect and prefer to focus on God's support of Rachel and Leah, the slave-owning women. Generally, scholars approve of God's support because they disregard Bilhah and Zilpah. For instance, commentator Hermann Gunkel expresses relief about God helping Leah and Rachel when he elaborates: "That Yahweh cares for the despised is a comforting belief: Yahweh helps the poor, the despised, the despairing, the fugitive slave (16.7ff.), the rejected child and his unfortunate mother (21.17ff.), the shamefully sold and slandered (39.2, 21ff.)."[13] To Gunkel, the fact that Leah and Rachel receive God's help while they also hold slaves does not enter his discussion.

Similarly, Gerhard von Rad highlights God's role in Leah's life: "After all the thoroughgoing worldliness of the previous story, God is again the subject of the event. He is the one who blesses and comforts the neglected wife."[14] Like Gunkel, von Rad focuses on the fact that God brings fertility to one of the wives, ignoring that she forces her slave to have sexual intercourse with her husband. Even feminist interpreter, Elyse Goldstein, does not relate the fate of Bilhah and Zilpah to God's one-sided support of Leah and Rachel. She writes: "God rewards Leah with fertility to make up for her troubles with her husband, and the women are now equalized. One gets a man's love; the other gets a child's love. One woman gains status through her husband, the other woman status through her children."[15]

These and other interpreters appreciate God's option for the "despised" but they disregard the complex social position in which the narrative places Leah and Rachel. In other words, scholars regard Leah's fertility as a blessing and are pleased that God supports Leah and Rachel while they disregard Bilhah's and Zilpah's situation. Ultimately, however, divine care does not benefit Leah or Rachel, as Fuchs stresses. Communication between God and the women functions merely as divine justification for the institution of motherhood. Like other stories, Genesis 29–30 describes androcentric and hierarchical order as divine order. Once the women, free or enslaved, give birth to sons, they become superfluous in the world of the narrative. They disappear or die eventually. The story does not endorse feminist values, except perhaps when it is understood as an illustration about the traps of androcentric and class-driven ideology for women, free or enslaved.

Wagner, Gerdi Nützel and Martin Kick (eds), *(Anti-)Rassistische Irritationen: Biblische Texte und interkulturelle Zusammenarbeit* (Berlin: Alektor Verlag, 1994), 140.

13. Hermann Gunkel, *Genesis*, trans. Mark E. Biddle (Macon, GA: Mercer University Press, 1997), 324.

14. Gerhard von Rad, *Genesis: A Commentary* (Philadelphia: Westminster, 1972), 294.

15. Elyse Goldstein, *ReVisions: Seeing Torah Through a Feminist Lens* (Woodstock, Vermont: Jewish Lights Publishing, 1998), 65. For the idea of God as the equalizer between the women, see also John Calvin, *Genesis*, trans. John King (Carlisle, PA: The Banner of Truth Trust, 1992), 140.

Androcentrism par excellence

There is little dispute over the fact that Genesis 29–30 represents an androcentric story par excellence. Scholars assert that the narrative depicts Leah and Rachel as embracing androcentric values in their struggle for children and husband. Athalya Brenner holds that the story is a "male-oriented, male-written judgment on female sociability and potential of socialization." To Brenner, Leah, and Rachel are like other biblical mothers who eventually give birth to "heroes," and are portrayed as rivals who are mostly concerned with motherhood.[16] Sharon Pace Jeansonne also maintains: "The struggle between Rachel and Leah clearly arises from a context of patriarchal structures and expectations."[17] Similarly, Peter Pitzele recognizes that Genesis 29–30 "dramatize[s] in the starkest possible terms the worst features of the patriarchal system. Women bear sons for men. Motherhood has been co-opted in the interests of lineage and class …. Two sisters are corrupted by a system that prizes sons."[18] Francine Klagsbrun also acknowledges the androcentric character of the narrative when she writes: "From a feminist point of view, we would say that they [Leah and Rachel] have incorporated patriarchal values, and certainly their stories are presented from a male perspective."[19]

Yet Klagsbrun hesitates to "dismiss these women simply as products of patriarchy." Do Leah and Rachel sense that they follow "a divinely directed destiny" which would make their children into the founders of a great nation? Klagsbrun believes so, alleging that "an intimacy with the divine … perhaps lay at the heart of their desire for children."[20] Leah and Rachel are figures full of strength and determination who play crucial roles for the destiny of their people. To Klagsbrun, one may learn a great deal from this story despite, or rather because of, the obvious androcentrism. Although her position tolerates, perhaps too easily, Leah's and Rachel's co-optation into androcentric and class oppression, Klagsbrun's concern is important. The story can be read as an illustration for why some women endorse patriarchal structures. Their class privilege makes Leah and Rachel eager to conform to the patriarchal goal of having sons. They are willing to use their class privilege and to force other women into helping them to maintain it. Thus read, the narrative illuminates the societal forces that make class-privileged

---

16. Athalya Brenner demonstrates that the story in Genesis 29–30 follows the "birth-of-the-hero" paradigm, which pursues androcentric interests, see her article "Female Social Behaviour: Two Descriptive Patterns Within the 'Birth of the Hero' Paradigm," *Vetus Testamentum* 36 (3) (1986): 273.

17. Sharon Pace Jeansonne, *The Women of Genesis: From Sarah To Potiphar's Wife* (Minneapolis, MN: Fortress, 1990), 79.

18. Peter Pitzele, "The Myth of the Wrestler," in *Our Fathers" Wells: A Personal Encounter with the Myths of Genesis* (San Francisco: HarperSanFrancisco, 1995), 181.

19. Francine Klagsbrun, "Ruth and Naomi, Rachel and Leah," in Judith A. Kates and Gail Twersky Reimer (eds), *Reading Ruth: Contemporary Women Reclaim a Sacred Story* (New York: Ballantine Books, 1994), 271.

20. Ibid., "Ruth and Naomi," 271.

women accept and actively support androcentric hierarchies prevalent in society even today.

The Story's Literary Structure

A closer look at the literary structure uncovers the particularities of this dynamic. Four literary scenes structure the story. The first scene, Genesis 29:31-5, establishes the situation: Leah is unloved, but fertile, giving birth to four sons: Reuben, Simeon, Levi, and Judah. Their names receive explanatory comments from the mother. Although the relationship between the sons" names and Leah's explanations are etymologically mostly incorrect,[21] Leah's statements are significant. Except for the explanation of the name of Levi (v. 34), they refer to God. After the first birth, Leah acknowledges, "Yahweh saw my misery; now my husband will love me" (v. 32). After the second birth, she remarks: "For Yahweh heard that I was unloved, and so God has given me this one too" (v. 33). After the fourth birth, she exclaims: "Now I shall praise Yahweh!" (v. 35). In other words, Leah correlates her fertility to the divinity although her goal—to gain the love of her husband— remains unattained. Initially, Leah believes to gain love for her fertility, but after the fourth son she recognizes that her God-given fertility will not provide her with Jacob's love, and so she praises God without a reference to her husband (v. 35).

The second scene, 30:1-8, reports Rachel's infertility which leads to Bilhah's rapes. When Rachel realizes that she has not become pregnant, she instructs Jacob: "Give me children, or I shall die!" (v. 1). He, however, is more cautious than his wife: "Am I in the position of God, who has denied you the fruit of the womb?" (v. 2). Jacob does not respond to his wife's sorrow and refuses responsibility for her infertility. He defends himself because infertility is not his problem but ultimately God's. His brisk response startled the rabbis of the early centuries CE. A midrash lets God intervene: "Said the Holy One, blessed be He, to Jacob: Is that a way to answer a woman in distress?"[22] The rabbis reprimand Jacob for his unsympathetic response. Yet in the narrative Jacob's answer leaves it up to his favorite wife to determine what to do next.

She takes action. "Here is my slave, Bilhah. Sleep with her, and let her give birth on my knees. Through her, then, I too shall have children" (v. 3). Without another comment from her husband, the deal is done. "Jacob came into her" (v. 4). When Bilhah becomes pregnant and gives birth to a son, Rachel invokes the divinity for the first time: "God has done me justice. Yes, God has heard my voice, and God has given me a son" (v. 6). Rachel learned her lesson. She believes

---

21. For a discussion about the etymologies of the names, see, e.g. Ephraim A. Speiser, *Genesis: Introduction, Translation, and Notes*, The Anchor Bible Commentary (Garden City, NY: Doubleday, 1964), 231–3; Claus Westermann, *Genesis 12–36: A Commentary*, trans. John J. Scullion (Minneapolis: Augsburg, 1985), 473–7.

22. Isaac Unterman, *The Five Books of Moses: The Book of Genesis: Profoundly Inspiring Commentaries and Interpretations Selected from the Talmudic-Rabbinic Literature* (New York: Bloch, 1973), 250.

that the divinity provides offspring through any means available. Forcing another woman to have intercourse with her husband, Rachel takes advantage of her class and later thanks God for the child. This is disturbing theology because it imagines Rachel as classifying gendered class oppression as God's will. Is God, indeed, the provider and denier of fertility under such conditions? Rachel affirms this question which demonstrates her co-optation into androcentric ideology. She wants a son, no matter what, and since the process works for her, she forces Bilhah a second time to have intercourse with the husband (v. 7). After the birth of another son, Rachel invokes God again, exclaiming: "I have wrestled a wrestling of *Elohim* with my sister, and I have won" (v. 8). To Rachel, her success in fulfilling patriarchal expectations means that God is on her side. This theology is not only disturbing but, worse, it is dangerous because it assumes patriarchy and classism as divinely sanctioned.

Rachel's exclamation in v. 8 raises many questions. At stake is the noun "God/ elohim." Interpreters often reject translating the Hebrew phrase as "a wrestling of elohim" and recommend alternatives. For instance, Nahum M. Sarna proposes: "A fateful contest I waged with my sister," explaining that his translation is based "on the occasional use of elohim, 'God,' as an intensifying or superlative element." However, he also writes that the phrase could be translated as "a contest for God."[23] Many interpreters follow Sarna's grammatical advice and consider the noun "God" in v. 8 as an intensifying adjective.[24] One of them is Terence E. Fretheim whose translation attempts to communicate the intense effort of Rachel. Deleting the terminological reference to the divinity in Hebrew, Fretheim translates the sentence as, "With mighty wrestlings I have wrestled with my sister."[25] Likewise Victor P. Hamilton compares Rachel's experience of wrestling "with Jacob's in Genesis 32.25f. and considers God in v. 8 'as an intensifying epithet.'" He translates v. 8: "I have been entangled in a desperate contest with my sister."[26] Other interpreters, such as Everett Fox, suggest a translation closer to the Hebrew text: "A struggle of God have I struggled with my sister."[27] It is indeed remarkable that the narrative relates the conflict between her sister and herself to the divinity. Does the Hebrew indicate more clearly than many vernacular translations that the women are deeply co-opted into androcentric theology?

The third scene, 30:9-13, switches back to Leah who, now infertile, resorts

23. Nahum M. Sarna, *Genesis* (The JPS Torah Commentary Series; Philadelphia: JPS, 1989), 208.

24. See also Victor P. Hamilton, *The Book of Genesis: Chapters 18–50* (Grand Rapids, MI: Eerdmans, 1995), 271–2.

25. Terence E. Fretheim, "The Book of Genesis," in Leander E. Keck et al. (eds), *The New Interpreter's Bible* (Vol. 1; Nashville, TN: Abingdon Press, 1994), 546.

26. Hamilton, *The Book of Genesis*, 271–2.

27. Everett Fox, *The Five Books of Moses: Genesis, Exodus, Leviticus, Numbers, Deuteronomy* (New York: Schocken Books, 1995), 139. Francis I. Anderson also argues that the noun "God" should remain visible in Gen. 30:8, see his brief comment, "Note on Genesis 30:8," *Journal of Biblical Literature* 88 (June 1969): 200.

to having her slave raped twice. Unlike Rachel (Gen. 30:1), Leah does not react to her sister's success in getting two sons; she worries about herself. Thus, v. 9 does not state: "When Leah saw that Rachel had two sons," but observes instead: "When Leah saw that she had ceased to bear children." Hated by her husband and co-opted into androcentrically defined class privilege, Leah establishes her social status through fertility. For different reasons, then, Leah resorts to the method earlier applied by Rachel. "Leah took her slave, Zilpah, and gave her to Jacob as a wife (*'issah*)" (v. 9). One interpreter, the Jewish medieval commentator Nachmanides (Ramban) points to the unusual nature of Leah's decision, commenting: "I do not know what motivated this deed of Leah and why she gave her handmaid to her husband for she was not barren that she should hope to have children through Zilpah, and it is not natural for women to increase the number of their husbands' wives."[28]

Importantly, the terminology of v. 9 relies on the slave-owner's perspective. Zilpah, the slave, is not treated like a wife, as Nachmanides suggests, but reduced to the physical functions of her body. Sexually violated, she gives birth to a child that she probably did not want and is not able to call her own. Later, Zilpah is raped another time (Gen. 30:12). Both times, Leah names the child and comments on the name. Similar to her statement about her fourth son, Leah does not invoke the name of God (Gen. 29:32-5) but refers only to luck and her social recognition: "What good fortune!" and "What blessedness because women will call me blessed!" (30:11-13). The enslaved woman herself does not speak since she is a prop giving birth to two sons. Even Jacob obeys quietly. Does he actually enjoy having sex with so many women? The text is silent on the matter and perhaps this silence exposes Genesis 29–30 as an androcentric fantasy that imagines wives inviting their husbands to have sex with enslaved women.

The fourth scene, 30:14-24, depicts the negotiation between Leah and Rachel that leads to more children for Leah and, eventually, to a son for Rachel. The severity of the hostility between the sisters finds expression in their first and last conversation. When the eldest son of Leah, Reuben, finds a special fruit and brings it to his mother, Leah exchanges the fruit for a night with Jacob. When Rachel wants the fruit, Leah replies bitterly: "Is it not enough to have taken my husband? You take my son's mandrakes as well?" (v. 14). Embroiled in rivalry over husband and children, Leah vents her feelings of loss. Rachel hears the disappointment in her sister's voice and easily relinquishes the man for the fruit: "Very well, he can sleep with you tonight in return for your son's mandrakes" (v. 15). Without objection, Jacob obeys Leah's order at the end of the day: "You must come to me" (v. 16). In this narrative the husband does not care with whom he sleeps, going wherever his wives tell him. Is this text a realistic description of slave-owning women or rather an androcentric fantasy? Jacob must have gone to Leah at least twice more because Leah gives birth to another son (vv. 19–20) and to her first and only daughter, Dinah (v. 21). After the births of the sons, Leah praises the

---

28. Ramban (Nachmanides), *Commentary on the Torah: Genesis,* trans. and annotated with index by Charles B. Chavel (New York: Shilo, 1971), 368.

divinity again. She believes that God rewarded her (v. 18), having given her a true gift (v. 20). The birth of her daughter, Dinah, does not receive such praise (v. 21), yet another indication of the narrative's androcentrism.

When the scene turns again to Rachel (v. 22), she becomes pregnant herself. "God remembered Rachel; God heard her, and God opened her womb; and she became pregnant, and she gave birth to a son" (v. 23). The race for fertility has found a preliminary end. Rachel names the son "Joseph" and exclaims: "God has taken away my disgrace!" and "May Yahweh add another son for me" (vv. 23, 24). This painful story about the co-optation of two sisters into androcentric class structures ends with the request to God for yet another son. Eventually, the belief in God as the provider and denier of fertility destroys Rachel (35:16-19). The story of Bilhah, her slave, however, continues in another fragmentary narrative.

Another Story of Bilhah

Bilhah appears once more in a verse in which the destructive relational pattern of Leah and Rachel moves reportedly to the next generation (Gen. 35:22). This, at least, is the sad conclusion based on an incident that involves Reuben, the oldest son of Leah, and Bilhah, Rachel's enslaved woman. The story demonstrates what Reuben learned: enslaved women are property to be raped without repercussion. Here is the short description of the event:

> It happened when Israel lived in that land,
> Reuben went,
> and he laid Bilhah, the concubine of his father,
> and Israel heard of it. (Gen. 35:22a)

Rarely mentioned in scholarly discussions, this brief report about Bilhah appears after Rachel dies during the birth of her second son. Indirectly the verse refers to rape. The Hebrew verb, *šakab*, is not followed by the preposition with (*'im*) but by the Hebrew object marker *'et*, as in other rape stories such as the rape of Dinah (Gen. 34:2) or Tamar (2 Sam. 13:14). The grammatical observation has consequences for the verse's meaning. Reuben does not sleep "with" Bilhah, a translation that feigns consent by Bilhah. Rather he "laid" her. He is the subject of the action and she the object. As a concubine and slave, Bilhah is sexually violated, raped.

George G. Nicol and Mordechai Rotenberg discuss the verse in some detail and thus their readings merit closer scrutiny. First, George G. Nicol rejects E. A. Speiser's idea that Genesis 35:22 is an ethnographic explanation for the decline of the tribe of Reuben in the course of Israelite history. Speiser proposes that "[t]hese scattered hints suggest that the tribe of Reuben once enjoyed a pre-eminent position, only to fall upon evil days."[29] Nicol claims instead that the story

---

29. Ephraim A. Speiser, *Genesis: Introduction, Translation, and Notes,* The Anchor Bible Commentary (Garden City, NY: Doubleday, 1964), 274.

remembers how Reuben avenges his mother whom Jacob never loved. Bilhah is the slave of Rachel, the loved wife. By raping Bilhah, Reuben challenges his father's authority, as other royal sons do when they "take possession" of another man's concubines.[30] Nicol elaborates: "This incident must therefore be considered to have caused deep humiliation to Jacob, who … had been usurped in the bed of [Rachel's] slave." To Nicol, Reuben introduces "an element of justice into the narrative" when he takes revenge in unexpected ways. Earlier, Leah calls the birth of Reuben "the reversal of my humiliation" (Gen. 29:32). Even though Reuben is not able to reverse Jacob's hatred for her into love, the son reverses his father's fortune by humiliating his father "at precisely the time when he is emotionally at his weakest and least able to resist."[31] In short, Nicol suggests that Reuben tries to destroy his father by targeting Bilhah.

Read accordingly, Genesis 35:22 depicts a struggle over power between two men, son Reuben and his father Jacob. Such an androcentric interpretation shows little concern for Bilhah's perspective and minimizes Reuben's activity as "sexual inter-course," "his offence against his father" or "taking possession of Bilhah." Indeed, in Nicol's view, the story demonstrates "a certain tastefulness in the fact that Genesis xxxv.22a associates Rachel's slave, and not Rachel herself, with Reuben's action." Reuben challenges Jacob's authority by "committing his offence" and shows "good taste" because Reuben attacks his aunt's slave and not directly his aunt.

Rotenberg, meanwhile, discusses Genesis 35:22 as an example of the "rehabili-tative story telling" method of the ancient rabbis.[32] The ancient rabbis noted that certain stories report particularly troubling activities of central biblical figures. Such a figure is Reuben, whose "sin" is explicitly described in Genesis 35:22 and remembered by Jacob in Genesis 49:3-4. The rabbis are aware of Reuben's problematic behavior and try to "rehabilitate" him. They want the story to be seen as "a righteous deed of honoring his [Reuben's] mother Leah," and so they explain: "He stood up against the humiliation of his mother by saying: If my mother's sister was a rival to my mother, shall the bondsmaid of my mother's sister be a rival to my mother? He thus arose and transposed the beds."[33] According to the ancient rabbinic view, Reuben defends his mother by raping Bilhah, which is a rather precarious "rehabilitative" effort, one that excuses Reuben for "his deed."

Many centuries apart, the interpretations of Nicol and the ancient rabbis are quite similar. Both focus on the male characters and soften the sexual violence perpetrated by Reuben. Both also ignore Bilhah's perspective. Perhaps unsurpris-ingly, then, Genesis 35:22 belongs to a list of biblical texts, the so-called "forbidden targumim," that the ancient rabbis advise not to explain to lay people. These "forbidden" texts "may be read [in Hebrew] but not translated [into the language of

30. See, e.g. 2 Sam. 3:6-11, 15-19; 1 Kgs 2:13-25.

31. George G. Nicol, "Genesis xxix.32 and xxv.22a Reuben's Reversal," *Journal of Theological Studies* 31 (1980): 536-9.

32. Mordechai Rotenberg, "The 'Midrash' and Biographic Rehabilitation," *Journal for the Scientific Study of Religion* 25 (1) (1986): 41-55.

33. Quoted ibid., 46. The quote from the Babylonian Talmud is in Shabbat 55b.

the congregation, e.g. English]."[34] This approach is similar to the Christian strategy. Even today, Christian lectionaries exclude Genesis 35:22 from the recommended list of sermon texts so that the verse is not read aloud during Christian worship. An influential interpreter like Gerhard von Rad indirectly endorses this ecclesiastical silence when he comments: "The crime itself is condemned by the narrator, without the necessity for his expressly stating it. The note is brief and fragmentary that one can form no opinion about what is told in vs. 21f."[35] When a renowned scholar such as von Rad does not have an opinion on this passage, a preacher will certainly refrain from choosing it as the basis for a sermon. Other Christian scholars, too, avoid direct references to v. 22. Richard J. Clifford and Roland E. Murphy state: "The details of this ugly incident are not given; in fact, the text breaks off at this point."[36] To these Christian scholars, Genesis 35:22 is too short, unclear, and "ugly" to merit further comment. Neither interested in Bilhah nor the issue of rape, many Jewish and Christian readers prefer to overlook Reuben's rape of Bilhah.

Yet another aspect of the verse deserves mention. Bilhah is characterized as Jacob's "concubine" (*pilegeš*). The terminology is unusual since Bilhah is Rachel's slave and the majority of biblical references consider her "a slave of Rachel." In Genesis 29:29, Rachel's father, Laban, gives Bilhah as a slave to his daughter Rachel when she marries Jacob. In 30:3,4,7, and 35:25, Bilhah is called Rachel's slave. Also Genesis 46:25 refers to Bilhah as a slave of Rachel, given as a wedding gift. Yet in 1 Chronicles. 7:13, Bilhah is neither Rachel's nor Jacob's possession. There her sons are identified as "the descendants of Bilhah." Bilhah appears in relationship to Jacob only one more time, namely in Genesis 37:2. The verse calls her and Zilpah "the wives of his [Joseph's] father."

Immersed in androcentric bias, commentators take for granted the term "concubine." They presume that Bilhah turns automatically into Jacob's concubine after Rachel's death, and so the switch from "slave" to "concubine" does not bother them. Has she not "slept with" him before? Indeed, the difference between an enslaved woman and a concubine is small. Like concubines, enslaved women are used to give birth to children who will be taken from them.[37] Both concubines and slaves have to submit to the orders of their superiors, whether this person is a slave-owner, a husband or a king. Sometimes the tasks of concubines and slaves can also be different. A concubine's primary role is to provide children, whereas a slave also fulfills other functions.

Furthermore, a concubine gives a man more prestige than a slave. A concubine may also reconcile political power struggles at royal courts whereas a slave never

---

34. Michael L. Klein, "Not to be Translated in Public," *Journal of Jewish Studies* 39 (1) (Spring 1988): 80–91.

35. Von Rad, *Genesis*, 341.

36. Richard J. Clifford and Roland E. Murphy, "Genesis," in Raymond E. Brown, Joseph A. Fitzmyer and Roland E. Murphy (eds), *The New Jerome Biblical Commentary* (Englewood Cliffs, NJ: Prentice Hall, 1990), 36.

37. For a brief discussion on "slave concubines," see Westbrook, "The Female Slave," 215–20.

interferes into such affairs.[38] Yet overall the roles of concubines and female slaves are similar so that the term "concubine" in Genesis 35:22 does not necessarily indicate a socially higher status than the term "slave." Even as a concubine, Bilhah is owned by Jacob who has unrestricted sexual access to her. She remains the property of the Jacob family whether she is concubine or slave, and so Reuben challenges his father's property rights when he rapes Bilhah. The narrative also illustrates an important idea about rape: men rape women to mark their territory over other men, which makes the raped women arbitrary in the androcentric story world and in the world of interpreters.

In such a world, then, men regard women as objects available for sexual violation. A narrative's focus on men and their behavior exposes the destructive consequences of androcentrism. Women, especially when they are enslaved or concubines, are acted upon by men who view them as symbols of male power. Whether raped or not, the women are quickly forgotten, as the long history of androcentric interpretations demonstrates abundantly. Yet when we identify these texts as rape stories the fate of the women is exposed for what it is: a fate that either devastates women's lives or co-opts women into androcentrism. The narratives do not offer optimistic answers and there is no Thelma and Louise tale in the Hebrew Bible, but there are enough biblical stories of rape to make visible some of the dynamics that shape women's and men's lives even today.

The City as a Raped Woman: Sexual Violence in Biblical Poetry

The issue of rape is not only a prominent issue in biblical narratives but it also shapes biblical poetry. Some of the poems appear in the prophetic literature and deserve special mention. We turn our focus now to those poems that pronounce God to be an angry punisher of idolatrous actions against the biblical and ancient Near Eastern cities of Jerusalem, Babylon, and Nineveh. Written during the time of the Babylonian exile in the sixth century BCE,[39] the poems depict cities as the main culprits for the Israelite disaster. Each city appears as a woman who prostitutes herself and enjoys her sexual prowess but whose end has come. Crude, brutal, and violent vocabulary prevails. The poems present the male god as a

---

38. For further explanations, see Karen Engelken, "*pilaegaes*," in G. Johannes Botterweck, Helmer Ringgren et al. (eds), *Theologisches Wörterbuch zum Alten Testament* (Vol. 6; Stuttgart: W. Kohlhammer, 1987), 586–90. See also Karen Engelken, *Frauen im Alten Israel*, 101, 124, where Engelken argues for a sharp distinction between the position of a concubine and a slave. For the opposite view, see Raymond Westbrook, "The Female Slave," 233, who finds the term *pîlegeš* "totally inappropriate" and considers it as the author's effort "to spare Reuben, whose crime in sleeping with Bilhah would have been far more heinous if she were Jacob's wife."

39. Perhaps Isa. 3:16-17 is a pre-exilic text although some commentators question an early date. For instance, Joseph Blenkinsopp is uncertain if Isaiah or a later writer composed the passage, see Joseph Blenkinsopp, *Isaiah 1–39* (New York: Doubleday, 2000), 201.

husband who condemns his wife. He curses and insults her, wishing upon her attacks of sexual violence. The poetry promotes imagery that relies on sexual violence as just and divinely ordained punishment. It is prophetic speech gone awry. The following sections explain the theological and ethical problems when metaphors rely on sexual violence as a divinely sanctioned punishment, when God turns into a rapist.

The Initial Victim: Jerusalem

In Isaiah 3:16–17, Jeremiah 13:22,26, Ezekiel 16 and 23, God prescribes sexual attacks and rape for Jerusalem and its female inhabitants. For instance, the prophetic poem in Isaiah characterizes the daughters of Zion as "haughty" and "walk[ing] with outstretched necks, glancing wantonly with their eyes, mincing along as they go, tinkling with their feet" (Isa. 3:16). Fashion-conscious in look and posture, women of Jerusalem are the recipients of androcentric mockery. They are viewed as "serious infractions of the social order,"[40] and their exaggerated obedience to androcentric standards of femininity makes them fair game for sexual attacks, at least according to the prophetic imagination. After the poem of Isaiah 3 establishes the women's arrogance and pride, God appears as the authorizer and executer of pornographic attacks. Verse 17 describes God's action over the women:

> YHWH will afflict with scabs the heads of the daughters of Zion, and YHWH will lay bare their secret parts. [NRSV]

The sexual candor of this poem makes many translators nervous, particularly those who translate the second line as a reference to the head rather than the genital area, "and Yahweh will lay bare their forehead."[41] They substitute sexual violence with a description that views captive women as being humiliated by having their hair shorn off. Grammatical ambiguity enables this change of meaning. At stake is the Hebrew noun *pot* that appears only one more time in 1 Kings 7:50 as a reference to a "door socket." Some scholars recognize that the text offers "coarse language"[42] and regard the noun as a reference to female genitals in a vulgar and colloquial expression. Moreover, metaphoric language is always ambiguous, particularly in a theologically problematic setting in which God is portrayed as the violator of Jerusalem's women. Why be clear and direct when the image of a door socket in which a door swings will do?

Another prophetic passage contains similarly troubling metaphors. In Jeremiah 13:22,26 God announces the rape of the woman Jerusalem—here the city is

---

40. Ibid.

41. See, e.g. Otto Kaiser, *Isaiah 1–12: A Commentary* (2nd edn; Philadelphia: Westminster, 1983); Gene M. Tucker, *Isaiah*, The New Interpreter's Bible (vol. 6) (Nashville, TN: Abingdon Press, 2001), 81.

42. So Blenkinsopp, *Isaiah*, 201.

imagined as a woman. In v. 22 the verb appears in the passive voice which avoids mentioning the identity of the rapist. Yet in v. 26 the verb is active and God its subject; God is the sexual violator. The following translation stays closely with the syntax of the Hebrew text:

> (22) On account of the greatness of your iniquity
> exposed/uncovered are your skirts,
> violated are your heels/genitals ... .
> (26) and also I myself shall strip your skirts over your face,
> so that is seen your shame.[43]

The passage is part of a larger poem in 13:20-7. The personal pronouns in vv. 22 and 26 are in the second person feminine singular ("you"). God addresses the feminine city in this speech in which God invokes sexual punishment for her transgressions. In v. 24, the two verbs, "to uncover" and "to violate," are in the passive voice, and so the focus is on the woman's situation. It is ambiguous who the perpetrator is although the scene is "clearly" one of rape.[44] The violator is identified later in v. 26; it is God. Yet because Jeremiah's predictions often warn about the Babylonian siege and ultimate victory, interpreters usually assume that in v. 24 the rapists are the victorious Babylonian soldiers. As a whole, the poem proclaims that the woman brought this fate upon herself and she is to be blamed for it. The prophet sides with the sexually violent perpetrators and views the attack as deserved and God as justifying it. Interestingly, commentators acknowledge freely that the passage is loaded with sexual metaphors. The nouns "skirt" and "heels" carry unambiguous sexual connotations and the verbs appear also in other contexts of sexual violence, such as in Isaiah 47:3, Ezekiel 16:36,37, and 23:29.[45] The prophetic poem in Jeremiah 13 envisions God as relishing in the rape of woman Jerusalem, a rape that is perpetrated by the presumed Babylonian army and supported by the male God. It represents a climax of androcentric fury regarding women, and it is a major theological problem because the prophet proposes the metaphor of God as a rapist.

Although commentators are uncomfortable with this passage, sometimes recognizing it as a rape scene, they do not question the prophetic claim that these poems are God's speech. Robert Carroll, for instance, recognizes the brutality of the image in vv. 22 and 26. He emphasizes the suffering of the women who are brutally raped by the invading army, and he also recognizes the difficulties in excusing the poem as metaphoric speech. In the poem the metaphoric rapist is still a rapist and he is God. Carroll thus writes, "metaphors and reality combine

---

43. This translation is taken from Angela Bauer, *Gender in the Book of Jeremiah: A Feminist-Literary Reading* (New York: Peter Lang, 1999), 101–2.

44. So, e.g. William L. Holladay, *Jeremiah: A Commentary on the Book of the Prophet Jeremiah Chapters 1–25* (Philadelphia: Fortress, 1986), 414

45. See, e.g. ibid., 103–4; Robert P. Carroll, *The Book of Jeremiah: A Commentary* (Philadelphia: Westminster, 1986), 303; Holladay, *Jeremiah*, 414.

to portray a sickening picture of battered sexuality and torn flesh, an image of a culture invaded, raped and devastated."[46] Even though Carroll emphasizes the link between metaphor and reality, he does not question the poet's sense of justice in which the poet depicts God as a sexual predator. Carroll accepts this image about God and he is not alone. Other interpreters, too, do not challenge the notion that Jeremiah 13 presents an acceptable theology, even when they wonder: "Why are these outrages Yahweh's portion for the city?"[47] Many commentators tolerate the fact that in these poems God punishes Jerusalem with sexual violence, and they side with the prophet. For instance, R. E. Clements explains:

> [T]he people were eagerly placing the blame for their tragic misfortunes upon God and regarding themselves self-pityingly as the unfortunate victims of a fate that they had not deserved. It was the concern of the prophet, as well as of his editors and followers, to show that the people could not evade the acceptance of responsibility for what they had suffered.[48]

Clements, like other interpreters, does not reject androcentric extremism that characterizes God as the perpetrator of rape. He finds it a fitting illustration of the prophet who criticizes his contemporaries for their mistaken political analysis. The prophet tells them that they are not victims, as they believe, but responsible for the national disaster of foreign occupation. Their own actions lead to war, national annihilation, and exile because they are promiscuous and do not follow God. They bring this fate upon themselves like a sexually violated woman. Interpreters, caught in the prophetic perspective, endorse this theology that might be called a theology of the rapist. Perhaps they find it too frightening to contradict biblical prophecy and take for granted its androcentric assumptions.

Yet some commentators are disturbed by the depiction of God as a sexually violent retaliator. One of them is Gracia Fay Ellwood who acknowledges the conflict between the androcentric poems and their portrayal of God.[49] Ellwood surmises that probably God speaks through these texts but "in a different sense than we had thought." To her, the prophetic texts cannot mean what they seem to imply because God would not command the rape of women. There has to be another way of reading but, curiously, Ellwood does not provide an alternative.

Other prophetic poems promote a similarly problematic view on God's relationship to rape. Ezekiel 16 and 23 are perhaps among the most extreme passages reporting divine commandments for the metaphoric rape of cities. Again, Jerusalem is the target of verbal threats of rape and abuse. This time, the prophet Ezekiel claims the following words as those of God:

Thus says YHWH God, Because your shame was laid bare and your nakedness

---

46. Carroll, *The Book of Jeremiah*, 304.

47. Ibid., 304.

48. R. E. Clements, *Jeremiah* (Atlanta: John Knox Press, 1988), 88.

49. See Gracia Fay Ellwood, "Rape and Judgment," *Daughters of Sarah* 11 (1985): 13

uncovered in your harlotries with your lovers, and because of all your idols, and because of the blood of your children that you gave to them, therefore, behold, I will gather all your lovers, with whom you took pleasure, all those you loved and all those you loathed; I will gather them against you from every side, and will uncover your nakedness to them, that they may see all your nakedness .... And I will give you into the hand of your lovers, and they shall strip you of your clothes and take your fair jewels, and leave you naked and bare. They shall stone you and cut you to pieces with their swords .... So will I satisfy my fury on you, and my jealousy shall depart from you; I will be calm, and will no more be angry. (Ezek. 16:26-37, 39-40, 42)

These harsh words obscure the perspective of the woman so that readers view the accusations only through the eyes of the accuser, Yahweh.[50] God speaks whereas the woman is only the recipient of the action. Since the woman is not given an opportunity to reply, her point of view is absent. She is imagined as naked, tortured, even murdered, and God is described as approving of these violent acts. The woman's body is the focus of the attention, as is the treatment that Yahweh curses upon her, and repetitive terminology hammers it home. She is to be stripped naked. Stoned and cut into pieces, the woman is ordered to be killed, and God expresses satisfaction about the prospect of her being thus punished.

The emphasis on the woman's nakedness stimulates androcentric porno-graphic fantasy. The objectified and naked woman is the forbidden sight of the perverse desire for more, which culminates in sexual violence and murder. She is imagined as being beaten and killed, all of which is commanded and justified by God. At the end of the poem, the woman is mutilated, raped, and slaughtered and God is satisfied. "So will I satisfy my fury on you, and my jealousy shall depart from you; I will be calm and will not more be angry" (Ezek. 16:42). The prophetic poem also turns the sexually violated woman into a sign of warning for women in general. Ezekiel 23:48 warns women about the dangers of sexual independence and self-determination, stating: "Thus will I put an end to lewdness in the land, that all women may take warning and not commit lewdness as you have done."

Some commentators reflect on the consequences of portraying God as a sexually violent punisher. Mary E. Shields observes that many commentators empathize with the deity, downplay divine rage, and jealousy, and consider God's rage as a sign of love for the woman.[51] This dysfunctional notion about love and relationship promises death to her. Shields thus insists that "it is dangerous ... to let the male figure off the hook here, even if that figure is God ... ."[52] She encourages readers to look closely and to endure "to be repelled by what we see"

---

50. So Mary E. Shields, "Multiple Exposures: Body Rhetoric and Gender in Ezekiel 16," in Athalya Brenner (ed.), *Prophets and Daniel: A Feminist Companion to the Bible (Second Series)* (New York: Sheffield Academic Press, 2001), 140.

51. Ibid., 146–7.

52. Ibid., 148.

and "to call into question this text's validity as 'the word of God.'"[53] Shields also asks us to examine critically a metaphor in which God "does the wounding." Unlike Renita Weems who identifies with the abused and battered woman, Jerusalem,[54] Shields maintains that the image of a raping God does not leave any room for grace because the prophecy of Ezekiel does not envision reconciliation.[55] The prophet imagines God as a raping murderer of women. To prevent misunderstandings, Shields asks for the deconstruction of this image of God so that it cannot be read as a justification of sexual violence.[56]

While Shields does not offer a deconstructive reading of the sexually violent poems, she locates the metaphor firmly within the male prophetic psyche. This androcentric imagination links God with misogyny and sexual violence. It is not God speaking but men enhancing male power. They picture God as a sexually violent punisher of women because it allows men to be violent and abusive towards women, children, and even other men. Hence, Shields insists that Ezekiel 16 and 23 are words of the prophet who speaks his androcentric truth, but they are not the words of God.

The Other Victims: Babylon and Nineveh

Prophetic androcentrism does not rest with viewing Jerusalem as a woman cursed by God with rape, abuse, and murder. The cities of Babylon and Nineveh, as well as their female inhabitants receive similar metaphoric treatment. For instance, a divine oracle against Babylon in Isaiah 13:16 presents the women of Babylon as threatened with rape. The verb used to connote sexual violation is šagal, which also appears in Deuteronomy 28:30 and Zechariah 14:2 in the sense of "being violently taken."

In another passage, Isaiah 47:2-3,10-15, the prophet envisions God as cursing the city Babylon personified as a young woman. She is stripped of her clothes and forced to expose her genitals.

> (2) Take the millstones
> and grind meal,
> put off your veil,
> strip off your robe,
> uncover your legs,
> pass through the rivers.
> (3) Your nakedness shall be uncovered
> and your shame shall be seen.
> I will take vengeance,

53. Ibid., 150.

54. Renita J. Weems, *Battered Love: Marriage, Sex, and Violence in the Hebrew Prophets* (Minneapolis, MN: Augsburg Fortress, 1995), 113.

55. Shields, "Multiple Exposures," 152.

56. Ibid., 153.

and I will spare no human. (Isa. 47:2-3)

Interestingly, the metaphor of sexual violence exhibits the same features with which prophetic speech also characterizes Israelite cities.[57] The metaphor depicts Israelite and foreign cities as women whom God threatens to strip, to lead around naked, and to expose their genitals. In the prophetic mind, woman is woman whether she is Israelite or a stranger.

Accordingly, the metaphor is not only applied to Babylon but also to Nineveh, another ancient Near Eastern city. This Assyrian city appears in Nahum 3:5-7 as a woman who receives threats of sexual violence.

(5)Behold, I come over you, says Yahweh of hosts,
and I will lift up your skirts over your face;
and I will let nations look on your nakedness and kingdoms on your shame.
(6) I will throw filth at you
and I will sexually violate you,[58] and I will make you a gazing stock.
(7) And all who look on you will shrink from you and say, Wasted is Nineveh,
who will bemoan her?
Whence shall I seek comforters for you?

Familiar imagery dominates in this poem. God is said to act as a sexually violent force. The terms "skirts," "nakedness," and, "shame" are references to female genitals.[59] The translation of the sentence "I will sexually violate you" uses the Hebrew verb *nabal* in the pi'el, which connotes a clear-cut sexual violation. The verb also appears in rape narratives such as Genesis 34:7, Judges 19–21, and 2 Samuel 13:12.[60] In the entire poem (3:1-19) Nineveh is unable to withstand the military attack. The enemy's horses overrun the city. Citizens die by the sword, fire destroys the houses in the town, and nobody is available to help. As in other prophetic poems, sexual violence intermingles with sexual harassment and murder. Rape appears as a predictable ingredient of the complete destruction, as the climax of this gruesome prophetic poetry.[61] The prophets see no greater penalty, no bigger depiction of total humiliation and destruction than to characterize it as rape. Rape

---

57. Gerlinde Baumann, *Love and Violence: Marriage as Metaphor for the Relationship between YHWH and Israel in the Prophetic Books*, trans. Linda M. Maloney (Collegeville, MN: Liturgical Press, 2003), 192

58. See Baumann's translation of this verse in her German book: *Liebe und Gewalt: Die Ehe als Metapher für das Verhältnes JHWH–Israel in die Prophetenbüchern* (Stuttgart: Verlag Katholisches Bibelwerk, 2000), 218 n.629: "Ich will dich schänden." The English translation of the German text offers a weak translation of v. 6 on p. 209: "and I will defile you." See also Gerlinde Baumann, *Gottes Gewalt im Wandel: Traditionsgeschichtliche und intertextuelle Studien zu Nahum 1,2–8* (Neukirchen–Vluyn: Neukirchener Verlag, 2005).

59. Ibid., 52–5; 210.

60. Ibid., 209.

61. Elke Seifert, *Töchter und Väter im Alten Testament: Eine ideologiekritische*

is so abhorrent that it is God's ultimate punishment, and with such a reading of the poem, perhaps a feminist reader can even agree.

A Sacred Witness? Concluding Remarks

Once we recognize that biblical literature addresses the topic of sexual violence, it is difficult to comprehend how interpreters have been able to ignore this topic for so long. It seems likely that their exegetical silence was based on indifference to women's welfare. After all, androcentric bias and perspective have permeated Western society, culture, and religion for centuries. Only since the 1970s, when feminists began to speak out against sexual violence, did feminist Bible scholars discover the urgency of the issue. Many people are still not comfortable in placing responsibility for sexual violence where it belongs: with the perpetrators, with patriarchal assumptions about women and gender, with other forms of oppression such as classism, and even with women's co-optation into androcentric standards. It certainly also belongs with the prophetic imagination that speaks of God as a sexually violent husband who uses rape as the ultimate form of punishment. Thus biblical narrative and poem address the phenomenon of sexual violence which makes it difficult to limit these texts to a bygone past alone. They seem to speak so directly to our time, in which rape-prone attitudes and behavior still harm women, children, and men. They are eerily relevant in the twenty-first century.

In that sense, then, the Hebrew Bible is a witness to sexual violence perpetrated in the past and present. Some interpreters maintain that biblical narratives and poems have contributed to the prevalence of sexual violence. For people of this conviction, the Bible is a perpetrator justifying and legitimating the heinous crime. Yet ultimately the Bible is merely a collection of texts that are regarded as sacred in the Christian and Jewish traditions. Yet if interpreters acquiesce to biblical stories of violence or read them to justify or ignore the issue, it is not the texts that are problematic but the reader's complicity with them. Readers create biblical meanings, and, with this hermeneutical principle in mind, the Hebrew Bible emerges as a sacred witness. It refuses compliance with sexual violence because it contains so many passages addressing the topic. If readers are willing to engage it, the Hebrew Bible contains countless narratives and poems to tackle it. The topic also requires feminist attention and care, and if we proceed accordingly, we can read biblical literature as a critique of androcentric and hierarchical structures of domination, in their intersectional manifestations, as they obfuscate, excuse, and even endorse sexual violence with the help of so many past and present interpreters. This reading process of biblical rape texts will also help contemporary readers to take sexual violence seriously as a religious, social, cultural, and political problem to this very day.

Untersuchung zur Verfügungsgewalt von Vätern über ihre Töchter (Neukirchen–Vluyn: Neukirchener Verlag, 1997), 308.

Chapter 5

RUTH, JEZEBEL, AND RAHAB AS "OTHER" WOMEN: INTEGRATING POSTCOLONIAL PERSPECTIVES

Throughout its entire history, the focus on the oppression and discrimination of women by patriarchal institutions and traditions in Western societies has pushed women of great intellect to examine the contributions of the Hebrew Bible to gender discrimination. For most of this time, the main social category applied to the biblical canon was gender, which led to significant observations and discoveries, as we have learned in the previous chapters of this book. Rarely, however, did feminist biblical interpreters relate their studies to other forms of social, political, economic, or religious forms of oppression. Yet this is exactly the direction that feminist biblical research has taken at the beginning of the twenty-first century. Women scholars from Two-Third World countries have urged the connection of the feminist with a postcolonial analysis of the Bible.

Postcolonial feminist Bible scholars have often experienced several forms of oppression that link sexism with racism, classism, or religious and other forms of discrimination. Thus they insist on analyzing gender oppression with other social categories and they firmly promote the interpretation of the Bible with them. Their countries have usually suffered through the political, economic, and social realities of colonialism and postcolonialism, and they know first hand that a monolithic analysis based on gender alone is insufficient for understanding histories, cultures, politics, and traditions of past and present geo-political dynamics.

The insistence on linking various forms of oppression in biblical analysis is not entirely new. For instance, we have seen from Marie-Theres Wacker's work that German feminist scholars of the Bible correlate examinations on gender oppression with anti-Jewish stereotypes. Similarly, African–American womanist interpreters emphasize the need for dismantling sexist and racist assumptions in biblical text and interpretation, as for instance the work of Renita Weems on the midwives in Exodus 1 illustrates.[1] The efforts of Two-Third World feminist scholars are thus among the most recent developments of feminist reading the

---

1. Renita Weems, "The Hebrew Women Are Not Like the Egyptian Women: The Ideology of Race, Gender and Sexual Reproduction in Exodus 1," *Semeia* 59 (1992): 25–34. See also Renita Weems, "Re-reading for Liberation: African American Women and the Bible," in

Hebrew Bible with multiple categories in mind. Their interpretations challenge the oppressive status quo, be it in terms of gender or socio-political and international relations. Postcolonial feminist work also reinforces the early feminist conviction that it is not enough to study the Bible only for academic purposes. They promote biblical exegesis as a way of fostering political, economic, social, and religious change in women's lives. After forty years of feminist biblical interpretations in the academy the conversation has turned global and again demands social responsibility and political change.

The Postcolonial Imagination

Since the late 1980s, the study of the postcolonial experience or "imagination," as some scholars call it,[2] has become prevalent outside and inside biblical studies. This theoretical move considers the study of imperialism as a crucial element for the academic examination of literatures, including the Bible. The interest in postcolonial critical thought is not an accident but must be understood as a result of the increasing presence of Two-Third World scholars.[3] The Bible has only slowly been included in postcolonial research and theory as prominent proponents of postcolonial studies have been working in other academic disciplines, such as literary studies and philosophy. Most, if not all, postcolonial theorists are of non-Western heritage, such as Edward Said who was born in Palestine, and Homi Bhabha, Gayatri Spivak, and Chandra Talpade Mohanty all of whom are of Indian origins.[4] They are Western-educated and have taken for granted a secular perspective, which marginalizes religion, and so the academic study of religion was not at the forefront of their minds. Yet they and others have challenged Western complacency to postcolonial dynamics, requiring scholarly

Silvia Schroer and Sophia Bietenhard (eds), *Feminist Interpretation of the Bible and the Hermeneutics of Liberation* (London and New York: Sheffield Academic Press, 2003), 19–32.

2. See Kwok Pui-lan, *Postcolonial Imagination and Feminist Theology* (Louisville, KY: Westminster/John Knox Press, 2005).

3. Some U.S.-American postcolonial scholars consider the change of the U.S.-immigration act of 1965 under Lyndon Johnson as the reason for the change; see Gayatri Chakravatry Spivak, *Death of a Discipline* (New York: Columbia University Press, 1993), 3. For a discussion on the terminology of "Two-Third World" and "Third World," see R. S. Sugirtharajah, *The Bible and the Third World: Precolonial, Colonial and Postcolonial Encounters* (Cambridge: Cambridge University Press, 2001), 2–3.

4. Among influential publications are: Edward W. Said, *Orientalism* (New York: Vintage, 1979); Edward W. Said, *Culture and Imperialism* (New York: Knopf, 1993); Homi K. Bhabha, *The Location of Culture* (London: Routledge, 1994); Gayatri Spivak, "Can the Subaltern Speak?" in Cary Nelson and Larry Grossberg (eds), *Marxism and the Interpretation of Culture* (Chicago: University of Illinois Press, 1988), 271–313; Chandra Talpade Mohanty, "Under Western Eyes: Feminist Scholarship and Colonial Discourses," *Feminist Review* 30 (Autumn 1988): 60–88.

scrutiny of the histories, politics, traditions, and ongoing worldwide effects of the colonial era. Two-Third World scholars in biblical studies have joined this project and published influential works on the impact of colonialism on the Bible in non-Western countries. One of the most prolific writers is R. S. Sugirtharajah, who has written ground-breaking work on the Bible in Southeast Asia, as well as several theoretical treatises on postcolonialism in biblical studies.[5]

Male thinkers initiated the theoretical debate on postcolonial analysis, but feminist scholars also made important contributions on the link between postcolonialism and gender oppression. Already in 1988, Chandra Talpade Mohanty criticizes the Western feminist inclination to universalize the analytic category "woman" as if all women, anywhere and at any time, face the same traditions, structures, and histories of gender oppression. Characteristic for postcolonial theorists, Mohanty rejects a monolithic gender analysis, especially since the Western feminist tendency to generalize about Third-World women has contributed to the eradication of differences among women in terms of race, class, ethnicity, religion, or national identity. According to Mohanty, this universalizing tendency is part of the intellectual tradition dominant in the colonizing West. Mohanty criticizes Western white women's research as standing in this tradition, a damning judgment, and her work has demonstrated that Western white feminist studies often perpetuate the political, economic, and social exploitation of Two-Third World countries. Mohanty explains:

> The relationship between Woman—a cultural and ideological composite Other constructed through diverse representational discourse (scientific, literary, juridical, linguistic, cinematic, etc.)—and women—real, material subjects of their collective histories—is one of the central questions the practice of feminist scholarship seeks to address. [...] I would like to suggest that the feminist writing I analyse here discursively colonize the material and historical heteroge-neities [differences] of the lives of women in the third world, thereby producing/ representing a composite, singular "third-world woman"—an image which appears arbitrarily constructed but nevertheless carries with it the author-izing signature of Western humanistic discourse. I argue that assumptions of privilege and ethnocentric universality on the one hand, and inadequate self-consciousness about the effect of Western scholarship on the "third world" in the context of a world system dominated by the west on the other, characterize a sizable extent of Western feminist work on women in the third world.[6]

---

5. Among his publications are: R. S. Sugirtharajah, *Postcolonial Criticism and Biblical Interpretation* (Oxford and New York: Oxford University Press, 2002); *The Bible and the Third World: Precolonial, Colonial, and Postcolonial Encounters* (Cambridge and New York: Cambridge University Press, 2001); (ed.), *Vernacular Hermeneutics* (Sheffield: Sheffield Academic Press, 1999); *Asian Biblical Hermeneutics and Postcolonialism: Contesting the Interpretations* (Maryknoll, NY: Orbis Books, 1998); (ed.), *The Postcolonial Bible* (Sheffield: Sheffield Academic Press, 1998).

6. Mohanty, "Under Western Eyes": 62–3.

Initially, Mohanty's sharp criticism of the totalizing tendencies in Western feminism surprised many Western feminists but many have come to understand and agree with her on the limitations of a monolithic gender analysis.[7] Postcolonial feminist theory, then, has significantly contributed to the growing acceptance of understanding gender dynamics in the context of other forms of oppression.

Postcolonialism and Biblical Studies

During the past fifteen years, postcolonial theories have also entered the field of biblical studies. After all, as especially African exegetes have repeatedly stated, "When the white man came to our country he had the Bible and we had the land. The white man said to us, 'let us pray.' After the prayer the white man had the land and we had the Bible."[8] The Bible had a huge impact on European colonial ambitions and territorial realities in many Two-Third World countries, and even in our own postcolonial time this influence continues to be felt. The Western Christian missionary movements propagated the reading of the Bible, and the plethora of biblical translations into the vernacular languages of the African, Asian, and Australian peoples demonstrates the success of distributing the Bible and thereby bringing Western mores, politics, and economics to these societies. R. S. Sugirtharajah summarizes the impact of the Bible on non-Western lands when he writes that "[a]long with gunboats, opium, slaves and treaties, the Christian Bible became a defining symbol of European expansion."[9] The task of postcolonial scholars is to understand this colonial expansion in biblical history, tradition, and interpretation.

The term "postcolonial" requires definition because it does not only describe the period *after* the end of colonialism as if it were a linear chronological sequence. Postcolonialism stands for a whole range of historical and cultural geopolitical dynamics that are reflected in textual practices, psychological conditions, and historical processes of the peoples involved. Fernando F. Segovia distinguishes five ways in which the term postcolonialism defines the "relationship between center and margins, metropolis and periphery, on a global political scale."[10] First, the term is a strictly temporal description and refers to the period of time after colonial occupation and domination. Second, the word indicates the complicated nature of the political stage called "independence" in which a former colony may, and often must, continue entertaining close socio-political and economic ties with

7. See, e.g. also the work of Judith Butler who criticizes universalizing and essentializing references to the category "woman" based on postmodern assumptions; see her *Gender Trouble: Feminism and the Subversion of Identity* (London: Routledge, 1990).

8. Quoted in Musa W. Dube, *Postcolonial Feminist Interpretation of the Bible* (St. Louis, MI: Chalice, 2000), 3.

9. Sugirtharajah, *The Bible and the Third World*, 1.

10. Fernando F. Segovia, *Interpreting Beyond Border* (Sheffield: Sheffield Academic Press, 2000), 12.

the former colonizing power. Thus defined, the noun refers to the experience of today's "neo-"colonialism. Third, the term describes "anti-discourses of opposition and resistance" to colonial doctrine and domination, and requires the studying of the literatures, documents, and artifacts of the colonized. Fourth, the term indicates the various phases of the colonizing dynamics: the pre-, post- and neo-colonial stages. Fifth, the word refers to the imperial exercise of power and, accordingly, postcolonial theories examine the histories and politics of imperialist domination.[11]

When postcolonial criticism emerges in the late 1980s,[12] it takes almost another decade before it reaches biblical studies. Yet when it finally does, its "greatest single aim ... is to situate colonialism at the center of the Bible and biblical interpretation"[13] because modern biblical exegesis develops exactly within the same 400 years in which Western colonization sweeps over many Two-Third World countries. To Sugirtharajah, postcolonial biblical criticism examines the imperialist traditions in biblical texts and interpretations and so contributes to a general understanding of the epistemology of empire. It requires that the analysis of geopolitical exploitation, expansion, and domination be the center of biblical research, urging biblical scholars to relinquish postures of political neutrality and intellectual aloofness. They are asked to get involved in the problems of the contemporary world in which these geopolitical dynamics are still present. Sugirtharajah states:

> What postcolonialism makes clear is that biblical studies can no longer be confined to the history of textual traditions, or to the doctrinal richness embedded in texts, but needs to extend its scope to include issues of domination, Western expansion, and its ideological manifestations, as central forces in defining biblical scholarship.[14]

In the demand for political involvement and contemporary relevance, then, postcolonial biblical studies overlap with feminist goals, and so feminist postcolonial scholars have also begun investigating the Bible's contributions to colonial history, politics, and culture.

Postcolonial Feminist Studies of the Bible

To date, the most comprehensive theoretical voice for studying the Bible from postcolonial feminist perspectives comes from Musa W. Dube.[15] Criticizing both the postcolonial omission of gender analysis and the Western feminist

---

11. Ibid., 12–13.

12. Sugirtharajah, *Postcolonial Criticism*, 23.

13. Ibid., 25.

14. Ibid., 74.

15. Dube, *Postcolonial Feminist Interpretation.*

co-optation into imperialist cultural strategies, she advances an approach that includes a critical reading of both imperialist agendas and gender stereotypes. Her call for postcolonial feminist Bible studies is grounded in the insight that the Bible is neither a Western nor a gender-neutral book but requires critical examination grounded in postcolonial and feminist theories. Dube is convinced that the problem of imperialism is "bigger" than patriarchy,[16] but she does not allow her investigations to be biased in favor of postcolonial critique, nor to neglect a gender analysis. She wants biblical interpreters to expose both androcentric and imperial ideologies in text and interpretation. If they do not bring both analytical categories to their work, they fall prey to the imperial imagination and leave unchallenged colonizing strategies and agendas in culture, politics, and religion.

Like other postcolonial feminist theorists,[17] Dube is cautious of a homogenizing and universalizing use of the category "woman" in Western feminism and encourages research that examines patriarchal and imperial conditions in history and culture. Patriarchal oppression takes many different forms and women of different social locations experience it differently. Like feminist postcolonial theorists in general, Dube also assumes that women who live under imperial oppression, who are the colonized, are doubly oppressed. Their colonization overlaps with patriarchal domination by the colonized native males and the patriarchal structures of the colonizing power. Dube wants feminist biblical interpreters to be aware of these differences among women that create the experience of "double colonization"[18] for some. A multivalent analysis of gender and postcolonialism enables such awareness, Dube asserts.

Since the Bible has to be interpreted with these crucial assumptions in mind, Dube develops the concept of "Rahab's reading prism." Many commentaries characterize Rahab as a Canaanite prostitute who collaborates with the Israelite spies in Joshua 2. Dube, however, emphasizes that Rahab submits to the imperial power of ancient Israel and her story illustrates the complex positioning of Two-Third World women. Rahab is a politically problematic female character with whom postcolonial feminists should not identify. Yet she is significant for her story illustrates the multiple positioning of colonized women. A colonized woman is thus the model for what Dube calls "Rahab's reading prism."

It is "a postcolonial feminist eye of many angles and of seeing, reading, and hearing literary texts through resisting imperial and patriarchal oppressive structures and ideologies … [It] enlightens women on how to form political coalitions that do not invite double-colonized women to the table as parroting Rahabs [i.e. women submitting to colonizing forms of oppression] … [It] demands the radical transgression of boundaries by embracing a multicultural canon, which

---

16. Ibid., 79.

17. Laura E. Donaldson, *Decolonizing Feminisms: Race, Gender, and Empire Building* (Chapel Hill: University of North Carolina Press, 1992). See also Laura E. Donaldson and Kwok Pui-lan (eds), *Postcolonialism, Feminism & Religious Discourse* (New York and London: Routledge, 2002).

18. Ibid., 121.

does not continue to privilege imperializing canons." Rahab's reading prism aims "at revolutionizing the structural oppression, at cultivating readings-writings of liberative interdependence, where differences, equality, and justice for various cultures, religions, genders, classes, sexualities, ethnicities, and races can be subject to constant reevaluation and celebration in the interconnectedness of our relationships."[19]

In short, Dube's hermeneutics defines feminist and postcolonial perspectives as crucial for biblical interpretation, and it demands attention to the multiple perspectives with which biblical literature can and should be interpreted in the effort of opposing the many forms of social, political, and economic forms of exploitation. This broad and all-inclusive goal for biblical interpretation engages actively the political, cultural, and religious conditions of our time. It is not content to reduce the reading of biblical literature into the distant past or to limit its revolutionary potential to gender only. As Dube states, postcolonial feminist interpreters of the Bible recognize the multilayered dimensions of human structures of power and participate in liberationist and justice-seeking projects of politically and socially progressive movements in today's world.

Yet despite these wide-ranging goals postcolonial feminist readers are very specific in how they read biblical texts and the histories of interpretation, and the following discussion introduces a sampling of their works in three sections. One section illustrates how postcolonial feminist interpreters relate stories of biblical women to their own experiences of imperial and androcentric oppression. Another section presents the work of postcolonial feminist interpreters who read the Bible with "ordinary readers,"[20] i.e. lay and usually Christian women living in Two-Third World countries and reading the Bible in community settings. Yet another section examines how some postcolonial feminist scholars analyse biblical literature within imperial history, politics, and tradition.[21]

The discussion demonstrates the wide range of postcolonial feminist interpretations that women from Africa, Asia, and Latin America·have developed so far. All of them read with political and social conviction, exegetical skill, and intellectual fervor towards a world beyond androcentrism and imperial exploitation. Among popular biblical women characters are Hagar, Ruth, Rahab, and Esther, as well as the gang-raped and murdered "concubine" in Judges 19, and Orpah, the sister-in-law of Ruth. Attention to gender and imperial positioning nurtures new

19. Ibid., 123.

20. For the expression "ordinary readers," see, e.g. Gerald O. West and Muse W. Dube Shomanah (eds), *"Reading With": An Exploration of the Interface Between Critical and Ordinary Readings of the Bible: African Overtures* (Atlanta, GA: Scholars Press, 1996); Gerald O. West, "And the Dumb Do Speak: Articulating Incipient Readings of the Bible in Marginalized Communities," in J. W. Rogerson, M. Davies, M. Daniel, and R. Carroll (eds), *The Bible in Ethics: The Second Sheffield Colloquium* (Sheffield: Sheffield Academic Press, 1995), 174–92.

21. For a different organization of postcolonial feminist interpretations, see Kwok, *Postcolonial Imagination and Feminist Theology*, 81–4.

meanings in the reading of biblical texts, as well as the hope toward postcolonial gender justice in the world.[22]

She is Like Us: Textual Alignments with the "Other" Women

A popular strategy among feminist postcolonial interpreters correlates the lot of biblical women with the socio-political context of their societies. Readers connect the biblical stories to their societies so that biblical texts are freed from the prison of historical meaning and speak to the contemporary needs of women in Two-Third World countries. Four interpretations will illustrate this approach.[23] Judith McKinlay interprets the book of Ruth in the context of Aotearoa New Zealand.[24] Athalya Brenner links her reading of the book of Ruth with the situation of contemporary Israel's foreign workers from Eastern Europe and the Far East. Laura E. Donaldson compares Orpah with the fate of Native American women, and Yani Yoo correlates the story of the concubine in Judges 19–21 to the Korean "comfort women."

Judith McKinlay interprets the book of Ruth as "a twentieth-century woman reader from Aotearoa New Zealand. She comes from a country that purports to live by a bicultural treaty guaranteeing rights and respect to two cultures."[25] McKinlay is part of the dominant culture of European heritage in New Zealand and she knows her country's colonial history well. Because she understands the ongoing dynamics of postcolonial rule in her native country, she reads Ruth against her own cultural position of privilege as "a New Zealand *Pakaha/ Palagi*."[26] Already the first verse in Ruth makes her suspicious about the perspective promoted in the story, "when the judges ruled" (Ruth 1:1). This is a story about land wars, and McKinlay remembers such stories from her childhood when she listened to them from one side only. She cautions her

22. For a recent analysis of feminist postcolonialism, see Jeremy Punt, "Dealing with Empire and Negotiating Hegemony: Developments in Postcolonial Feminist Hebrew Bible Criticism," in Susanne Scholz (ed.), *Feminist Interpretation of the Hebrew Bible in Retrospect* (Sheffield: Sheffield Phoenix Press, 2016), 278–303.

23. For additional examples, see Julie Li-Chuan Chu, "Returning Home: The Inspiration of the Role Dedifferentiation in the Book of Ruth for Taiwanese Women," *Semeia* 78 (1997): 47–53. See also Sarojini Nadar, "A South African Indian Womanist Reading of the Character of Ruth," in Musa W. Dube (ed.), *Other Ways of Reading: African Women and the Bible* (Atlanta and Geneva: Society of Biblical Literature/WCC Publications, 2001), 159–75; Kwok, "Finding Ruth a Home: Gender, Sexuality, and the Politics of Otherness," in *Postcolonial Imagination and Feminist Theology*, 100–21.

24. The Maori people are the indigenous population in New Zealand.

25. Judith McKinlay, "A Son Is Born to Naomi: A Harvest for Israel," in Athalya Brenner (ed.), *Ruth and Esther: A Feminist Companion to the Bible (Second Series)* (Sheffield: Sheffield Academic Press, 1999), 153.

26. Ibid., 161.

readers, "Be alert," and she questions by whom, to whom, and for whom the book of Ruth is told.[27]

McKinlay's attention to the national identities of Ruth the Moabite, of Naomi and Boaz the Israelites, and of the Israelite storytellers and their listeners creates an innovative and highly intriguing interpretation of the book of Ruth. Gone is the romantic comedy in which Ruth follows her mother-in-law to find love and a new home, culminated by the birth of a son who will be the ancestor of King David. In McKinlay's retelling the book of Ruth turns into a xenophobic and imperialistic confirmation of Israelite superiority and national hegemony with an insider mythos that scares her. In fact, McKinlay worries that this book, reinforcing colonizing tendencies in New Zealand and elsewhere, is read as sacred scripture in her country where "racial politics are alive and well."[28] McKinlay warns women of the colonized and the colonizer: "Moabite mothers beware! *Pakeha/palagi* women read very carefully."[29]

Another interpretation that focuses on national identities comes from Athalya Brenner. She compares the situation of Ruth to the migration of workers from primarily Eastern and Far Eastern countries into contemporary Israel, particularly by single, female, and foreign workers.[30] Reading the book of Ruth in this contemporary context, Brenner posits that Ruth is "a prime example" for the difficulties of foreigners, especially single, low income women, to cross cultural boundaries with the hope of full integration in the host culture. Yet they have little chance of gaining full and equal status in the new country even when they are exemplary like Ruth, Brenner states. After all, Ruth is only "absorbed" rather than "integrated" into ancient Israel, she disappears in Chapter 4, and her son is recognized as Naomi's and not hers.[31] Similar to McKinlay's interpretation, therefore, Brenner does not view the book of Ruth as an idyllic, romantic narrative about a Moabite woman finding love and a home. Rather, she observes that "read against the reality of foreign female work today,"[32] the story illustrates the ongoing struggles of immigrant women who are sometimes desperate for a cross-cultural marriage. They hope to find financial security and cultural acceptance in a new society in which "full integration … is in fact impossible."[33]

Different from these two readings that focus on Ruth, one postcolonial feminist interpretation sheds light on the neglected female character, Ruth's sister-in-law, Orpah, by comparing this woman's fate with Two-Third World women. A scholar of Cherokee heritage, Laura E. Donaldson places the book of Ruth in her Native

27. Ibid., 161.

28. Ibid., 157.

29. Ibid.

30. Athalya Brenner, "Ruth As a Foreign Worker and the Politics of Exogamy," in Athalya Brenner (ed.), *Ruth and Esther: A Feminist Companion to the Bible (Second Series)* (Sheffield: Sheffield Academic Press, 1999), 158–62.

31. Ibid., 161.

32. Ibid., 162.

33. Ibid.

American context, arguing that in this story intermarriage is promoted as an assimilationist strategy.[34] The tale reminds Donaldson of white European settlers and their descendants who promoted this strategy with Native Americans. For instance, Thomas Jefferson, the second president of the United States, proposed mixed marriages because "in time, you will be as we are; you will become one people with us."[35] The social absorption had, however, disastrous consequences for American Indian society, as it destroyed indigenous matrilineal customs and bonds within families and tribes. To Donaldson, intermarriage in the book of Ruth must thus be viewed as an assimilationist strategy to colonial power and not as an appealing act of benevolence. From a native feminist perspective, Ruth is a negative symbol of silent collaboration with the colonizer, and so Donaldson rejects the identification with Ruth as a viable option for colonized people, especially when they are women.

Since the figure of Ruth does not present an identification model for native readers, Donaldson rediscovers Orpah, the sister-in-law of Ruth, who returns home after the death of her husband (Ruth 1:14). Orpah's story is a "counter-narrative"[36] because she upholds her heritage and origins. Like Cherokee women, she chooses her mother's house in contrast to Ruth who abandons it and assimilates to the "alien Israelite Father."[37] Donaldson's focus on Orpah transforms the traditional "colonizing" reading of Ruth from a positive to a negative character whereas Orpah turns from a negative to a positive one. Ruth is not a role model to Donaldson who resists "imperial exegesis" and aims to contribute to the "empowerment of aboriginal peoples everywhere."[38] Her interpretation of the book of Ruth is innovative and unique.

A fourth and final example comes from Yani Yoo who compares the story of the unnamed concubine in Judges 19–21 with the fate of the Korean "comfort women" during the Japanese colonization of Korea from 1910 to 1945.[39] To Yoo, all of these women are "victims of imperialism, militarism, racism, and patriarchy"[40] who have experienced *han* after the great injustice done to them. *Han* is a Korean expression for feelings of pain, sorrow, helplessness, and desire for revenge to right the wrong. In six concise points Yoo describes how the biblical story and the story

34. Laura E. Donaldson, "The Sign of Orpah: Reading Ruth through Native Eyes," in Athalya Brenner (ed.), *Ruth and Esther: A Feminist Companion to the Bible (Second Series)* (Sheffield: Sheffield Academic Press, 1999), 138. For another interpretation that highlights Orpah, see Musa W. Dube, "The Unpublished Letters of Orpah to Ruth," in Athalya Brenner (ed.), *Ruth and Esther: A Feminist Companion to the Bible (Second Series)* (Sheffield: Sheffield Academic Press, 1999), 145–50.

35. Quoted ibid., 137 n.24.

36. Ibid., 141.

37. Ibid., 144.

38. Ibid.

39. Yani Yoo, "Han-Laden Women: Korean 'Comfort Women' and Women in Judges 19–21," *Semeia* 78 (1997): 37–46.

40. Ibid., 44.

of the comfort women illuminate each other. First, in both stories the women are nameless and anonymous which adds to their being demeaned. Yoo explains that Japanese soldiers invented derogatory nicknames to force comfort women into prostitution and rape. Similarly, the women in Judges 19–21 remain nameless, adding to their silence and humiliation. Second, in both stories comfort women and the biblical woman are reduced to their physical bodies; they "are treated as 'things' which have genitals."[41] They are there for rape, especially when they are sexually inexperienced, and so both the Japanese army and the male Benjaminites kidnap and rape virginal women. Third, in both cases the violence perpetrated on the women is systematic and collective, as well as "state-organized,"[42] reaching genocidal dimensions. Fourth, tribal or state-wide wars precede systematically organized sexual violence in which men fight for their interests and women are their victims. The comfort women were at the mercy of Japan that sought to colonize Korea. Similarly, Judges 19–21 reflect tribal conflicts from the formative period in early Israel when war among the tribes of Israel raged. Fifth, in both stories women are viewed as "gifts and scapegoats" for men.[43] The comfort women were given as gifts of "comfort" by the Japanese emperor to his soldiers, and the concubine and the women of Jabesh-Gilead and Shiloh turn into gifts for the Benjaminite soldiers. Sixth, both the comfort women and the women in Judges 19–21 are quickly forgotten. Only feminist efforts recover their lost histories and bring back the women's pain and suffering. Because women are still sexually violated all over the world and due to the persistence of "the deep-seated diseases like militarism, imperialism, and patriarchy," Yoo urges women "around the world" to continue fighting "to prevent all evil powers from causing *han*." She believes that "[o]nly then will the spirit of *han* recede from the world and the spirit of peace and justice prevail."[44] In all of these interpretations, then, postcolonial feminist readers align biblical meaning with the socio-political contexts of their societies and create new meanings of biblical stories, characters, and events.

In Favor of Ordinary Two-Third World Women

Another strategy has gained increasing popularity among postcolonial feminist Bible readers that is closely aligned with the development of interpretations in support of ordinary Two-Third World women who are not academically trained in biblical studies. Postcolonial feminist scholars propose that ordinary readers have much to contribute to the biblical meaning-making process and that academics better listen to their readings. For too long, biblical scholars dismissed ordinary readers and the disregard has led to dominating and oppressive interpretations. It is thus urgent to correlate biblical meanings to the needs and sensibilities of

41. Ibid., 42.
42. Ibid.
43. Ibid.
44. Ibid., 45.

ordinary readers, especially when they have much to contribute to liberatory and egalitarian views on the Bible.

The following description highlights two proposals that interpret the Hebrew Bible with ordinary Two-Third World women readers in mind. A first proposal, advanced by Musa W. Dube, uses the method of divination, popular among the Botswanian people, for the interpretation of the book of Ruth. A second proposal, mentioned by Dora R. Mbuwayesango, outlines the historical effects of translating biblical terminology for God into the vernacular languages of the Zimbabwean people. In both cases a concern for ordinary Two-Third World readers, especially women, shapes the interpretation of the Hebrew Bible.[45]

One way of engaging ordinary women readers of Botswana, according to Musa W. Dube, is to imitate their popular divination method. Originally, southern African people used divination sets with bones, coins, or beads, but later they also began to use the Bible as the "talking book" after their Christianization by Western missionaries. Thus even today the Bible is often part of divination readings among many Christian spiritual healers. The goal of consulting a diviner-healer is to diagnose problems as part of a systemic spiritual, social, and physical whole. Professional diviner-healers read the Bible to suggest remedies for broken relationships and ill health. Dube explains: "Healing physical illness thus begins with attending to all the social relationships of the CR's [consulting reader's] life, before medication is offered for obvious physical ailments. One's physical body is regarded as part of the larger social body."[46] Biblical meaning emerges from the relationship between the healer and the person consulting with the healer, as well as from the questions brought to the text and from the difficult situation experienced by the requesting person.

Dube proceeds to use the divination method, applying it to her interpretation of the book of Ruth. Her goal is to understand the international relations between ancient Judah and Moab, the two nations featured in the biblical tale, and so to attend to the social relationship pattern exhibited in this biblical book, as consulting readers would do on the basis of the divination method. Dube explains:

> The book of Ruth will be my divining set, and I will be a CR [consulting reader]. I regard all other published readers of Ruth as divine-readers. As a CR, my reading is in communication therefore with published readers of Ruth, although my reading of the divining set remains my own …. As a CR, the issues that bring me to read Ruth as a divining set are: (1) I seek to decolonize the production of knowledge in biblical studies that tends largely to use Western

45. Musa W. Dube, "Divining Ruth for International Relations," in Musa W. Dube (ed.), *Other Ways of Reading: African Women and the Bible* (Atlanta and Geneva: Society of Biblical Literature/WCC Publications, 2001), 179–95; Dora R. Mbuwayesango, "How Local Divine Powers Were Suppressed: A Case of Mwari of the Shona," in Musa W. Dube (ed.), *Other Ways of Reading: African Women and the Bible* (Atlanta and Geneva: Society of Biblical Literature/WCC Publications, 2001), 63–77.

46. Dube, "Divining Ruth for International Relations," 181.

modes of conceptualization and analysis. (2) I am committed to an interdisciplinary approach in biblical studies, and, with this essay, I seek to focus on international relations, southern African divination systems and practices, and Ruth. (3) My focus on international relations relates largely to my social standing as a citizen of Botswana, indeed, of Africa as a whole ... .[47]

Based on these guidelines and assumptions, Dube sets out to read the book of Ruth. The result is an interpretation quite different from others, whether androcentric or feminist. It highlights the discrepancies in the characterization of Judah as a fertile and nourishing land in contrast to Moab, a land of death, hunger, and loss. In Moab, three husbands die and two of them die childless, leaving behind their young wives, Ruth and Orpah, without a future. In Judah, however, two women find not only food but the younger woman remarries and gives birth to a son who is the beginning of a long lineage important to ancient Israel.

Dube's interpretation emphasizes that the relationship between the two countries is not healthy because it is imbalanced. One country is praised as a land with a future, offering much blessing, whereas the other is a land of death and silence. Subordination and domination define Moab's and Israel's relationship and this hierarchical pattern harms both countries. To remedy the death-creating imbalance, Dube wants to see "liberating interdependence" between Judah and Moab in which Judah encourages mutual and open contact with Moab. The story, however, does not allow for such mutuality and openness because it is stuck in an unwell state in which one country rejects the other. This is a mistake, Dube suggests, because "[n]ations are never pure or independent, but they are interdependent, interconnected, and multicultural."[48] Dube's innovative reading, based on a guiding principle of ordinary women readers in southern Africa, advances an understanding of the book of Ruth that aims to heal imbalanced international relations between Moab and ancient Israel as well as among countries of our time.

While Dube creatively adapts a method popular among Botswanian women to biblical interpretation, another postcolonial feminist scholar, Dora R. Mbuwayesango from Zimbabwe and who teaches in the United States, discusses the hermeneutical problems involved in supporting ordinary African women readers. She explains that it is a difficult process because colonization has infiltrated every aspect of religious life, including vernacular Bible translations. What is needed are new translations that do not colonize indigenous concepts and belief systems unlike the Bibles distributed in African countries like Zimbabwe during the past century. Mbuwayesango demonstrates the severity of the problem by analyzing Bible translations used by the Shona peoples who live in a region in Zimbabwe called Mashonaland. They have experienced religious and cultural devastation throughout the twentieth century, also due to the missionary Bible translations that destroyed the Shona peoples' sense as a collective with a succinct cultural and religious identity and heritage.

47. Ibid., 184.
48. Ibid., 194.

Mbuwayesango explains that Western Christian missionaries who were part of the colonizing powers of Zimbabwe since the late nineteenth century faced the challenge of making the Bible relevant to the Shona peoples. Initially, biblical terminology meant little to the people, especially when the Bible referred to God. The missionaries then began substituting biblical vocabulary with Shona terms. This translation strategy was particularly successful after translators substituted the biblical word for God with the Shona term, Mwari. At first, this idea did not find unanimous approval from missionary translators and organizations. They insisted on distinguishing between the Shona gods and the biblical God because they considered the former unworthy of being associated with Elohim or Yahweh.[49] Yet by the 1960s, Western missionaries accepted the assimilation of Shona terms into the Bible as the best strategy. The effect on the religious and cultural sensibilities of the Shona peoples resulted in the suppression of Shona stories and folktales.

Soon the Shona people regarded their myths and religious traditions as secondary to the Bible which came to dominate their cultural and social imagination. The Bible began to shape the meaning of Shona terms in ways that were alien and even contradictory to Shona tradition. For instance, Shona tradition depicts Mwari as absolutely apart from creation in which gods are unlike humans, but biblical creation stories anthropomorphize God (e.g. Gen. 1:26-7). Other biblical narratives, such as Genesis 18:22, identify God even as a *male* messenger, and in the prophetic text, Isaiah 63:16, God is addressed as "father," an impossibility for Shona belief. The anthropomorphic and androcentric bias of the biblical notions stands in direct opposition to the Shona view of Mwari as genderless and different from humanity. Mbuwayesango suggests that the increasing prevalence of the Bible in the vernacular languages of the Shona peoples has contributed to an increasing androcentric bias in Shona religion and culture. While androcentric beliefs increased in Shona culture due to the success of Christian missionaries, the genderless notion of Mwari disappeared gradually. Worst of all, the assimilation of indigenous terminology into biblical history and story destroyed the indigenous meaning of those terms, and over time the Shona peoples have come to remember Mwari as the biblical Christian God only. They forgot traditional ideas about Mwari as a Shona god and now take for granted its biblical connotations. Mbuwayesango explains:

> Mwari ceased to be the God of the Shona peoples and became the God of the Hebrews .... The missionaries, and the Bible as the missionaries interpreted it, thus had the final word on what is acceptable and not acceptable for Mwari's new identity; the ways of the Shona were deemed obsolete.[50]

According to Mbuwayesango, the only remedy for this oppressive and colonizing situation consists in developing new linguistic tools such as dictionaries and new

49. Mbuwayesango, "How Local Divine Powers Were Suppressed," 66.
50. Ibid., 71, 73.

Bible translations. These translations have to make a clear distinction between the traditions, stories, and terminologies of the Bible and the Shona peoples. Mbuwayesango rejects proposals of some Zimbabwean theologians to develop Bible versions that include Shona stories and traditions in the biblical canon because she is convinced that such comprehensive translations would "fall into the trap of making Mwari compatible with Christian concepts."[51] Instead she wants to see a clear distinction between Christian documents and Shona stories so that "the identification of Mwari with the genderless Shona deity will be reclaimed."[52] Consequently, ordinary readers, female and male, are currently unable to read biblical texts without succumbing to an inherently colonizing pattern. Their efforts to create decolonized interpretations depend on the future work of Mbuwayesango and her colleagues. Otherwise, ordinary readers find themselves unconsciously in the unfortunate, even tragic position of perpetuating oppressive biblical meanings because the linguistic fabric of their vernacular Bibles is entangled with the political, economic, and spiritual oppression of their land.

Spinning Hybrid Interpretations Within (Post)colonial Theory

Yet another strategy, locating feminist biblical meaning within (post)colonial history, is advanced by Judith E. McKinlay in a book that deals with a potpourri of biblical women. One of them is the Phoenician queen, Jezebel, who is married to the Israelite king, Ahab (1 Kgs 16). Through the Jezebel stories, McKinlay asserts, we are still able to detect a struggle in ancient Israel between the acceptance of hybridity and difference on the one hand and the promotion of homogeneity and sameness on the other.[53] For instance, King Ahab's marriage to the Phoenician Jezebel reflects a moment in Israelite history in which Phoenicians were "not regarded as evil-bringers" and a sharp distinction between Israelites and Canaanites did not yet exist.[54] Only a later ideological push in ancient Israel, supported by a move toward monotheistic thinking that was intolerant of other gods, resisted the earlier conviction. During this later era, in which the writings of the Deuteronomistic History and the books of Ezra and Nehemiah emerged, the strict distinction between insider and outsider defined a position that limited, regulated, and repressed otherness as described in the stories of Jezebel.

McKinlay finds such efforts toward "managing heterogeneity"[55] also present in the "settler narratives" of her country. "[J]ust as Phoenician and Israelite may have once lived together without conflict and with certain intermarriage, so it

---

51. Ibid., 75.

52. Ibid.

53. Judith E. McKinlay, *Reframing Her: Biblical Women in Postcolonial Focus* (Sheffield: Sheffield Phoenix Press, 2004), 75.

54. Ibid., 74.

55. Ibid., 75.

was initially with Maori and European settlers."[56] Initially, they did not fight each other, and one did not yet dominate the other. They shared the land. However, when the colonists gained power, they rejected "the space of hybrid togetherness" and tried to establish strict segregation between the two cultures, a difficult task because "settler cultures are inevitably 'sites of rehearsal, of (re)negotiation.'"[57] After all, McKinlay knows, grounded in her understanding of the history of her country, colonized and the colonizer share space and resources. Contact between them is inevitable. Social, legal, and economic connections exist, and attempts to repress them succeed only temporarily. McKinlay explains that therefore "traces and signs of fracture soon appear." Her own family history illustrates the impossibility for a strict and lasting separation between two peoples living in the same land. McKinlay elaborates:

> As I have already stated, my own identity is as *Pakeha*, yet one of the Maori politicians in parliament is descended from the same Scottish stock, and is thus a distant cousin. And while our mutual Scottish forebears settled here in New Zealand as a self-contained Gaelic speaking community, they had spent sufficient time in Canada on the way here for a marriage with a Canadian indigenous woman, my great-great-grandmother, so that my family identity as Scottish had fractured even before the arrival in New Zealand. But the memory of this was soon silenced and only the genealogical searching of a cousin has recently brought it once again to light. Renegotiation continues … .[58]

When McKinlay reads the Naboth tale in 1 Kings 21, in which Queen Jezebel kills the Israelite owner, Naboth, to acquire his vineyard for her husband, McKinlay relies on postcolonial feminist insights to create an unusual interpretation. It depicts Jezebel as "the silenced 'subaltern.'" She is silent although she speaks in the story.[59] McKinlay surmises that words might have been put into Jezebel's mouth and "may well have been part of the mechanics of silencing an historical Jezebel."[60] Hostile Israelite writers, censoring foreign influence among their people, perhaps invented her words. It is thus possible to conjecture that Jezebel was not involved in the theft of Naboth's vineyard. Yet regardless, the story's final version made Jezebel famous as the "evil foreign murdering queen"[61] who did not only steal from a God-fearing Israelite but also contributed to the quick demise of her husband and son. In other words, McKinlay does not trust the colonizing perspective of the writers because to them "Jezebel was a useful cipher in the deliberate polemic of a religio-political movement within Israel or Judah or Yehud."[62]

56. Ibid., 76.
57. Ibid.
58. Ibid.
59. Ibid., 77.
60. Ibid.
61. Ibid.
62. Ibid., 79.

Jezebel's story, ending with her gruesome death in 2 Kings 9, illustrates that the queen is viewed from a perspective that is ready to kill the "other," especially when she is female. The scene about her death emphasizes her made-up eyes and hair and how she stands proudly in the window frame. She is a *femme fatale*. To McKinlay, these details are part of an "Othering" strategy in which the enemy is feminized to establish inferiority. Feminization of the enemy, the foreigner, signifies weakness, and so Jezebel is killed like an enemy. McKinlay asserts that the queen's murder resembles a "military coup d'état"[63] rather than the killing of a weak woman. Thrown down from the window and eaten by the dogs, she is killed in one quick and brutal swoop. Readers, trapped by this colonizing perspective, rarely understand the dynamics of this imperial storytelling and therefore they do not usually sympathize with Jezebel's gruesome death.

In the end, then, McKinlay is convinced that the Jezebel stories are told from the perspective of the Israelite winners who opposed mingling with Canaanites and Phoenicians. Theirs are settler narratives that claim dominance in the land, and they describe the queen from "the politics of the religious and cultural 'Othering' processes of Israel."[64] The stories want to create a clear-cut distinction between Israelites and Phoenicians and teach: "[L]ook to yourselves, Israel. Israelites are Israelites and Phoenicians are Phoenicians. Or even more explicitly, Baal and Asherah worshipers are one people, Yahweh worshipers are quite another. Don't confuse the two. Take great care that you are not falling into the sin of Ahab!"[65] The Jezebel stories envision a radical segregation between insider and outsider in ancient Israel, and even today they are not often read through this postcolonial feminist lens.

While McKinlay correlates female characters of biblical literature with (post)colonial insights mostly derived from her New Zealand history, other interpreters pursue different links between the Hebrew Bible and (post)colonialism. One of them is Musa W. Dube who connects close readings of biblical story with postcolonial history and theory. A New Testament scholar, Dube also uses the Hebrew Bible to develop hybrid meanings from biblical literature interpreted in postcolonial contexts, often within African traditions. The strength of her approach is based on a successful blending of postcolonial feminist theory with textual interpretation. For instance, Dube presents the narratives in Exodus and Joshua 1–12 as an illustration of what postcolonial theorists call patterns of "anti-conquest" and "contact zone" in literatures of imperial settings.[66] Anti-conquest patterns enable colonizers to claim innocence for the colonial violence perpetrated onto foreign people and to assert simultaneously their right for travelling into foreign land and acquiring its resources. Contact zone patterns appear in colonial literature to describe "the space of colonial encounters"[67] when geographically and

---

63. Ibid., 81.
64. Ibid., 84.
65. Ibid.
66. Dube, *Postcolonial Feminist Interpretation*, 57.
67. Ibid., 58.

historically separated peoples meet in a land that the colonizer is in the process of colonizing. To Dube, the exodus narratives are "excellent examples" of these literary-rhetorical patterns that sanction imperialist oppression.[68]

The exodus narratives begin by establishing the "innocence" of the Israelites. Previously, Joseph had developed good relations with Pharaoh (Gen. 45ff.) and the Israelites were initially welcomed in the Egyptian empire. According to the narratives, this happened thanks to God's intervention (Gen. 45:5-7), and so the exodus story establishes God as the ultimate power behind the events. Predictably, the exodus events begin with God's "mighty acts of liberation." They affirm the notion that the slaves need their own land, and they suggest, according to Dube, that the victimized rightly turns into the victimizer.[69] To Dube, this is anti-conquest ideology at its best.

Moreover, the exodus narratives also sanction the need for the Israelites to travel to a foreign land. Repeatedly, Moses urges Pharaoh "to let my people go" (Exod. 5:1, 14; 8:1, 20; 9:1, 13). The struggle persists over several chapters, and dramatic elements such as the ten plagues underline the tension over the demand for travel. In this anti-conquest narrative God is the ultimate authorizer. God supports the Israelites to get freedom and to reach the Promised Land. The story also describes the Israelites as a special people to God, who is portrayed as justifying their need for land—all typical features of colonizing literature. The emphasis is on "God, gold and glory" to claim and eventually to own the new land. "God" authorizes that the Israelites reach the new land, "gold" is defined as the Promised Land that is "flowing with milk and honey," and "glory" emerges from the people's ability to be freed from slavery, journeying to the land and taking it into possession. Dube explains: "In every way, Israel's story in Exodus-Joshua highlights the literary-rhetorical strategies of colonial subjugation of distant land."[70]

In addition, the exodus story is dominated by patriarchal ideology in which men, such as Moses, feature centrally[71] while female characters are portrayed as being complicit in the narrative's colonizing patterns. This, too, is typical for colonizing narratives. In them women are not innocent bystanders but support the promise for land and the quest for national power. This dynamic appears, for instance, in the stories of the midwives (Exod. 1:15-21), the mother and sister of Moses (2:1-10), Pharaoh's daughter (2:5-10), and the wife of Moses (2:15-22; 4:24-6). There, too, women help men in reaching power and control. Yet women who support the colonial expansion of men are not only women of the colonizers but also come from the colonized people. In colonizing narratives, they, too, support the goals of the male colonizers. A biblical story, best illustrating this dynamic, is the story of Rahab (Josh. 2) who is a colonized woman in co-operation with the Israelite colonizers.

68. Ibid.
69. Ibid., 60.
70. Ibid., 70.
71. Ibid., 73.

To Dube, the story of Rahab exemplifies "the dangers of reclaiming women's roles without naming its imperialistic agendas."[72] The narrative describes Rahab, the Canaanite prostitute, as a supporter of two Israelite spies who visit her house in the middle of the night and receive important information from her. It enables the Israelites to successfully attack and occupy the town. Viewed from a postcolonial feminist perspective, Rahab is a problematic figure because, as a symbol for the distant land, she "willingly and openly accept[s] and proclaim[s] the colonizers" superiority and pledge[s] ... loyalty to them."[73] She is co-opted into the colonizing project, and as such she represents the domestication of the distant land. The only solution for a feminist postcolonial reader is to uncover both patriarchal and imperial agendas of biblical literature and not to fall prey to either one, a problem of Western feminist scholarship, Dube maintains.[74]

Nevertheless, the story of Rahab is crucial for Dube's approach to biblical interpretation because her story serves as a model for "Rahab's reading prism," a decolonizing and anti-patriarchal reading strategy, as outlined earlier in this chapter. Illustrating the four Gs of empire building (God, gold, glory, gender), Rahab reminds readers of the intertwined forms of oppression: sexism and colonialism. Accordingly, any feminist reading should include both depatriarchalizing and anti-imperializing strategies to avoid Rahab's fate, the co-optation into imperial goals and agendas. Dube writes: "Theorizing Rahab's story as a reading strategy, therefore, offers a model that takes seriously both patriarchal and imperial oppression of the past and present and thus provides an understanding that can advance strategic coalitions between international feminist movements in the postcolonial era ..."[75] Dube's postcolonial and feminist interpretation of biblical literature is not content to stay within or behind the text but it seeks to articulate "relationships of liberating interdependence between genders, races, ethnicities, continents, cultures, nations, and the environment."[76] The goal is justice and peace on earth.

Beyond Subordination and Domination: In Conclusion

The broadening of feminist biblical studies to include scholars from around the world is one of the most energizing and significant developments in the field. It means, as this chapter illustrates, the inclusion of a diverse range of perspectives and voices that expand the conversation from a white male and Western defined horizon towards a politicized understanding of feminist biblical scholarship from Two-Third World scholars and Bible-readers, including women. Moreover, postcolonial feminist work brings the gift of a renewed emphasis on political,

72. Ibid., 76.
73. Ibid., 79.
74. Ibid., 80, 199.
75. Ibid., 201.
76. Ibid.

social, economic, and spiritual change that was widespread during the early stages of feminists reading the Bible but is often difficult to sustain in academic contexts. Christian women mystics and nineteenth-century suffragettes were always mindful of the connection between biblical meanings and social change. They did not only read biblical literature as historical or literary texts but they also wanted to develop interpretations that sought real changes in women's lives. In a professionalized, academic setting in which feminist scholars are encouraged and sometimes choose to forgo the relevance of their work for society, the call of feminist postcolonial interpreters serves as an important reminder of the long-standing tradition of feminists reading the Bible toward socio-political change.

Postcolonial feminist scholars demand that feminist work make connections with various forms of oppression, one of which is gender. They insist that the understanding of sexism be related to geopolitical analysis. As difficult as this may be for Western and white feminist and academic interpreters, postcolonial feminist scholars invite Western readers to join their struggle and not to perpetuate unjust relationships on any level of society. Postcolonial feminist interpreters then exert a highly politicized claim on biblical studies, one that might make some Western white academics and clergy uncomfortable. Gone is the option of retreating into the ivory towers of academia or into privatized and individualized piety. Postcolonial feminist scholars promote an engaged reading of biblical literature that is grounded in gender oppression and equally connected to imperial oppression and exploitation in the world.

Postcolonial feminist interpreters also connect biblical studies with the interdisciplinary intellectual and cultural discourses of our time. It seems that feminist readings, if placed within postcolonial feminist studies, have much to gain from the many conversation partners, all of whom are trying to understand women's and gender history, traditions, and lives in the global context. Examining how women read the Bible and how differently located women readers interpret biblical texts promises a comprehensive understanding into gendered lives, histories, and cultures. A traditionally defined approach to biblical studies cannot offer such breadth and depth of knowledge in the Hebrew Bible and its interpretation history.

Thus, once the task of biblical scholarship includes feminist and postcolonial studies, the reading of the Bible embraces manifold, wide-ranging, and diverse questions, skills and perspectives. It brings the field into conversations with other academic disciplines, discourses, and developments. It also turns biblical studies into a field of global significance in which researchers explore the Bible's global reach. Postcolonial feminist interpreters have begun to demonstrate the need for such work in which gender remains a crucial element as it integrates with other categories of socio-political analysis, such as imperialism and geopolitical dynamics of the postcolonial era.

Chapter 6

DENATURALIZING THE GENDER BINARY:
QUEER AND MASCULINITY STUDIES AS INTEGRAL
TO FEMINIST BIBLICAL HERMENEUTICS

The Bible is a queer book, but it is safe to say that this simple fact has been long forgotten. Scholars and lay readers of the Bible have invented all kinds of methods, methodologies, and interpretation strategies (also known as "hermeneutics") to normalize their views of what the Bible means to them. Thus, unsurprisingly, Bible courses are taught in colleges, universities, and theology schools with the goal to inform students about the proper, i.e. the scholarly sound, ways of reading biblical texts. Over the centuries, Bible scholars have developed different academic ways of reading the Bible, but it always comes down to this point: initially, those scholarly ways of reading challenge the hermeneutical norms, but eventually they become hegemonic ways of reading that endorse the socio-political, economic, socio-cultural, and religious-theological status quo of living in the world. Said differently, what today's readers take for granted were often marginalized and perhaps even revolutionary—queer—ways of reading the Bible in the past.

A good example for this dynamic is the historical-critical method. Baruch Spinoza (1632–77), a Jewish thinker of science and philosophy, raised historical questions about the Pentateuch's authorship when he anonymously published his work, entitled *Tractatus Theologico-Politicus*, in 1670. Although it was immediately vilified, his courageous inquiries into the authorship of the Pentateuch enabled later generations of Bible scholars to investigate the matter further. Nowadays, the idea that Moses is not the Pentateuch's author is mainstream, except among the most fundamentalist Christian apologists who defend God's authorship of the Bible. What was marginal and "other" during the seventeenth century CE is the dominant viewpoint in biblical scholarship today. Spinoza's "queer" investigations into the historicity of the Bible have become normative.

In biblical studies the use of the term "queer" is notable only since 1999 when a few scholars began investigating the Bible as a queer book.[1] They were engaged in

---

1. For the first scholarly article in biblical studies with the word "queer" in it, see Mona West, "Reading the Bible as Queer Americans: Social Location and the Hebrew Scriptures," *Theology & Sexuality* 10 (March 1999): 28–42.

the socio-political and intellectual discussions within the LGBTIQ[2] and feminist movements that had emerged since the late 1960s, and wanted to connect queer theories with the scholarly study of the Bible. Nowadays, the commitment to queering both the Hebrew Bible and the New Testament has led to many heterodox interpretations. They contest normalized, essentializing, binary, and naturalized meanings of the Bible. Often queer exegetes engage with philosophers and theorists important in queer and feminist studies, such as Michel Foucault, Teresa de Lauretis, Judith Butler, Eve Sedgewick, and Adrienne Rich.[3] Queer exegetes have exposed hegemonic discourses about "homosexuality" as pathologizing, and they have opened up exegetical conversations about gender, sexuality, and sexual orientations in a field adhering to phallogocentric and heteronormative assumptions and belief systems. Since the 1990s, queer exegetes have destabilized and subverted the exegetical foundations of the academic study of the Bible. They have recovered the Bible's queerness although many of these exegetes have also remained committed to standard methods and exegetical procedures of mainstream biblical studies.

This chapter presents the developments that have redefined the Bible as queer literature. First, it discusses the emergence and significance of queer theories in general. Second, it explains why and how queer Bible scholars have contested methodological, and hermeneutical heteronormativity of mainstream Bible meanings. Third, the chapter turns to a related development, namely critical masculinity studies or CMS. This newest hermeneutical approach focuses on the positionality of males and maleness in biblical texts and the interpretation history. Biblical masculinity studies focus on linguistic, methodological, and hermeneutical assumptions about maleness to establish masculinity as an explicitly socio-political category that stands in contrast to hegemonic androcentric scholarship. A conclusion offers ideas about some of the challenges that queer and masculinity biblical scholarship faces today.

Why Queer Theories Matter

The term "queer" became prominent in academic circles in the early 1990s. In the wake of the gay and lesbian liberation movement of the late 1960s, the term "homosexuality" had fallen out of favor as a pathologizing concept that arose at

---

2. For further details on this list of acronym, see, e.g. https://internationalspectrum. umich.edu/life/definitions (accessed December 12, 2016).

3. See, e.g. Michel Foucault, *The History of Sexuality: An Introduction (vol. 1)*, trans. Robert Hurley (New York: Random House, 1978); Teresa de Lauretis, "Queer Theory: Lesbian and Gay Sexualities (Introduction)," *differences* 3 (2) (1991): iii–xviii; Judith Butler, *Gender Trouble: Feminism and the Subversion of Identity* (London: Routledge, 1990); Eve Sedgewick, *Epistemology of the Closet* (Berkeley and Los Angeles, CA: University of California Press, 1990); Adrienne Rich, "Compulsory Heterosexuality and Lesbian Existence," in *Blood, Bread, and Poetry: Selected Prose 1979–1985* (London: W. W. Norton, 1986), 23–75.

the end of the nineteenth century. It was replaced by "gay," a successful reappropriation of the word's original meaning of "happy," "carefree," or "bright and showy." The term "queer" also reappropriated a less cheery term that prior to the 1980s meant "strange," "odd," "peculiar," or "eccentric."

More specifically, the term "queer" first appeared in academic discourse when Teresa De Lauretis used it in a conference in February 1990.[4] Scholars liked the term so much that it coined an innovative theoretical development of deconstructing and eliminating binary distinctions about sexuality and gender. Since then, queer theorists have dismantled the distinction between "natural sexuality" or heterosexuality on the one hand and homosexual practices considered transgressive, abnormal, deviant, or sick on the other hand. Often, queer theorists hold ambiguous views about the field of gay and lesbian studies because it presupposes the binary notion of heterosexuality that queer theorists want to eliminate. They argue that both homosexuality and heterosexuality are symbiotically dependent upon each other because the term heterosexuality, presumably the "natural" expression of human sexuality, did not even exist until the end of the nineteenth century.[5] Furthermore, the differentiation between heterosexuality and homosexuality includes another assumption, namely the superiority of heterosexuality to homosexuality ("deviant" sexuality), defining homosexuality as an identifiable pathology or a lifestyle option. Consequently, queer theorists reject the binary definition of heterosexuality as the norm and homosexuality as the deviant, the transgression, and the "Other" to be tolerated or punished by law, and they urge to eliminate the very assumptions upon which this binary distinction rests.

When the binary distinction is rejected, queer sexualities emerge in their own right. Accordingly, as De Lauretis explains, "male and female homosexualities—in their current sexual-political articulations of gay and lesbian sexuality, in North America—may be reconceptualized as social and cultural forms in their own right, albeit emergent ones and thus still fuzzily defined, undercoded, or discursively dependent on more established forms."[6] No longer understood as part of a binary, queer sexualities are respected as independent "social cultural forms." They participate in social processes that are "both interactive and yet resilient, both participatory and yet distinct, claiming at once equality and difference, demanding political representation while insisting on its material and historical specificity."[7] In short, queer sexualities step out of the hegemonic shadows of heteronormative discourse, and queer theorists have focused on them ever since De Lauretis proposed so in 1990.

The success of De Lauretis's conference was probably also related to the fact that it connected street talk with academic talk. It enabled queer theorists to deconstruct hegemonic heteronormativity, looking at sexual identities in their

4. De Lauretis, "Queer Theory," iii–xviii.

5. See, e.g. Jonathan Katz, *The Invention of Heterosexuality* (Chicago and London: University of Chicago Press, 1995).

6. Lauretis, "Queer Theory," iii.

7. Ibid.

intersectional manifestations, expressions, and performances.[8] At the heart of queer theorizing lies a deep suspicion about hegemonic norms and essentializing foundations. For instance, Jonathan Kemp defines queer studies as deconstructing and reconfigurating the existing paradigms about sexuality. He acknowledges that "queer is nothing new" when it is understood that "[t]he gay movement has always been torn by a conflict of interests between those who want social reform and those who want revolution." He states: "[Q]ueer is just another name for those who want revolution, those who choose to live outside of and thereby challenge society's norms,"[9] and so queer theories represent a "sophisticated level of theoretical engagement." Queer theorists borrow from post-structuralism in their resistance to normativity and hegemonic powers that shape people's thoughts and lives. They challenge essentialized notions of sexual identities in their intersectional manifestations, and they move into "a realm of experimentation with alternative ways of structuring society."[10] As Laurel Schneider explains: "Queer theory is not just for or about so-called homosexuals. It is critical theory concerned principally with cultural deployments of power through social constructions of sexuality and gender."[11]

In this sense, then, queer theories do not merely aim for intellectual discourse; they promote radical change in society. Kemp observes that "[q]ueer is whatever is at odds with the norm." It is an "inherently political motivation"[12] that includes "a practice or process of critique."[13] Queerness stands "for different things and [can] be used to critique different aspects of contemporary life."[14] Importantly, it is not limited to the study of sexualities. As a field, queer studies are "transdisciplinary" and do not have "a fixed referent."[15] Queer theorist, David M. Halperin, elaborates on this view of queer studies as a generic critique of various hegemonies of power, writing:

> "Queer," ... does not designate a class of already objectified pathologies or perversions; rather, it describes a horizon of possibilities whose precise extent and heterogeneous scope cannot in principle be delimited in advance. It is from the eccentric positionality occupied by the queer subject that it may become possible to envision a variety of possibilities for reordering the relations

8. For an influential discussion on the performance of gender that does not yet use the term "queer" but elaborates on the construction of sexuality, see Judith Butler, *Gender Trouble: Feminism and the Subversion of Identity* (New York and Routledge: Routledge, 1990).

9. Jonathan Kemp, "A Queer Age: Or, Discourse Has a History," *Graduate Journal of Social Science* 6 (1) (2009): 11.

10. Ibid., 11.

11. Laurel C. Schneider, "Queer Theory," in A. K. M. Adam (ed.), *Handbook of Postmodern Biblical Interpretation* (St. Louis: Chalice Press, 2000), 206.

12. Kemp, "A Queer Age," 12.

13. Ibid., 13.

14. Ibid.

15. Ibid.

among sexual behaviours, erotic identities, constructions of gender, forms of knowledge, regimes of enunciation, logics of representations, modes of self-construction, and practices of community—for restructuring, that is, the relations among power, truth and desire.[16]

Queerness is thus a future-oriented practice and a theoretical process of embodied criticism. It envisions and embraces innovations and possibilities beyond the current mainstream, and it challenges the dominant socio-political, economic, cultural, or religious norms, the manifold hegemonies of power, and the persistent status quo. Put another way, queer theory's resistance to assimilation directly contrasts the Borg's famous assertion in *Star Trek*: "Resistance is futile." Queerness "disturb[s] the order of things,"[17] it "reconfigure[es] counterhegemonic sexualities," and it re-appropriates "queer" as "a badge of honor."[18] The persistent threat to queer success is the "threat of institutionalization that occurs when a critical term enters the academy, a taming of the critical energy, a domestication, a declawing and detoothing of its sharpest assets."[19] The temptation to become the normative is real. Queer theorists stress repeatedly, as if to warn readers not to forget, that "[q]ueer, if it names anything, names a critical impulse that can never, must never settle."[20] As it turns out, to never settle, to never acquiesce, and to never be content with the current state of affairs poses a significant challenge even for the most fervent revolutionaries, whether they are queer or otherwise. The relative success in legalizing same-sex marriage, adoption rights, and related non-discriminatory laws in many Western societies is a case in point.

Despite the problem of assimilatory tendencies in LGBTIQ practices in Western societies during the past few decades, the notion of queerness as "outlaw" is repeatedly reaffirmed. For instance, Jasbir K. Puar develops the analytic category of "homonationalism" to argue that queer sexualities have, in fact, assimilated in U.S.–American national and international discourse.[21] Puar explains that "[t]he emergence and sanctioning of queer subjecthood is a historical shift condoned only through a parallel process of demarcation from populations targeted for segregation, disposal, or death, a reintensification of racialization through queerness."[22] Accordingly, Western countries and especially

16. David M. Halperin, *Saint Foucault: Towards a Gay Hagiography* (New York and Oxford: Oxford University Press, 1995), 62.

17. For the phrase, see Michel Foucault, *The Order of Things: An Archaeology of the Human Sciences* (New York: Random House, 1970).

18. Kemp, "A Queer Age," 18, 19, 20.

19. Ibid., 22.

20. Ibid.

21. Jasbir K. Puar, *Terrorist Assemblages: Homonationalism in Queer Times* (Durham, NC: Duke University Press, 2007). See also David L. Eng, Judith Halberstam and Jose Estaban Munoz, "What's Queer about Queer Studies Now? Introduction," *Social Text* 23 (3–4) (Fall–Winter 2005): 1–17.

22. Ibid., xii.

the United States are in the process of assimilating sexual queerness so that queer sexualities are no longer seen as Other. Simultaneously, entire population groups and "civilizations" emerge as deviant and Other, not for their sexualities, but for their racial, ethnic, and even religious identities. Assimilationist views of queer sexualities in Western countries have thus come to protect the powers of the nation state and they help constitute a profound reorientation of the relationship between the state, capitalism, and sexuality. To Puar, it is high time to expose "the geopolitical and historical forces, neoliberal interests in capitalist accumulation both cultural and material, biopolitical state practices of population control, and affective investments in discourses of freedom, liberation, and rights."[23] The hegemony of neoliberal capitalism absorbs queer sexualities into Western national normativity to enable the "tactics, strategies, and logistics of our contemporary war machines."[24]

The domestication of queer rights privatizes queer sexualities, enabling the legal acceptance of gay marriage and the adoption of children but at the expense of "other" populations. Puar observes that "[t]he narrative of progress for gay rights is thus built on the back of racialized others, for whom such progress was once achieved, but is now backsliding or has yet to arrive."[25] This process is particularly apparent in the intensification of Islamophobia in Western societies. This sociopolitical and cultural-religious development stands in direct correlation with the neocolonial and neoliberal suppression of all Muslims as potential terrorists, Puar explains. Their bodies have become "nonheteronormative, if we consider nation and citizenship to be implicit in the privilege of heteronormativity, as we should."[26] Consequently, so Puar, "the (American imperialist) nation" characterizes terrorist bodies as sexually perverse, doing the unnatural, the forbidden, and the "queer." They "disobey normative conventions of 'appropriate' bodily practices and the sanctity of the able body."[27]

Puar's "queer re-reading of the terrorist bodies" also contests political-intellectual conventions in queer studies by refusing to accept terrorist bodies as culturally, ethnically and religiously nationalist, fundamentalist, patriarchal, and often even homophobic. Puar insists on reshuffling the "with U.S. or against U.S." public discourse on the war on terror. Her queer theoretical approach "allows for a scrambling of sides that is illegible to state practices of surveillance, control, banishment, and extermination."[28] Significantly, Puar's redefinition of the queer body as not grounded in sexual practices or identities rejects queer liberalism or, what Lisa Duggan calls, "the new homonormative."[29] It rejects classifying

---

23. Jasbir K. Puar, "Rethinking Homonationalism," *International Journal Middle Eastern Studies* 45 (2013): 337.

24. Puar, *Terrorist Assemblages*, xiv.

25. Puar, "Rethinking Homonationalism," 337.

26. Puar, *Terrorist Assemblages*, 221.

27. Ibid.

28. Ibid.

29. Lisa Duggan, "The New Homonormativity: The Sexual Politics of Neoliberalism," in

sexualities as queer as they adapt to heteronormative family life while simultaneously ignoring the hegemonic structures of empire. Queerness has moved on and, according to Puar, it has re-emerged in the assemblages of neoliberalism and terrorist movements.

Clearly, this analysis offers a radical point of view, and so some theorists propose "the end of queer theory."[30] Still, queer theorists are well advised to remain suspicious of quick and easy identifications of the queer critical impulse either in mainstream adaptations to Western socio-cultural life or among suicide bombers. What seems certain is the fact that, in light of political and religious conservative mobilization against queer justice, the queer critical impulse is much needed even after more than twenty-five years of queer theorizing.

About the Emergence of Queer Bible Hermeneutics

The insistence to connect queer analysis with the full spectrum of dominating structures of oppression has also made its way into queer Bible scholarship. For instance, Teresa J. Hornsby addresses the status of biblical scholarship in light of feminist, gender and sexuality issues.[31] She suggests that the development from a women-centric focus to a broadly conceptualized gender and queer agenda is not indicative of a subversive positioning of feminist biblical studies, as suggested by Deryn Guest.[32] Rather, according to Hornsby, both women-centric and queer approaches need to be understood as accommodating the dominant forces in the economic-capitalist globalized world in which we live, since "sexuality and gender are constructed in collusion with capitalistic power."[33] Accordingly, as capitalism changes, sexual and gender norms also shift, and so Bible scholars merely mirror the larger cultural trajectories when they engage feminist, gender, and sexuality issues.

Hornsby bases her analysis on three assumptions: namely, that "power produces sexual normatives," "the dominant form that this power takes in Western Euro cultures is neoliberal capitalism" and "Christianity (indeed, organized religion) is an arm of power that aids in this production."[34] Calls for change in feminist, gender, and queer biblical scholarship, as well as in other

Russ Castronovo and Dana D. Nelson (eds), *Materializing Democracy: Toward a Revitalized Cultural Politics* (Durham, NC: Duke University Press, 2002), 177.

30. James Penney, *After Queer Theory: The Limits of Sexual Politics* (London: Pluto Press, 2014).

31. Teresa J. Hornsby, "Capitalism, Masochism, and Biblical Interpretations," in Teresa J. Hornsby and Ken Stone (eds), *Bible Troubles: Queer Reading at the Boundaries of Biblical Scholarship* (Atlanta, GA: SBL, 2011), 137–55.

32. Deryn Guest, *Beyond Feminist Biblical Studies* (Sheffield: Sheffield Phoenix Press, 2012).

33. Hornsby, "Capitalism, Masochism, and Biblical Interpretations," 137.

34. Ibid.

areas of culture and society, are linked to the shift from a "closed, centrally powerful, and industrial" economic system to one that is "open, globally diverse, and electronically based."[35] Consequently, theoretical inclusions of non-heteronormative and queer sexualities in culture, theology and biblical interpretation are not deconstructive moves that will overcome worldwide oppression but they are "capitalism's use of Christian theology to construct the types of sexual/economic subjects it needs."[36] Neoliberalism needs bodies willing to submit and enjoy masochistic positions in the societal-economic interplay of power. Feminist, gender, and queer biblical exegesis assists in this process even if its help is provided unintentionally; such is the power of the neoliberal capitalist system over every body and thing.

In other words, Hornsby maintains that the move of queering the Bible does not automatically present a challenge to neoliberalism because "queer sexualities are manufactured and serve power just as much as a sanctioned sexuality."[37] Capitalism requires people with "more open, fluid, ambivalent sexual identities," willing to suffer for this elastic and promised space. In turn, feminist, gender, and queer readings of the Bible (and culture) accommodate the production of these non-normative bodies. In Hornsby's assessment, then, resistance to neoliberalism is an illusion because the feminist agenda is always already part of economic neoliberalism.

Not every queer Bible interpreter shares this dystopian explanation that takes on almost totalitarian proportions without any alternatives. Especially during the early phase when queer terminology and theory made it into biblical scholarship, biblical interpreters emphasized the positive impact of queer voices for biblical meanings. Mona West, for instance, stresses that LGBTIQ people embrace the term "queer" as a definition for "the radical and important nature of our existence as persons who will not be silent and who will question (query) the systems that oppress us."[38] She recognizes the heterolithic composition of queer communities as well as the Bible as a common signifier used to justify "our demonization and oppression" that has culminated into labelling queer people as an "abomination." West outlines four reading strategies to interpret the Bible in queer ways. They are "a defensive stance toward Scripture, an offensive stance toward Scripture, outing the Bible, and reading the Bible from the social location of being Queer."[39] It should be noted that her explanations about a queer Bible hermeneutics come from a Christian gay-affirming church context, the UFMCC, that locates itself within the queer community as a socio-politically and religiously outsider position.

35. Ibid.

36. Ibid., 141–2.

37. Ibid., 153.

38. Mona West, "Reading the Bible as Queer Americans," *Theology & Sexuality* 10 (1999): 31. See also Robert E. Goss and Mona West (eds), *Take Back the Word: A Queer Reading of the Bible* (Cleveland: Pilgrim, 2000).

39. Ibid., 32.

Other early adopters of an explicitly "queer" stance contrast with a biblical hermeneutics that tries to decipher "what the Bible says about homosexuality."[40] They integrate the discussions as they have emerged in queer theoretical works, suggesting to move beyond the issue of what the Bible says about "same-sex relations." They propose to subject biblical literature to "queer commentary" with the goal of producing "helpful effects among a particular group of contemporary socially-located readers referred to by West as 'queers.'"[41] In addition, queer Bible readers problematize the efforts of developing biblical meanings that accommodate queer-identified Christians and Jews. They take their cues from queer theorists who deconstruct normative approaches to sexuality and extend them to "alternative ways of organizing sexual practice that do not necessarily stress the gender of the sexual partners."[42]

For instance, Ken Stone illustrates such an approach in a study on Jeremiah 20:7. There, the prophet appears within a sado-masochistic relationship with God.[43] Calling for a "hermeneutics of sadomasochism," Stone asserts that "the text can therefore be construed, I think, as replicating dynamics at least associated with an S/M scene."[44] Stone's reading takes seriously the theoretical insight that "queer" does not refer to sexuality only but nurtures a hermeneutical stance of resistance against hegemonic powers. A queer Bible hermeneutics questions a whole range of social conventions of normality in which even the biblical deity has the potential of being a queer character.[45] In short, every biblical text, character, and topic can be queered, and so the entire Bible offers a feast for queer readings. Publications, such as the *Queer Bible Commentary* and *Torah Queeries*, illustrate the enormous breadth of making connections between queer theories and biblical interpretation.[46]

40. For a discussion of this issue from a queer stance, see, e.g. Ken Stone, "Homosexuality and the Bible or Queer Reading? A Response to Martti Nissinen," *Theology & Sexuality* 14 (2001): 107–18.

41. Ken Stone, "Queer Commentary and Biblical Interpretation: An Introduction," in Ken Stone (ed.), *Queer Commentary and the Hebrew Bible* (Cleveland: The Pilgrim Press, 2001), 18.

42. Ibid., 27.

43. Ken Stone, "'You Seduced Me, You Overpowered Me, and You Prevailed': Religious Experience and Homoerotic Sadomasochism in Jeremiah," in Lisa Isherwood (ed.), *Patriarchs, Prophets and Other Villains* (London and Oakville: Equinox, 2007), 101–9.

44. Ibid., 107.

45. See, e.g. Roland Boer, "Yahweh as Top: A Lost Targum," in Ken Stone (ed.), *Queer Commentary and the Hebrew Bible* (Cleveland: The Pilgrim Press, 2001), 5–105. See also Stephen D. Moore, *God's Beauty Parlor and Other Queer Spaces in and Around the Bible* (Stanford: Stanford University Press, 2001). For a theological treatise outside of biblical studies, see Marcella Althaus-Reid, *Indecent Theology: Theological Perversions in Sex, Gender, and Politics* (London and New York: Routledge, 2000).

46. Deryn Guest, Robert E. Goss, Mona West, Thomas Bohache (eds), *The Queer Bible Commentary* (London: SCM Press, 2005); Gregg Drinkwater, Joshua Lesser, and David

There are, however, also some concerned voices about reading the Bible through queer lenses. They hesitate to move away from feminist and lesbian hermeneutical perspectives, worrying that "queer" may be used to reinforce androcentric perspectives. This cautionary stance toward a queer hermeneutics appears especially in feminist and lesbian theoretical analyses.[47] They charge that assumptions about heteropatriarchal hegemonies are not only a problem of heteronormative discourse, but they also exist in queer theoretical works. Some feminist-lesbian theorists have contested the idea for decades that queer theories present new insight about gender binaries. For instance, already in 1978, Monique Wittig asserted that lesbians are not "women" in heteropatriarchal perspective, as they perform their lives outside the hegemonic gender binary of female and male, interrupting and transcending heteronormative gender categories.[48] Lesbian scholarship, having long challenged gender binaries decades before queer studies emerged, made visible lesbians who are far too easily subsumed and ignored in hegemonic heteropatriarchy, including in queer studies. Sheila Jeffreys observes poignantly that "[t]he appearance of queer theory and queer studies threatens to mean the disappearance of lesbians."[49] Disregarding feminism, queer theorists mask as counter narratives what is, in fact, a reinscription of heteropatriarchal normativities. They ignore the political and theoretical work of lesbian feminism that has maintained the centrality of resisting heteropatriarchal regimes of power since the early 1970s. Queer theorists ought to include lesbian theories because they address the very gender issues advertised as innovative theoretical discourse in queer studies.[50]

One biblical scholar, Deryn Guest, works on the front lines of queer and lesbian-feminist bible hermeneutics. She stresses the significance of a lesbian biblical hermeneutics that does not follow the idea of queer as "becoming committed to challenging that which is perceived as normal."[51] Although Guest acknowledges the potential danger of a lesbian biblical hermeneutics as reinforcing heteronormative binaries, Guest proposes its value for five reasons. First, feminist biblical scholars are "insufficiently cognizant" of queer theories as a critical tool and

---

Shneer (eds), *Torah Queeries: Weekly Commentaries on the Hebrew Bible* (New York: New York University Press, 2009).

47. For a famous articulation of this critique, see Adrienne Rich, "Compulsory Heterosexuality and Lesbian Existence," *Signs* 5 (1980): 631–60.

48. Monique Wittig, *The Straight Mind and Other Essays* (New York: Harvester Wheatsheaf, 1992), 32.

49. Sheila Jeffreys, "The Queer Disappearance of Lesbian Sexuality in the Academy," *Women's Studies International Forum* 17 (5) (1994): 459.

50. For an accessible survey of this and related positions, see Amy Goodloe, "Lesbian-Feminism and Queer Theory: Another 'Battle of the Sexes'?"; originally published at Lesbian.org in 1994; republished in 2014, online: http://amygoodloe.com/papers/lesbian-feminism-and-queer-theory-another-battle-of-the-sexes/ (accessed December 12, 2016).

51. Deryn Guest, *When Deborah Met Jael: Lesbian Biblical Hermeneutics* (London: SCM Press, 2005), 45.

might perceive queer works as further masculinizing the field. This worry is not completely groundless, according to Guest, given that some queer theorists are indeed reticent to destabilize "the male dominance inherent in heterosexism."[52] An explicitly lesbian biblical hermeneutics is central because it reminds feminist Bible scholars to critique heteropatriarchy as well as essentialized gender notions. Second, Guest insists that lesbian and gay studies have contributed favorably to the development of queer studies, and so lesbian hermeneutics is certainly part of the queer project. Third, Guest cautions that, in contrast to lesbian hermeneutics, queer theories do not "sufficiently engage with the contemporary grassroots concerns."[53] While queer scholarship questions, challenges, and critiques various problems, it does not usually offer "effective practical solutions." There is, however, a great need for "a political conscience" in light of the ongoing anti-lesbian and anti-gay oppression in the world. Guest stresses that "[r]emaining engaged in political and ecclesial discourse on these issues is vital for the well-being of lesbian, gay, bisexual and transgender, LGBTIQ-identified persons ...."[54] A lesbian Bible hermeneutics contributes to such an engagement. Fourth, Guest believes that a lesbian Bible hermeneutics respects those who have found homes in lesbian and gay communities. In her view, "an abandonment of 'lesbian' as an identity label" would create "bafflement, unease, anxiety, pain, anger and loss."[55] Since a "post-lesbian and gay era" is not in sight, Guest worries that a move beyond an explicitly lesbian Bible hermeneutics would seem like a betrayal of the feminist commitment to women's issues. Fifth, Guest warns that queer theories "will prove to be an elitist discourse" that is "hardly accessible to the lay person" if such discourse disconnects from its communities of accountability.[56] An explicitly lesbian Bible hermeneutics remains loyal to its accountability structure and must therefore be developed. In short, Guest explains that "the adoption of a lesbian identity is still a transgressive act."[57] It is "a brave act of independences from sex-gender norms," although it also "risks solidifying the lesbian label and thereby, paradoxically, endorsing normative heterosexuality."[58] Both insights need be held in tension when one develops "a specifically lesbian approach to biblical interpretation."[59]

Guest also makes demands on feminist Bible scholars. She calls upon them "to tool up and become even more expansively theory-rich, able to bring the critical studies of masculinities, queer studies, trans studies, intersex studies, and lesbian and gay studies into negotiation with feminist theory without necessarily

52. Ibid., 46.
53. Ibid., 48.
54. All quotes, ibid.
55. Ibid., 49.
56. Ibid., 51.
57. Ibid., 52.
58. Ibid.
59. Ibid., 53.

privileging what have been, to date, stalwart feminist positions."[60] She wants feminist exegetes to move beyond essentialized notions about women and to interrogate heteronormative assumptions in their intersectional manifestations as they permeate the readings of biblical texts. Furthermore, she urges feminist interpreters to write from lesbian vantage points because one does not have to live as a lesbian to write like one. Feminist exegetes need to genderqueer the practice of reading the Bible and to dismantle "the biblical construction of heterosexuality as an institution, as an apparently divinely sanctioned identity position, and, more importantly, as an apparatus of heteronormativity ...."[61] In this sense, then, biblical exegesis, whether done with queer or lesbian approaches, is a powerful political discourse that challenges not only how we see the Bible, but also the world in which it is grounded and within which its meanings are shaped.

Coming out of the Biblical Closet: The Prevalence of Hermeneutical Heteronormativity and the Queering of the Biblical Canon

When people reference the Bible in socio-cultural and religious disputes about the ordination of queer people or marriage equality, or when they try to figure out what the Bible "says" about "homosexuality," they often fall back to the so-called clobber passages. These are biblical texts from the Hebrew Bible and the New Testament that have traditionally been cited to authorize discrimination against the LGBTIQ community. Among them are the following passages: Genesis 1:27; Genesis 2:23-4; Genesis 19:1-29; Leviticus 18:22; Leviticus 20:13; Deuteronomy 23:17-18; Romans 1:26-7; 1 Corinthians 6:9; Timothy 1:10; Jude 1:7. When these verses are quoted, they are usually used to proof-text anti-gay positions. Traditional historical critics have, however, long maintained that these texts should not be quoted in contemporary discussions on same-sex practices.[62] Nevertheless, such scholarly argumentation has largely fallen on deaf ears in the public arena when the conversation turns to the Bible.[63] Stuck in what Mona West classifies as the "defensive" stance, the public assumes that it is required to argue for or against the clobber passages in justification of the Bible's position on queer sexualities. Queer Bible critics have certainly reminded contemporary Bible reading audiences that the proof-texting approach is limiting and unsatisfactory and that the entire canon

---

60. Deryn Guest, *Beyond Feminist Studies* (Sheffield: Sheffield Academic Press, 2012), 150.

61. Ibid., 162.

62. See, e.g. John Boswell, *Christianity, Social Tolerance, and Homosexuality* (Chicago: University of Chicago, 1980; Robin Scroggs, *The New Testament and Homosexuality* (Philadelphia: Fortress Press, 1983); Victor Paul Furnish, *The Moral Teaching of Paul* (rev. 3rd edn; Nashville, TN: Abingdon, 2009 [1985, 1979]).

63. See, e.g. Caleb Kaltenbach and Matthew Vines, "Debating Bible Verses on Homosexuality," *New York Times* (June 8, 2015), http://www.nytimes.com/interactive/2015/06/05/us/samesex-scriptures.html?_r=0 (accessed December 12, 2016).

of the Bible is a source for queer biblical meanings. This section elaborates on two specific biblical texts to present both approaches. One of them is Leviticus 18:22 and the discussion dismantles the heteronormative meaning on linguistic grounds. The other text, innovatively interpreted in queer hermeneutical communities, is Judges 3:12-30; it illustrates that the Hebrew Bible is a treasure trove for queer meanings.

Queering the Heteronormative Reading of Leviticus 18.22

Most interpretations insist that Leviticus 18:22 prohibits gay sex not only between men but by extension also between women. Predictably, the various English Bible versions offer translations cementing the heteronormative reading. For instance, the King James Version of 1611 commands: "Thou shall not lie with mankind, as with womankind: it is abomination." Contemporary translations follow suit. The New International Version (1984, U.S.A.) orders: "Do not lie with a man as one lies with a woman; that is detestable." The New Jerusalem Bible (1985) states: "You will not have intercourse with a man as you would with a woman. This is a hateful thing." The New Revised Standard Version (1989) instructs: "You shall not lie with a male as with a woman; it is an abomination." The JPS Tanak (1985) commands: "You shall not lie with a male as with a woman; it is an abomination." Even the inclusively inclined translation by the Priests for Equality (2007), eliminating any gender-specific vocabulary, charges: "Do not lie with a person of the same sex in the same way as you would lie with a person of the opposite sex; it is detestable." In light of the general agreement among these and many other translations, the conclusion seems unavoidable that Leviticus 18:22 prohibits same-sex intimacy.

Yet the eight Hebrew words of this verse are actually much more opaque than these and other Bible translations acknowledge. In a recent linguistic study K. Renato Lings examines the verse's grammatical ambiguities.[64] He highlights the grammatical ambiguities to suggest a very different meaning of the verse. For instance, he observes that the meaning of the noun *zākār*, which is usually translated as "man" or even as "mankind," refers to any member of the male sex regardless of his age. Lings thus argues that the noun should not be translated as "man" but as "male." This translation does not limit the meaning of *zakar* to an adult man because the noun does not specify age but only gender. Lings also points to the puzzling phrase of *miškevē 'iššâ* that is commonly translated in English as "as with a woman." Yet he shows that it ought to be translated as "the lyings of a woman" because it neither contains a comparative particle nor is its construct form a regular occurrence in the Hebrew Bible. In fact, the phrase appears only one other time in the Hebrew Bible, in Genesis 49:4 where it is usually translated as "bed." In light of the grammatical ambiguity, Lings proposes what he classifies as an "exotic" rendering of the verse: "And with a male you shall not lie down a woman's bed ...."[65] It is just not clear what the rendering means,

---

64. K. Renato Lings. "The 'Lyings' of a Woman: Male-Male Incest in Leviticus 18.22?" *Theology & Sexuality* 15 (2) (2009): 231–50.

65. Ibid., 238.

and this opaqueness is the point that translators should not attempt to smoothen out. The verb of the sentence, *šakav 'eth* that is normally translated as "to lie with" invites another important point in the translation of v. 22. The verb includes the object marker *'eth* to mark the ensuing noun, "a male," as its object. Importantly, this verb/object conjunction appears in several other biblical texts in which it depicts a rape. There the male rapist is the verb's subject who lays the object of the sentence, the woman, such as in Genesis 34:2 or 2 Samuel 13:14.

In other words, the grammatical analysis demonstrates that Leviticus 18:22 does not refer to gay sex among men or women. Rather, the verse prohibits male incestuous relations, as Lings proposes, or perhaps further, the verse prohibits male incestuous rape. The latter meaning gets grammatical support from Genesis 49:4. It mentions Jacob, complaining about Reuben's "activity." Jacob states in dismay that his son Reuben "mounted" his "father's bed" (*miškevē 'abika*), a euphemistic reference to Genesis 35:22c in which Reuben's "activity" is his "father's bed" occurs. There, in the same verb constellation as in Leviticus 18:22, Reuben "laid" (*šākab 'ēt*) Bilhah, the enslaved woman of Rachel, his aunt. An enslaved woman, Bilhah has no say in the matter; her consent does not matter, and thus Reuben "laid" her in the sense of raping her. As I explain elsewhere:

> Rarely mentioned in scholarly discussions, this brief report about Bilhah appears after Rachel dies during the birth of her second son. Indirectly, the verse refers to rape. The Hebrew verb, *šākab*, is followed not by the preposition (*'im*) but by the Hebrew object maker, *ēt*, as in other rape stories, for instance the rape of Dinah (Gen. 34:2) or the rape of Tamar (2 Sam. 13:14). The grammatical observation has consequences for the verse's meaning. Reuben does not sleep "with" Bilhah, a translation that feigns consent by Bilhah. Rather, he laid her. He is the subject of the action and she the object. As a concubine and slave, Bilhah is sexually violated, raped.[66]

In short, when one tries to make sense of the phrase *miškevē 'iššâ* in Leviticus 18:22, it becomes clear that the phrase resonates with tales of rape. It also appears in a literary context in which men are warned against heterosexual incestuous sex with women who are their relatives. Said differently, Leviticus 18:22 does not only prohibit male-on-male incest but it also hints at the non-consensual dimension of male-on-male incest, especially when one of the males is underage. When v. 22 is read in this queer way, it does not universally prohibit same-sex love at all. Rather, it forbids incestuous rape among males, including boys.

Perhaps, then, Leviticus 18:22 ought to be read in conjunction with other ancient Near Eastern legislation that prohibits male and female incestuous rape in one single law. For instance, Hittite law 189 states: "If a man violates his own mother; it is a capital crime. If a man violates his daughter; it is a capital crime.

---

66. For a more detailed discussion, see Susanne Scholz, *Sacred Witness: Rape in the Hebrew Bible* (Minneapolis, MN: Fortress Press, 2010), 72.

If a man violates his son; it is a capital crime."[67] This law mentions three cases of incestuous rape with the mother, the daughter, and the son. When one correlates this idea to Leviticus 18:22, the translation of the biblical verse turns into a queer meaning that prohibits male and female incestuous rape. It reads: "You (masculine singular) shall not rape a male; it is like the rape of a woman; it is an abomination."

The Gay-Terror Text of Judges 3:12-30

While a queer reading of Leviticus 18:22 deconstructs a homophobic agenda and transforms the verse into a much-needed prohibition about incest and sexual violence in the family, queer exegetes stress that the entire canon of the Bible awaits queer reading. Since biblical texts have multiple meanings due to their inherent ambiguity, elasticity, flexibility, and opaqueness, queer interpreters know that every text can be queered. Accordingly, other clobber texts have queer meanings, too. For instance, when Genesis 1:27a ("And God created the human being in God's own image") is read as an affirmation that every sexual orientation is part of the divine creation, v. 27b ("male and female God created them") also receives a queer-affirming meaning. Here is the argument: The nouns "female" and "male" in v. 27b constitute a merism, which is a figure of speech listing several parts as an illustration of the whole. Thus the two terms "female" and "male" exemplify the much wider spectrum of gender identities. They should not be considered as the exclusive parts of all of humanity. In light of this literary insight Margaret Moers Wenig suggests the following interpretation of v. 27b: "God created some humans male, some female, some who appear male but know themselves to be female, others who appear female but know themselves to be male, and others still who bear a mix of male and female characteristic." Accordingly, v. 27 recognizes that "God created humankind *zachar u'nikevah* male and female *and every combination in between.*"[68]

But these alternative meanings go far beyond the clobber passages. The entire biblical corpus constitutes readings ripe for queer interpretation. One such source, Judges 3:12-30 has, however, invited a far less exuberant queer reading than Genesis 1:27. In fact, a queer exegesis turns this narrative about Ehud, an Israelite judge, and King Eglon of Moab into "a text of terror for gay-identified readers."[69] The story reports a murderous male-on-male rape in which Ehud, the famous Israelite judge, seduces the Moabite king to spend time with him alone in a vaguely defined chamber (was it a bathroom?). Ambiguous vocabulary hints at a

---

67. For a detailed discussion of ancient Near Eastern rape laws, including this one, see Scholz, *Sacred Witness*, 105–33.

68. Margaret Moers Wenig, "Male and Female God Created Them: Parashat Bereshit (Genesis 1:1–6:8)," in Gregg Drinkwater, Joshua Lesser, and David Shneer (eds), *Torah Queeries: Weekly Commentaries on the Hebrew Bible* (New York and London: New York University Press), 16.

69. Deryn Guest, "Judges," in Deryn Guest, Robert E. Goss, Mona West, Thomas Bohache (eds), *The Queer Bible Commentary* (London: SCM Press, 2006), 176.

sexual encounter between the two men during which Ehud kills Eglon, with a knife shoved into the king's belly. The murderous deed enables the oppressed Israelites to successfully free themselves from Moabite oppression. Scholarly interpreters hail Ehud throughout the ages although they always sense something strange in Ehud's actions, his left-handedness, and his ethnic origins as a Benjaminite. When all is said and done, is he not a loner who is "peculiar, unnatural, devious, sinister," as many interpreters suggest? Is he not a rather "queer" character?[70] Foremost, he should not be exonerated as is popularly done, because even God, "a complicit collaborator,"[71] sides with Ehud, and the ethnic humor about the stupidity of the Moabites runs through the entire narrative. Gay-identified readers notice that Eglon is feminized; he appears to be a soft and fleshy man, characteristics that reinforce homophobic stereotypes about gay men as feminine, passive, and easily victimized. As Guest remarks: "Ehud is too easily forgiven and exonerated, given a quick box around the ears but then a smiling tousle of the hair for achieving something useful despite the methods used."[72] Rarely, if ever, do readers sympathize with the murdered king because "[t]o sympathize with Eglon's plight is simply not an expected readerly position."[73] Instead, readers accept the murderous rape as an acceptable way to side with the Israelite "hero," Ehud, and they overlook his murderous act and violence.

Yet the request to side with the Israelite judge is a terrifying proposition for gay-identified readers, as it teaches them to read against their own interests and to accept textual assumptions and rhetorical allusions about a possibly sexually violent encounter between two men that ends in the death of one of them. The story justifies physical, and sexual violence, even murder, as divinely sanctioned. It is thus not comical at all but a real "text of terror" for gay-identified readers.

In sum, Judges 3:12-30 is a murderous male-on-male rape story with deeply embedded assumptions about sexuality and ethnicity. It contains an abundance of clues, traces, and hints for queer interpreters looking to identify male-on-male sexual violence, even murder, in the Hebrew Bible. Certainly, this queer meaning is deeply buried in the socio-cultural and religious imagination of the text, not providing uncensored, truthful discourse on the topic. Yet it is remarkable that so many clues, traces, and hints appear when readers look for them. Queer readers thus maintain that the entire biblical canon can be turned into a rich resource for developing awareness and sensitivity about queer meanings, ethics, and theopolitical discourse far beyond defensive readings of the biblical clobber texts.

---

70. Ibid., 174.
71. Ibid., 176.
72. Ibid., 177.
73. Ibid.

And Then There Was a Man: From Feminist and Queer Interpretations to Critical Masculinity Studies

While queer theorists were busy defining, investigating, and evaluating how to queer society and its cultural artifacts, including the Bible, another area of study gained prominence. Standing on the metaphorical shoulders of the feminist and queer movements, the critical analysis of masculinities focuses on what it means to be a man in society, culture, and religion. Although males have dominated human endeavors, to the point that "masculinity" was never even considered as a question, scholars have, in recent years, developed methods which are used to critically investigate the significance of men, manhood, and normative masculinity throughout the ages. They have thus been quick to express their gratitude to "practitioners of feminism for inspiration,"[74] and sometimes they have even gone so far as to classify "masculist interpretation" as "parasitic"[75] to feminist analysis and as "a subcategory within the larger body of transdisciplinary gender studies," with feminist studies as "its historical precedent."[76]

Clearly then, without decades and, in the case of feminism, several centuries of feminist and queer critical discourse of heteronormativity, heteropatriarchy, and phallogocentrism, investigations into "hegemonic masculinity" would probably not have gotten off the ground. Like feminist and queer theories, masculinities studies challenge notions of essentialism and tend to reject binary gender divisions. Yet the field has also encountered feminist suspicion about perhaps being part of a backlash movement against feminist studies,[77] especially in light of the 1990s popularity of politically, religiously, and culturally reactionary popular publications and projects, such as Robert Bly's *Iron John: A Book about Men* or the Christian Right's movement called The Promise Keepers.[78] Over and over again, scholars in masculinity studies explain that they do not endorse or promote the popular celebration of manhood that essentializes men and moves the discourse

---

74. Stephen D. Moore, "'O Man, Who Art Thou…?' Masculinity Studies and New Testament Studies," in Stephen D. Moore and Janice Capel Anderson (eds), *New Testament Masculinities* (Atlanta, GA: Society of Biblical Literature, 2003), 2.

75. John Goldingay, "Hosea 1–3, Genesis 1–4, and Masculist Interpretation," *Horizons in Biblical Theology* 17 (1995): 37.

76. Björn Krondorfer, "Introduction," in Björn Krondorfer (ed.), *Men and Masculinities in Christianity and Judaism: A Critical Reader* (London: SCM Press, 2009), xiv.

77. For an early feminist articulation of this suspicion, see, e.g. Eve Sedgwick, "Gender Criticism," in Stephen Greenblatt and Giles Gunn (eds), *Redrawing the Boundaries: The Transformation of English and American Literary Studies* (New York: Modern Language Association of America, 1992), 272. See also Michael S. Kimmel, *The Politics of Manhood: Profeminist Men Respond to the Mythopoetic Men's Movement (and the Mythopoetic Leaders Answer)* (Philadelphia: Temple University Press, 1995).

78. See, e.g. Robert Bly, *Iron John: A Book about Men* (Reading, MA: Addison-Wesley, 1990). For a critical analysis of the Promise Keepers, see, e.g. Dane S. Claussen, *The Promise Keepers: Essays on Masculinity and Christianity* (Jefferson, NC: McFarland, 2000).

on masculinities toward the Right. Rather, they see their inquiries as being about the *critical* study of men that co-operates with feminist, gender, and queer theorists.

Belatedly and gingerly, Hebrew Bible scholars have begun to consider questions about the critical study of men in their exegetical explorations during the last two decades. The reticence of Hebrew Bible scholars to engage masculinity studies is obvious. Stephen D. Moore holds "the disciplinary specificity of feminist biblical studies" responsible for the unsubstantial presence of biblical masculinity studies in Hebrew Bible. He maintains that the field of feminist biblical scholarship did not change at such "a rapid pace" as feminist literary studies that opened up to deconstruction and other forms of poststructuralism, as well as to issues of race, ethnicity, class, colonialism, or imperialism, already in the mid-1980s.[79] In Moore's view, the lack of feminist biblical scholars to engage these theoretical developments prevented the field from working with masculinity studies, "except at the fringes of the discipline."[80] The general hesitation, however, did not mean that there have not been a few scholars who have read the Hebrew Bible in light of masculinity studies.

One of the first is Howard Eilberg-Schwartz who, in 1994, published a whole book on monotheism and phallogocentric depictions of God in the Bible.[81] A popularizing writer, Eilberg-Schwartz recognizes that it is shocking to focus on God's penis. Yet in his book he exposes the connection between male authority and the deification of masculinity in religious-biblical discourse. He explains: "Feminist and gender criticism convinced me that gender is not just another subject that intersects with religion, but is central to the work that religion accomplishes and the ways in which it goes about it .... More specifically, feminist criticism and gender theory impressed me with the importance of taking seriously the gender of God. God's imagined masculinity is critical to understanding many central rituals and myths of monotheism."[82] He explores these dynamics in which experiences of men as "the dominant figures in the social order are projected onto the one and only God."[83] Eilberg-Schwartz posits that in the Hebrew Bible the male divinity's phallus is always veiled or hidden, and thus the biblical God is not depicted as a male divinity. Rather God's phallus remains in the shadows of biblical thinking about God's gender although God is characterized in male terminology. Thus, according to Eilberg-Schwartz, biblical prose and poetry creates "a whole set of tensions"[84] within the biblical construction of masculinity.

---

79. Stephen D. Moore, "Final Reflections on Biblical Masculinity," in Ovidiu Creangă (ed.), *Men and Masculinity in the Hebrew Bible and Beyond* (Sheffield: Sheffield Phoenix Press, 2010), 241–2.

80. Ibid., 243.

81. Howard Eilberg-Schwartz, *God's Phallus and Other Problems for Men and Monotheism* (Boston: Beacon Press, 1994).

82. Ibid., 5.

83. Ibid., 21.

84. Ibid., 26.

The tension is, in fact, foundational to the divine-male relationship in the biblical rhetoric in which "masculinity and divinity are bound up with each other."[85] At the same time, every man fails to be like God because a man's penis is exposed, out in the open, and even circumcised, whereas the biblical God's phallus remains invisible. The resulting tension within biblical masculinity guarantees the ongoing failure for men. Eilberg-Schwartz explains: "[T]he symbol of a male God is not simply a legitimation of masculinity or an object of male desire. It is also an image against which men must measure themselves and by whose standard they fall short."[86] Human males do not measure up to divine masculinity as the latter is powerful and strong, but ultimately non-sexual. In this sense, then, Eilberg-Schwartz disagrees with feminist theorists about the link between the father God and male authority. In the biblical imagination God and males are fundamentally different. Eilberg-Schwartz explains:

> The disappearance of the phallus does not undo male domination in the social or symbolic system, but it does create a different kind of masculinity with its own distinctive problems. Human men, because they do have penises, can only partially assume the power invested in a sexless God. When it comes to a man's penis and his sexual desire, there is a fundamental difference between him and God.[87]

This fundamental tension in the biblical concept of divine and male masculinities, as outlined by Eilberg-Schwartz and as he articulates it in contrast to feminist positions,[88] has, however, not significantly influenced future biblical masculinity studies.[89] Still, the book opened the door for further scholarly explorations. One year later, in 1995, David J. A. Clines published an essay which investigates the masculinity of King David.[90] Clines acknowledges that his feminist colleague, J. Cheryl Exum, encouraged him to pursue this topic,[91] and so his study examines biblical depictions of David as a "fighting male," "a persuasive male," a "beautiful

---

85. Ibid.

86. Ibid., 199.

87. Ibid., 200.

88. For instance, Esther Fuchs made the powerful feminist argument: "Prophecy is the core and culmination of the monotheistic paradigm. The discursive intermingling of God's words and those of the male prophets represents the apotheosis of the andro-theistic relationship infrastructure of monotheistic ideology. This andro-theistic relationship must preclude female discourse." See her "Prophecy and the Construction of Women: Inscription and Erasure," in Athalya Brenner (ed.), *Prophets and Daniel: A Feminist Companion to the Bible (Second Edition)* (Sheffield: Sheffield Press, 2001), 54–69.

89. For a brief reference, see, e.g. Stephen Moore, "Gigantic God: Yahweh's Body," in *The Bible in Theory: Critical and Postcolonial Essays* (Atlanta, GA: SBL, 2010), 206.

90. David J. A. Clines, "David the Man: The Construction of Masculinity in the Hebrew Bible," in *Interested Parties: The Ideology of Writers and Readers of the Hebrew Bible* (JSOT Supplement 205; Sheffield: Sheffield Academic Press, 1995), 212–43.

91. Clines acknowledges her in a footnote of his essay where he writes: "I should like to

male," a "bonding male," a "womanless male," and a "musical male" in 1 Samuel 16 to 1 Kings 2. Clines also correlates the biblical characterization of David as a man with contemporary notions about masculinity and he challenges male commentators to become conscious of their utter adoration for David. They normalize, minimize or render as undisturbing any masculine trait of David that does not fit with contemporary notions of masculinity. They adore David against all odds.

Clines's discussion of hegemonic masculinities in the story of David has encouraged not only Clines but also other scholars to explore the possibilities of biblical masculinity studies.[92] Most recently, Stephen M. Wilson points to an expanded list of masculinity traits for biblical men. Wilson maintains that the Hebrew Bible does not only feature strength, wisdom and persuasive speech, beauty, and the avoidance of women as part of biblical masculinity, as Clines argues for David, but also self-control, fertility and marriage, honour, kinship solidarity, and legal manhood.[93] Other exegetes, such as Dennis T. Olson, emphasize the "continual seesaw between violence and reconciliation" in the portrayal of men in Genesis and elsewhere.[94] Two important anthologies provide a foundation

thank Cheryl Exum for advising me that this was the next paper I should write, though I doubt that I has turned out as she would have imagined it … ."; see ibid., 243 n.75.

92. For Clines's prolific scholarly output on the topic of biblical masculinities since 1998, see, e.g. "Ecce vir, or, Gendering the Son of Man," in J. Cheryl Exum and Stephen Moore (eds), *Biblical Studies/Cultural Studies: The Third Sheffield Colloquium* (Sheffield: Sheffield University Press, 1998), 352–75; "He-Prophets: Masculinity as a Problem for the Hebrew Prophets and Their Interpreters," in Alastair G. Hunter and Phillip R. Davies (eds), *Sense and Sensitivity: Essays on Reading the Bible in Memory of Robert Carroll* (London: Sheffield Academic Pres, 2002), 311–28; "Paul, the Invisible Man," in Stephen D. Moore and Janice Capel Anderson (eds), *New Testament Masculinities* (Atlanta, GA: Society of Biblical Literature, 2003), 181–92; "Being a Man in the Book of the Covenant," in J. Gordon McConville and Karl Möller (eds), *Reading the Law: Studies in Honour of Gordon J. Wenham* (New York and London: T&T Clark, 2007), 3–9; "Dancing and Shining at Sinai: Playing the Man in Exodus 32–34," in Ovidiu Creangă (ed.), *Men and Masculinity in the Hebrew Bible and Beyond* (Sheffield: Sheffield Phoenix Press, 2010), 54-63; "Final Reflections on Biblical Masculinity," in Ovidiu Creangă (ed.), *Men and Masculinity in the Hebrew Bible and Beyond* (Sheffield: Sheffield Phoenix Press, 2010), 234–9.

93. Stephen M. Wilson, *Making Men: The Male Coming-of-Age Theme in the Hebrew Bible* (Oxford: Oxford University Press, 2015), 29–46.

94. See, e.g. Dennis T. Olson, "Untying the Knot? Masculinity, Violence, and the Creation-Fall Story of Genesis 2–4," in Linda Day and Carolyn Pressler (eds), *Engaging the Bible in a Gendered World: An Introduction to Feminist Biblical Interpretation in Honor of Katharine Doob Sakenfeld* (Louisville and London: Westminster John Knox, 2006), 71–86. For brief rehearsal of masculinities in Genesis, legal texts, the Deuteronomistic History, and the prophetic literature, see Susan E. Haddox, "Is There a Biblical Masculinity? Masculinities in the Hebrew Bible," *Word & World* 31 (1) (Winter 2016): 5–14. See also Susan E. Haddox, *Metaphor and Masculinity in Hosea* (Studies in Biblical Literature 141; New York: Peter Lang, 2011).

for increased scholarly engagement of a wide range of biblical texts, topics, and characters, as well as explorations into the interpretation history. Hebrew Bible scholars have also come to differentiate various forms of masculinities, such as hegemonic, subordinate, marginal, imperial, subaltern, de-essentialized, queer, and even female.[95] Although it is probably too optimistic to state that masculinity studies have made it in biblical studies, a steady stream of publications offers important investigations about what makes men male in the Hebrew Bible.[96]

One last caveat about these developments in biblical masculinity studies. It is clear that "passion" and ethics that power feminist and queer studies are largely absent in masculinity studies of the Hebrew Bible. Both Clines and Krondorfer urge colleagues to deal with this problem.[97] I wonder if the lack of passion and ethics also relates to the fact that most works in biblical masculinity studies proceed without mentioning, no less seeking out, or engaging feminist biblical scholarship. In fact, many publications in biblical masculinity studies proceed as if feminist biblical publications did not even exist. Adherence to an empiricist-antiquarian methodology without reference to feminist biblical scholarship is pervasive although many, though certainly not all, feminist Bible scholars warn about the dangers of these epistemological and hermeneutical moves.[98] Instead,

95. Ovidiu Creangă (ed.), *Men and Masculinity in the Hebrew Bible and Beyond* (Sheffield: Sheffield Phoenix Press, 2010); Ovidiu Creangă and Peter-Ben Smit (eds), *Biblical Masculinities Foregrounded* (Sheffield: Sheffield Phoenix Press, 2014).

96. For surveys on the various publications and developments, see, e.g. Susan E. Haddox, "Masculinity Studies of the Hebrew Bible: The First Two Decades," *Currents in Biblical Research* 14 (2) (February 2016): 176–206; Joseph A. Marchal, "Queer Studies and Critical Masculinity Studies in Feminist Biblical Studies," in Elisabeth Schüssler Fiorenza (ed.), *Feminist Biblical Studies in the Twentieth Century: Scholarship and Movement* (Bible and Women: An Encyclopædia of Exegesis and Cultural History 9.1; Atlanta: Society of Biblical Literature, 2014), 261–80; Katherine Low, "Space for Women and Men: Masculinity Studies in Feminist Biblical Interpretation," in Susanne Scholz (ed.), *Feminist Interpretation of the Hebrew Bible in Retrospect: Methods* (vol. 3; Sheffield: Sheffield Phoenix Press, 2016), 345–63.

97. Clines observes: "Especially by comparison with the beginnings of feminist biblical criticism, masculinity studies in the Hebrew Bible seem strangely lacking in passion .... Perhaps there is no agenda in masculinity studies, other than intellectual curiosity." See Clines, "Final Reflections on Biblical Masculinity," in Ovidiu Creangă (ed.), *Men and Masculinity*, 238. Krondorfer comments: "In the general field of 'men's studies in religion,' we have moved away from a simple positivist reading of male figures in the Jewish and Christian traditions .... The analytical portion is grounded both in the tools of one's professional trade as well as the theory that guides the investigation .... A small step toward regaining a public voice, I have suggested, is to make explicit one's ethical and moral stance ...." See Krondorfer, "Biblical Masculinity Matters," in Ovidiu Creangă and Peter-Ben Smit (eds), *Biblical Masculinity Foregrounded*, 288, 292, 294.

98. See, e.g. Esther Fuchs, "Men in Biblical Feminist Scholarship," *JFSR* 19 (2) (Fall 2003): 93–114; Elisabeth Schüssler Fiorenza, *Power of the Word: Scripture and the Rhetoric*

many biblical masculinity publications naturalize, essentialize, and adapt biblical meanings to exegetical norms, obfuscating their own social locations and hermeneutical interests. The focus is stuck on a long line of well-known male characters, and few exegetical moves depart from normative biblical readings. Perhaps this exegetical situation would change if biblical masculinity scholars did not reinforce the gender binary of masculinity versus femininity but grounded themselves in feminist and queer hermeneutical challenges to concepts such as biblical androcentrism and heteronormativity. Even the key concept of the hermeneutics of suspicion that has served feminist interpreters so well is mostly absent in biblical masculinity studies which often looks a lot like androcentric and heteronormative exegesis. This development goes indeed against the "original intent" of the founding voices of masculinity studies in religion. Are exegetes in Hebrew Bible masculinity studies in the process of adapting to exegetical normativity, abandoning their hermeneutical sisters and brothers in feminist and queer biblical studies?

To Boldly Go Despite Exegetical, Professional, and Institutional Normativities: Concluding Remarks

The problem of adapting to hegemonic normativities is certainly not only a problem of exegetes in biblical masculinity studies. Queer Bible scholars also wrestle with it, as do feminist Bible interpreters. The delicate balance between the exegetical status quo and transformation is difficult to maintain because exegetes also want to eat, gain tenure and promotion, publish with prestigious publishing houses, and be part of the scholarly discourse in the field and the humanities in general. Feminist, genderqueer, and masculinity scholars are not alone in this tightrope balance. Some may think that the very endeavour of biblical interpretation is already always a game played within the halls of intellectual hegemony. After all, departments of theological and religious studies and Christian or Jewish schools of theology have not exactly been known to foster revolutionary progress throughout the ages. While this is certainly true, the institutional location within universities, colleges, and seminaries has also provided much needed support for exegetical innovation then and now. Although feminist, queer, and masculinity exegetes are not in the majority in any institution of higher education anywhere in the world, so far there have been some of them here and there who have kept critical thinking about the Bible going, sometimes even flourishing in challenge to gender normativities in their various manifestations, despite various educational and professional hassles, constraints, and even threats. Thus, over time, countless innovative readings have opened up exegetical, theo-religious, and intellectual spaces for many students and provided "queer" biblical meanings where previously none were found.

of Empire (Minneapolis, MN: Augsburg Fortress, 2007); Elisabeth Schüssler Fiorenza, *Democratizing Biblical Studies: Toward an Emancipatory Educational Space* (Louisville, KY: Westminster John Knox, 2009).

Chapter 7

ESSENTIALIZING "WOMAN": THREE NEOLIBERAL STRATEGIES IN CHRISTIAN RIGHT'S INTERPRETATIONS ON WOMEN IN THE BIBLE

The adaptation of biblical interpretation to hegemonic normativities enjoys rising popularity in various Bible-reading sectors. The Christian Right, which as an umbrella term includes the fundamentalist, conservative, and mainstream varieties of evangelicalism, features prominently as it has made itself heard in the larger U.S.–American public since the 1970s.[1] As Randall Balmer explains, "in the mid-1970s, evangelicals emerged from their subculture with a vengeance, seeking to make their presence felt in the media, in culture, and in politics."[2] They "made their mark on television, radio, and the music industry; spawned megachurches throughout the nation; and helped to elect Republican politicians to office, from school boards to the presidency."[3] They also developed an extensive network of biblical interpretations for the lay and academic public. By now, an evangelical reading of the Bible is even taken for granted as the dominant Christian voice about biblical views in the Western world and beyond.[4]

As Christian Right interpreters have intensified their systematic exploration of the Bible, they have increasingly become interested in the study of biblical women. At the same time, feminist exegetes had begun to challenge androcentric and heteronormative assumptions about biblical texts in the 1970s. Conservative Christian biblical scholars began feeling these hermeneutical challenges on their

1. For a historical survey on U.S.–American evangelicalism and the emergence of the Christian Right, see, e.g. Randall Balmer, *The Making of Evangelicalism: From Revivalism to Politics and Beyond* (Waco, TX: Baylor University Press, 2010). See also Axel R. Schäfer, *Countercultural Conservatives: American Evangelicalism from the Postwar Revival to the New Christian Right* (Madison: University of Wisconsin Press, 2011).

2. Ibid., 78.

3. Ibid.

4. For a discussion of Christian Right's positions worldwide, see, e.g. Philip Jenkins, "Believing in the Global South," *First Things* (December 2006), http://www.firstthings.com/article/2006/12/believing-in-the-global-south (accessed December 12, 2016). For a book-length treatment, see his book *The Next Christendom: The Coming of Global Christianity* (3rd edn; Oxford and New York: Oxford University Press, 2011).

normative readings and, true to form, turned their attention to gender issues. Although books on women in the Bible already enjoyed a certain popularity in the mid-twentieth century, as the above chapter on the history of feminist approaches to the Hebrew Bible explains, the renewed Christian Right's dedication to the topic has led to a virtual explosion of countless evangelical books on women in the Bible.[5]

A Conceptual Framework: Three Neoliberal Strategies

Feminist Bible scholars have critically commented on books about women in the Bible for decades. Already in 1983, Elisabeth Schüssler Fiorenza addresses the hermeneutical-exegetical problems of these kinds of books in her pioneering publication, *In Memory of Her*, although, at the time, conservative Christian publications on women in the Bible were not yet as abundantly produced as they are today. It is worth taking note of Schüssler Fiorenza's three observations on this genre of books. First, she explains that such collections "of so-called data and facts on 'Women in the Bible' … take the androcentric dynamics and reality constructions of patriarchal texts at face value."[6] Second, she notes that these books advance an apologetic hermeneutic legitimizing "societal and ecclesiastical patriarchy and … women's 'divinely ordained place.'"[7] Third, she clarifies that they aim to identify doctrinal truth in their readings of the Bible, and so turn the Bible into "an absolute oracle revealing timeless truth and definite answers to the questions and problems of all times."[8]

In short, conservative Christian readers of the late twentieth and early twenty-first century have a considerable tradition of clinging to an apologetic hermeneutic in defence of the Bible as the direct and unencumbered word of God. It enables interpreters to essentialize, naturalize, and universalize female characters, and to read biblical texts at face value in line with literalist-historicizing approaches. Most importantly, however, the feminist evaluation of books on women in the Bible makes painfully clear that not every biblical interpretation with a focus on women, gender, or sexuality advances feminist, and queer aligned analyses.

This central point is sometimes not even understood in feminist exegetical publications, as feminist Hebrew Bible scholar, Esther Fuchs, charges. In fact, she regards the essentializing, naturalizing and universalizing hermeneutical assumptions, prevalent in scholarly treatments on biblical women, as rooted

5. See, e.g. the online catalogues of Christian Right's presses such as Zondervan, Thomas Nelson, Baker Publishing Group, InterVarsity Press, Wipf and Stock, or Kregel Publications.

6. Elisabeth Schüssler Fiorenza, *In Memory of Her: A Feminist Theological Reconstruction of Christian Origins* (New York: Crossroad, 1983), xxiii–xxiv, 30.

7. Ibid., 7.

8. Ibid., 5.

in neoliberalist thought.[9] Fuchs shows that recognized feminist Hebrew Bible scholars, among them Ilana Pardes, Susan Ackerman, and Tikva Frymer-Kensky, exhibit three particular neoliberal strategies. First, these scholars focus on the "experience" of women within "widely used historical categories" that are "recognizable to social and political historians."[10] Fuchs charges that this focus does not challenge the academic framework within which the historical reconstructions of women appear, as they "highlight women's strength and power, autonomy and social status, distinct significance and cultural contribution" with the goal of delineating biblical "herstory."[11]

Second, another neoliberal strategy, found in feminist Bible scholarship, presents "woman" as "a natural, commonsense, 'real', collective, individual presence that claims ontological autonomy."[12] It presupposes gender as "a stable unchanging essence, or reality," enabling neoliberal feminist interpreters to conform to disciplinary boundaries. When feminist scholars rely on this neoliberal strategy, they describe "ancient women's 'strong' voices," Israelite women's "alleged independence," and their "social power," which, according to Fuchs, are "neoliberal desires and dreams" projected onto biblical texts.[13]

Third, yet another neoliberal strategy informs a considerable number of feminist Bible publications. Assuming the principles of "Western and European liberalism and humanism in Reason,"[14] this strategy enables interpreters to "separate power from knowledge."[15] It defines "woman" as "a gendered concept based on class advantage and Christian notions about the separation of body and mind." Accordingly, interpretations are "held up as a model of a universal 'human' intellectual pursuit of truth,"[16] while their deep complicities with the political infrastructures from which they emerge are concealed. Accordingly, interpretations appear to be "innocent, unmotivated or unshaped by political interests," and as advancing "human progress" because they include a formerly excluded part of human knowledge—women.[17] This neoliberal strategy also assumes "that biblical women can be studied 'outside' considerations of male power and hegemony."[18] Accordingly, the study of biblical women is seen as a mere matter of inclusion

9. For an introduction on neoliberalism, see, e.g. Manfred B. Steger and Ravi K. Roy, *Neoliberalism: A Very Short Introduction* (Oxford and New York: Oxford University Press, 2010).

10. Esther Fuchs, "The Neoliberal Turn in Feminist Biblical Studies," in *Feminist Theory and the Bible: Interrogating the Sources* (Feminist Studies and Sacred Texts; Lanham, MD: Lexington Books, 2016), 55.

11. Ibid., 55–6.

12. Ibid., 56.

13. Ibid.

14. Ibid.

15. Ibid.

16. Ibid.

17. Ibid.

18. Ibid.

that remedies previous omissions. When feminist Bible interpreters take this neoliberal strategy for granted, they accept patriarchy and ignore searching "for its historical roots and interrogating its origins."[19] Their scholarship claims to be descriptive, even objective, merely outlining "sexual difference rather than power." Yet, so Fuchs, such scholarship upholds the socio-political, cultural, and religious status quo and it re-legitimizes "the fathers of the field."[20]

Fuchs criticizes sharply the effect of these neoliberal assumptions in feminist Bible exegesis when she contends:

> Rarely do these works refer to feminist genealogies of knowledge, to their own indebtedness to feminist mothers, or even to their methodological or theoretical departure from feminist antecedents. Instead, there is much citing and genuflection to "discarded" fathers of the field, who were unfairly questioned by radical (poststructural) feminists.[21]

Further, Fuchs's critique of neoliberal strategies in feminist Hebrew Bible scholarship can also help readers understanding Christian Right's approaches to women in the Bible. Evangelical scholarship also upholds these particular strategies, failing to "investigate the discursive formations, the intersection of power and language in the construction of woman." They also do not "question the very notion and definition of 'women'"; they do not "trace the discursive emergence of this category in the text," and they do not "delineate the hierarchical power relations in the most basic representations of this subject, on the level of language."[22] Ultimately, what Fuchs and other feminist theorists define as a feminist hermeneutical posture in studying gender is conveniently ignored.

In other words, similar to neoliberal feminist scholarship, the Christian Right's interpretations on women in the Bible disregard the very notion of the text as a site in which the concept of woman is constructed. Instead, these scholars affirm "humanist notions of essentialist truths, attainable knowledge, rationalism, individualism, competitiveness, and economic success."[23] Fuchs quotes feminist theorist, bell hooks, who articulates why it is so important to take seriously the notion of "woman" as a construct. As hooks explains: "Many feminist radicals now know that neither a feminism that focuses on woman as an autonomous being worthy of personal freedom nor one that focuses on the attainment of equality of opportunity with men can rid society of sexism and male domination."[24] Consequently, it is insufficient for feminist readers to retrieve ancient Israelite women's lives or to legitimize women's equal inclusion in biblical

---

19. Ibid., 57.
20. Ibid.
21. Ibid.
22. Ibid., 67.
23. Ibid., 66.
24. Ibid., 66. For this quote, see also bell hooks, *Feminist Theory: From Margin to Center* (Cambridge: South End Press, 2000), 26.

retellings because such approaches do not contribute to the transformation of society toward gender justice. Instead, they accept the socio-political, cultural, economic, and religious parameters of the kyriarchal system.[25]

The following analysis takes Fuchs's conceptual framework seriously. It illuminates the silenced and hidden neoliberal strategies in Christian Right's works on women in the Bible. Accordingly, the first section investigates Christian Right's readings on women in the Bible as a rhetorical discourse that depicts biblical women's "experience" in support of androcentric and heteronormative hegemonies. The next section demonstrates how Christian Right's interpretations essentialize, naturalize, and universalize gender binaries, which in turn stabilizes them. Yet another section explores the separation of power from knowledge in Christian Right's retellings. Finally, the conclusion affirms the need to investigate women, gender, and sexuality as intersectional constructs so that feminist biblical scholarship aligns itself with the overall direction of feminist critical studies today.[26]

Biblical Women's "Experiences" in Alliance with Androcentrism and Heteronormativity

When evangelical readers focus on the experience of biblical women, they emphasize their familial roles as wives, mothers, daughters, or sisters. These readers also mention that some biblical women stand out in military, political, or even business leadership roles. In their opinion, the Bible provides spiritual-historical information that depicts women performing roles in support of androcentric and heteronormative norms.

Christian Right's approaches to women in the Bible illustrate this neoliberal strategy. For instance, the bestselling popular writer, Elizabeth George, presents a book on *The Remarkable Women of the Bible* that includes more than fourteen "remarkable" women of the Christian biblical canon. Among them are Eve as a "remarkable creation," Sarah of "remarkable faith," Rebekah who has a "remarkable journey," Miriam as a "remarkable leader," Deborah who has "remarkable wisdom," Ruth and Naomi who have "remarkable devotion," Hannah who makes a "remarkable sacrifice," and Esther who has "remarkable courage."[27] Classifying

25. For a detailed analysis of this dynamic, see, e.g. Elisabeth Schüssler Fiorenza, *The Power of the Word: Scripture and the Rhetoric of Empire* (Minneapolis, MN: Augsburg Fortress Publishers, 2007).

26. See, e.g. Uma Chakravarti (ed.), *Thinking Gender, Doing Gender: Feminist Scholarship and Practice Today* (New Delhi: Orient BlackSwan, 2016); Wendy Harcourt (ed.), *The Palgrave Handbook of Gender and Development: Critical Engagements in Feminist Theory and Practice* (New York: Palgrave Macmillan, 2016); Mary Evans, Clare Hemmings, Marsha Henry, Hazel Johnsteon, Sumi Madhok, Ania Plomien and Sadie Wearing (eds), *The SAGE Handbook of Feminist Theory* (Thousand Oaks, CA: Sage, 2014).

27. Elizabeth George, *The Remarkable Women of the Bible and Their Message for Your Life Today* (Eugene: Harvest House, 2003).

these biblical women as "remarkable" yet ordinary, George promises that readers, too, will be able to experience "God's life-changing power" by learning from these biblical women. George explains that these female figures loved God "passion- ately," teaching today's women to do the same. As biblical women "reveled" in their "lovely womanhood and femaleness"[28] in their roles as mothers, wives, or sisters, contemporary readers can learn from them. An utterly simplistic retri- bution theology undergirds George's retellings shaped by a literalist-historicizing, individualized, and sentimentalized hermeneutics that describes biblical women's experiences in alliance with androcentric and heteronormative hegemonies.

Another volume, written by Sue Poorman and Lawrence O. Richards, covers female biblical character from A to Z.[29] The table of content indicates a fuss-free organization with the majority of the book devoted to "Women of the Bible A–Z." It also includes appendices on "Historical Panorama of Women," "Women of the Old Testament," "Women of the New Testament," "Pauls," Teachings on Women," and, "Proverbs 31 Woman." The authors explain that they want their readers to "go back in time to experience the life and times"[30] of the many biblical women. Accordingly, historical-literalist retellings that begin with Abigail and end with Zipporah dominate the summarizing and simplifying descriptions of the female characters. Sometimes Poorman "and Richards also move into a semi-feminist mode when they emphasize that "the Genesis account is descriptive rather than prescriptive" and the narratives do not advocate "patriarchal" conventions as "God's will for humankind."[31] They explain that not all biblical laws and customs reflect "a totally accurate picture of women's place" in ancient Israel.[32] Wanting to show affinities between past and present women, the authors state, as many other authors do in similar books: "Both the wonderful gifts God gave human beings and the Fall's twisting of those gifts is revealed as powerfully in biblical women of this period as in the women of our own time."[33] They find in the biblical record "equal rights of husband and wives"[34] and they stress that in some Hebrew Bible texts, such as Proverbs 31, women are not depicted as "inferior to men by nature."[35] The book

---

28. Ibid., 12.

29. Sue Poorman Richards and Lawrence O. Richards, *Women of the Bible: The Live and Times of Every Woman of the Bible* (Nashville, TN: Thomas Nelson, 2003). For a similar but less comprehensive publication, see Ann Spangler and Jean E. Syswerda, *Women of the Bible: 52 Bible Studies for Individuals and Groups* (Grand Rapids, MI: Zondervan, 1999, 2002). The idea to include in one book "all" the women of the Bible is also found in scholarly feminist work; see the comprehensive volume by Carol Meyers, Toni Craven, and Ross Kramer (eds), *Women in Scripture: A Dictionary of Named and Unnamed Women in the Hebrew Bible, the Apocryphal/Deuterocanonical Books and New Testament* (Grand Rapids, MI: Eerdmans, 2001).

30. Poorman and Richards, *Women of the Bible*, vii.

31. Ibid., 281.

32. Ibid., 283.

33. Ibid.

34. Ibid., 285.

35. Ibid., 326.

thus underscores women's "faithfulness to God" as a solution to any circumstances in which biblical and contemporary women find themselves, whether it is Hagar's situation as a "slave," Rahab's life as a "harlot," or Samson's mother, Manoah's wife, in Judges 13.[36] Pietistic, sentimentalizing, and individualistic readings reinforce women's roles as loving mothers, obedient wives, and faithful believers in God.

The approach that features each biblical woman by name in a separate chapter has proven to be very popular in this genre of books. Numerous best-selling evangelical authors have pursued it with a vengeance. They have made careers out of composing biblical retellings that are heavy on spiritual-moralizing advice and present biblical women in gender-stereotypical roles, interspersed with this or that exceptional heroine or "wicked" woman. One highly successful author is Ann Spangler who calls herself "an award–winning writer" with a background in "Christian publishing."[37] She has enjoyed a prolific publishing career, writing on the Bible within a Christian spiritual framework. Her first book, *Dreams: True Stories of Remarkable Encounters with God*,[38] retells the stories of male dreamers, such as Abraham, Jacob, Daniel, Solomon, and Joseph, without making gender a prominent issue. This emphasis changes in 1999 when she and her co-author, Jean E. Syswerda, publish their first book on *Women of the Bible: A One-Year Devotional Study of Women in Scripture*,[39] which has been republished in 2002, 2007, and 2015, a testament to the book's popularity in evangelical circles. Spangler and Syswerda also produce several follow-up titles that contain a reduced number of women characters, such as *Women of the Bible: Eve to Pricilla* and *Mothers of the Bible*.[40] Noticeably, in these works motherhood and marriage feature prominently. For instance, Spangler and Syswerda present Eve as the first woman, listing her as

36. Ibid., 81, 180, 208–12.

37. See her website at http://www.annspangler.com/about/. Another popularizing and best-selling writer on women in the Bible is Liz Curtis Higgs. For a list of her books and related activities, see her website at http://www.lizcurtishiggs.com/ (both accessed December 12, 2016). She describes herself as an "author of more than thirty books, with 4.6 million copies in print," who is dedicated to "platform ministry." Higgs received some academic recognition, according to her webpage, which states: "Her alma mater, Bellarmine University, presented her with a Distinguished Alumni Award in 2005. And she received an Honorary Doctorate from Georgetown College in 2010."

38. Ann Spangler, *Dreams: True Stories of Remarkable Encounters with God* (Grand Rapids, MI: Zondervan, 1997).

39. Ann Spangler and Jean E. Syswerda, *Women of the Bible: A One-Year Devotional Study of Women in Scripture* (Grand Rapids, MI: Zondervan, 2015 [2007, 2002, 1999]). See also their *Prayer through the Eyes of Women of the Bible* (Grand Rapids, MI: Inspirio, 2000); *Blessings and Promises through the Eyes of Women of the Bible* (Grand Rapids, MI: Inspirio, 2001).

40. Jean E. Syswerda, *Women of the Bible: 52 Bible Studies for Individuals and Groups* (Grand Rapids, MI: Zondervan, 2002); Ann Spangler and Jean E. Syswerda, *Mothers of the Bible: A Devotional* (Grand Rapids, MI: Zondervan, 2006); Ann Spangler, *Women of the Bible: Eve to Pricilla* (Grand Rapids, MI: Zondervan, 2010);

"The Mother of All Who Have Life"[41] and the "first woman to conceive a child, the first to harbor a fertilized egg in her womb."[42]

For the next fifteen years, Spangler writes women-centered books, some of which are co-authored and all of which are translated into numerous languages.[43] In 2002, she co-authors with Robert D. Wolgemuth, the chair of the Evangelical Christian Publishers" Association, a volume on *Men of the Bible: A One-Year Devotional Study of Men in Scripture*, followed by *Fathers in the Bible* in 2006.[44] Both publications indicate the remarkable rise of father-oriented devotional books, such as Robert Wolgemut's *The Father's Plan: A Bible Study for Dads* and Ed Strauss's *Bible Prayers for Fathers: A Devotional*.[45]

These kinds of books are marketed as faith-deepening spiritual literature about women (and men) in "Scripture." Presenting biblical women with concerns similar to contemporary women, the authors offer their retellings as bridges across the "thousands of years"[46] of chronological separation. The books also promise "a deeper love for God's Word and its truth in your life,"[47] while they never engage feminist or much of any other biblical scholarship. The sentimental-fictional retellings of biblical narratives include countless clichéd theological doctrines, such as the indwelling of the Holy Spirit when reading the Bible. These

41. Spangler and Syswerda, *Women of the Bible* (2015), 17.

42. Ibid. 20.

43. Several of her books are translated into Spanish, French, German, and Chinese, indicating a certain ecclesial global reach: *Les femmes de la Bible: une année d'études bibliques sur les femmes dans l'Écriture* (Nîmes: Vida éd 2004); *Mütter im Buch der Bücher: ein Andachtsbuch* (Asslar, Gerth Medien, 2007); *Sheng jing zhong de nv ren* (with Jean Syswerda and trans. Wanlan, He; Taibei: Dao sheng chu ban she, 2007); *Madres de la Biblia* (Miami, FL: Editorial Vida, 2008); *Frauen im Buch der Bücher: ein Andachtsbuch für das ganze Jahr* (Assler: Gerth Medien, 2012).

44. Ann Spangler and Robert D. Wolgemuth, *Men of the Bible: A One-Year Devotional Study of Men in Scripture* (Grand Rapids, MI: Zondervan, 2007 [2002]); *Fathers in the Bible: A Devotional* (Grand Rapids, MI: Zondervan, 2006). This book is translated into Spanish in 2008: *Padres de la Biblia* (Miami, FL: Vida, 2008).

45. Robert Wolgemut's *The Father's Plan: A Bible Study for Dads* (Nashville, TN: Thomas Nelson, 2010); Ed Strauss, *Bible Prayers for Fathers: A Devotional* (n.p.: Barbour Books, 2016). For the many derivatives on this topic, see, e.g. Robert Wolgemut, *NIV, Dad's Devotional Bible* (Grand Rapids, MI: Zondervan, 2016). The explicit focus on biblical men is not new; see, e.g. Herbert Lockyer, *All the Men of the Bible: A Portrait Gallery and Reference Library of More than 3000 Biblical Characters* (Grand Rapids, MI: Zondervan, 1958, 1988); J. Sidlow Baxter, *Mark These Men: A Unique Look at Selected Men of the Bible* (Grand Rapids, MI: Kregel, 1992, [1960]); Edward M. Bounds, *Bible Men of Prayer* (Grand Rapids, MI: Zondervan, 1964 [1921]). Many similar titles exist as any search on any major online book-selling site illustrates, leading to a long list of countless books for Christian Right's congregations and lay readers.

46. Spangler and Syswerda, *Women of the Bible*, 9.

47. Ibid., 10.

are pietistical, moralizing, and simplistic spiritual-theological publications that do not care about scholarly credentials and do not look for academic approval. Many authors collaborate closely with their publication houses, sometimes having previously been employed by them. The collaboration often leads to various iterations and republications of the same titles—once it is clear they sell. In fact, there seems to be an almost insatiable appetite for these kinds of biblical retellings in the Christian Right's market.

In light of Spangler's disregard for feminist scholarship, it is perhaps unsurprising that Ann Spangler has also written several books on prayer. She even comments on a Bible translation published by the Nations Bible Mission Society.[48] Since audience pleasure and not intellectual rigor define Spangler's writing, she easily accepts exclusive language conventions for God ("Lord," he), and in these kinds of projects she is only marginally concerned with biblical or contemporary women. Yet these books, too, reach international audiences.[49] In 2015, she published another book, this time on the *Wicked Women of the Bible*.[50] It contains many of the same female characters that already appear in her previously co-written books, but in this latest book the list of biblical women is relatively short. It is organized by the adjective "wicked" in its "literal and ironic sense,"[51] such as "Wicked Lies: The Story of Eve," "Wicked Old: The Story of Sarah," "A Wicked Disguise: The Story of Tamar," or "Wicked Smart: The Story of Abigail." As usual, Spangler does not engage biblical scholarship, focusing her retellings instead on the question why "God put" these "wicked" women into the Bible and

48. See, e.g. Ann Spangler, *Praying the Names of God: A Daily Guide* (Grand Rapids, MI: Zondervan, 2004); *The Names of God* (Grand Rapids, MI: Zondervan, 2009); with LaVonne Neff, *The Names of God Bible* (Grand Rapids, MI: Revell, 2011). Predictably, this Bible translation was produced by the theologically conservative Nations Bible Mission Society (http://godsword.org/) (accessed December 12, 2016) with many board members affiliated with the Lutheran Church—Missouri Synod (LCMS). As she has done throughout her entire publishing career, Spangler selects theologically conservative publishers, in this case it is Revell, a division of the Baker Publishing Group.

49. See, e.g. Ann Spangle and Wendy Bello, *Dulces palabras de Dios, con amor, para ti: una guía diaria* (Miami, FL: Editorial Vida, 2011).

50. Ann Spangler, *Wicked Women of the Bible* (Grand Rapids, MI: Zondervan, 2015). See also an online interview with Spangler on this book conducted by Jonathan Petersen, the manager of marketing for Bible Gateway, the evangelical-conservative Bible website provider. The interview is entitled "Wicked Women of the Bible: An Interview with Ann Spangler" (September 22, 2015), and can be found at https://www.biblegateway.com/blog/2015/09/wicked-women-of-the-bible-an-interview-with-ann-spangler/. The topic seems to be popular in Christian Right's circles, as other authors also write on it; see, e.g. Liz Curtis Higgs, *Bad Girls of the Bible, and What We Can Learn from Them* (Colorado Springs, CO: WaterBrook Press, 2013 [2007, 1999]). Interestingly, feminist Bible scholars also write on it; see, e.g. Gale A. Yee, *Poor Banished Children of Eve: Woman as Evil in the Hebrew Bible* (Minneapolis, MN: Augsburg Fortress, 2003).

51. Spangler, *Wicked Women of the Bible*, 11.

allowed "these unpleasant stories to be commemorated."[52] Spangler creates total fiction[53] on the selected biblical women whom she characterizes as disobedient, doubting, or faithless wives, mothers, sisters or daughters, as well as women with questionable professions, such as the so-called "Medium of Endor," whom Spangler classifies as "A Wicked Sorceress," or as women who are inherently evil, such as Jezebel whom Spangler labels as "Wickedness Personified." In this and in many other books the experiences of women are reduced to being mothers, wives, sisters, women after menopause, or women with love-life issues, and sometimes they are leaders, usually queens, who follow or do not follow God.[54] Women's roles are essentialized, as if they characterized all women regardless of place and time and illustrated every woman's strength, power, and social status throughout the ages.

Attributing "Woman" with Ontological Autonomy

The second neoliberal strategy attributes ontological autonomy to the category of "women." Accordingly, "woman" is not a construct shaped by time and place but has an essential, stable, and unchanging identity. As Fuchs explains, this neoliberal strategy posits that the category of woman is not subject to "discursive formations."[55] Consequently, biblical women appear within the naturalized, essentialized, and universalized heteronormative gender binary. In short, gender categories are not historically, politically, culturally, and religiously located. They are presented as if they had been there since the creation of the world.

Many Christian Right books on women in the Bible follow this neoliberal strategy which reinforces enthusiastically the gender binary. Even further, these

52. Ibid.

53. Some authors acknowledge that their interpretations are fictions; see, e.g. Donna Herbison, *Through My Eyes: Women of the Bible* (Bloomington: Authorhouse, 2015)

54. See, e.g. Liz Curtis Higgs, *It's Good to Be Queen: Becoming as Bold, Gracious, and Wise as the Queen of Sheba* (Colorado Springs, CO: WaterBrook Press, 2015); J. Lee Grady, *Fearless Daughters of the Bible: What You Can Learn from 22 Women Who Challenged Tradition, Fought Injustice and Dared to Lead* (Bloomington, MN: Chosen Book, 2012); Kathi Macias, *Mothers of the Bible Speak to Mothers of Today* (Birmingham, AL: New Hope Publishers, 2009); Carolyn Custis James, *The Gospel of Ruth: Loving God Enough to Break the Rules* (Grand Rapids, MI: Zondervan, 2008). For general-advice books that include biblical women, see, e.g. Debra Evans, *Six Qualities of Women of Character: Life-Changing Examples of Godly Women* (Grand Rapids, MI: Zondervan, 1996). The six qualities are "brokenness, belief, surrender, obedience, devotion and service." See also Debra Evans, *Women of Courage: Inspiring Stories of Faith, Hope, and Endurance* (Grand Rapids, MI: Zondervan, 1999). The six virtues are affiliated with particular biblical women: "humility (Esther), patience (Anna), trust (Hagar), vision (Deborah), love (the repentant woman), and vocation (Priscilla)."

55. Fuchs, "The Neoliberal Turn," 56.

works seemingly fortify the gender binary even when they tackle sexuality issues.[56] One of the authors who strengthens the gender binary in this fashion is Herbert Lockyer (1886–1984). He began his career as a minister in Scotland and England for more than two decades before coming to the United States, and he published many popularizing books on the Bible. Part of a British holiness movement, called the Keswick Higher Life Movement, he was invited by the Moody Bible Institute for a lecture in 1936 which led him to expanding his ministry in the U.S.A. He spent his final years in Colorado Spring, Colorado, and his son, Herbert Lockyer Jr., a Presbyterian minister, edited many of his father's books.[57] The elder Lockyer published more than fifty books that have been republished even after his death due to the son's editorial commitment to his father's work.[58]

In 1958, Lockyer published his first book on a gendered topic, entitled *All the Men of The Bible: A Portrait Gallery and Reference Library of More Than 3000 Biblical Characters*.[59] The volume contains short entries on countless biblical men, setting the tone for his imaginative and diligent biblical retellings. In 1967, Lockyer produced the companion volume, *All the Women of the Bible: The Life and Times of All the Women of the Bible*,[60] and with the help of his son both volumes were published posthumously in one volume in 1996, with another printing in 2006.[61]

56. See, e.g. Russell D. Moore and Andrew T. Walker, *The Gospel & Same-Sex Marriage* (Gospel for Life; Nashville, TN: B&H Books, 2016); Roy E. Gane, Nicholas P. Miller, and H. Peter Swanson (eds), *Homosexuality, Marriage, and the Church: Biblical, Counseling, and Religious Liberty Issues* (Berrien Springs, MI: Andrews University Press, 2012).

57. For additional biographical details, visit http://www.whitakerhouse.com/DeskTop. aspx?page=AuthorInfo&author=399.

58. The son also publishes his own books with similar titles but with a different publisher; see, e.g. Herbert Lockyer, Jr., *All the Music of the Bible: An Exploration of Musical Expression in Scripture and Church Hymnody* (Peabody, MA: Hendrickson Publishers, 2004). He continues editing his father's work posthumously; see, e.g. Herbert Lockyer, *All About the Second Coming*, ed. Herbert Lockyer, Jr. (Peabody, MA: Hendrickson Publishers, 1997).

59. Herbert Lockyer, *All the Men of the Bible: A Portrait Gallery and Reference Library of More Than 3000 Biblical Characters* (Grand Rapids, MI: Zondervan, 1988 [1958]). In 1949, he had already published a book on the Holy Spirit; see *All about the Holy Spirit* (Peabody, MA: Hendrickson Publishers, 1995 [1949]). For a brief online biographical note, visit http://www.whitakerhouse.com/DeskTop.aspx?page=AuthorInfo&author=399 (accessed December 12, 2016).

60. Herbert Lockyer, *All the Women of the Bible: The Life and Times of All the Women of the Bible* (Grand Rapids, MI: Zondervan, 1967).

61. Herbert Lockyer, *All the Men of the Bible; All the Women of the Bible* (Grand Rapids, MI: Zondervan, 2006 [1996]). See also James B. Hurley, *Man and Woman in Biblical Perspective* (Grand Rapids, MI: Zondervan, 1981).

The back cover promotes the book in vivid language:

> Bringing together two books in one convenient volume, *All the Men/All the Women of the Bible* is a portrait gallery and reference library of over 3,400 named biblical characters. Taken from the time-honoured 'All' series by Dr. Herbert Lockyer, this book mines the wealth of Scripture to give you characters you can learn from, teachings you can apply, and promises you can stand on.
>
> *All the Men* This monumental book puts comprehensive information on the men of the Bible at your fingertips, including a list of major characters. Besides named individuals, it also classifies the thousands upon thousands of unnamed men. It includes a guide to the often complex pronunciations of biblical names. And it explores the attributes of Jesus, God's model for biblical manhood.
>
> *All the Women* From Abi to Zipporah, discover how the lives and character of different biblical women, named and unnamed, mirror the situations of women today. More than 400 profiles offer fascinating insights into the Bible's multi-dimensional women. Wives, mothers, single women, prophetesses, queens, leaders, villainesses, and heroines—all are portrayed in rich, thought-provoking detail.[62]

The construct of woman and man remains firmly locked in the heteronormative gender binary. Accordingly, essentialized femaleness and maleness characterize Lockyer's interpretations. In addition, his literalist-historicizing hermeneutics presents gender as a commonsense notion that is as real in biblical times at it is today. Predictably, women are wives, mothers, and queens, even villains and heroes, while Jesus is the model of biblical manhood. To make the nuclear family complete, Lockyer authored a book on *All the Children in the Bible* in 1970.[63]

Importantly, then, Christian Right books on women in the Bible take the binary of female and male for granted. Gender is divinely ordained in Genesis 1, and so these books accept the construct of woman or man as a fact. Seemingly when a popularizing author writes a book on biblical women, a book on biblical men is not far off. Many evangelical authors advance the

---

62. Backcover, *All the Women of the Bible*, 2006.

63. Herbert Lockyer, *All the Children in the Bible* (Grand Rapids, MI: Zondervan, 1970). Interestingly, Lockyer rarely diverted from his early idea to use the adjectival "all" in the many titles of his books; see, e.g. *All the Kings and Queens of the Bible: Tragedies and Triumphs of Royalty in Past Ages* (Grand Rapids, MI: Zondervan, 1961); *All the Messianic Prophecies of the Bible* (Grand Rapids, MI: Zondervan, 1973); *All the Divine Names and Titles in the Bible: A Unique Classification of All Scriptural Designations of the Three Persons of the Trinity* (Grand Rapids, MI: Zondervan, 1975); *All the Holy Days and Holidays or, Sermons on All National and Religious Memorial Days* (Grand Rapids, MI: Zondervan, 1968); *All the Books and Chapters of the Bible: Combination of Bible Study and Daily Meditation Plan* (Grand Rapids, MI: Zondervan, 1966).

binary viewpoint because, to them, it is natural, self-evident, and biblical. That youth audiences need to learn about it, too, is equally clear. Thus, a book like Laurie Polich's *Creative Bible Lessons from the Old Testament: 12 Character Studies on Surprisingly Modern Men & Women* makes sure that teenagers, too, learn to never question the ontological autonomy of the gender binary in their churches.[64]

The essentializing framework within which the construct of woman is upheld also prevents the possibility for difference among women. Very few books, published by the Christian Right's various publishing houses, explore intersectional issues of class, race, ethnicity, or geopolitics in the retellings of biblical women's stories. Almost all authors privatize, sentimentalize, and spiritualize concerns that women of color may face, similar to general biblical women's books. For instance, the anthology, *God's Words of Life for Women of Color*, targets an audience of African-American Christian women. It includes "enriching devotions from the African American Devotional Bible" with "uplifting and encouraging" biblical texts from the King James Version, as well as "devotionals ... written by well-known African-American men and women, in cooperation with the 19-million-member Congress of National Black Churches."[65] It is curious that the publisher, Zondervan, produced the volume on the corporate level, not seeking an individual author for the book. Did Zondervan test the waters to see if there is a market among African–American Christian women for Bible-oriented books that focus on biblical women without addressing racism, poverty, or other forms of structural oppression?

The 2013-volume by Michelle Clark Jenkins suggests that perhaps Christian Right's publishers are indeed in the process of explicitly addressing evangelical women of color.[66] Jenkins follows the tried-and-proven format of individual women portrayals. The volume, written in the first-person singular voice of various biblical women, begins with a chapter on "I am Eve," followed by chapters on "I am Sarah," "I am Hagar," "I am Rebekah," "I am Rachel," "I am

64. Laurie Polich, *Creative Bible Lessons from the Old Testament: 12 Character Studies on Surprisingly Modern Men & Women* (Grand Rapids, MI: Youth Specialties/Zondervan, 2005). For additional titles for adults, see, e.g. Nancy M. Tischler, *Men and Women of the Bible: A Reader's Guide* (Westport, CT: Greenwood Press, 2002); Jim George, *10 Minutes to Knowing the Men and Women of the Bible* (The Bare Bones Bible Series; Eugene, OR: Harvest House Publishers, 2010); *Once-A-Day Men and Women of the Bible Devotional (NIV): 365 Insights from Scripture's Most Memorable People* (Grand Rapids, MI: Zondervan, 2012); Andreas J. Köstenberger, *God's Design for Man and Woman: A Biblical-Theological Survey* (Wheaton, IL: Crossway, 2014).

65. Snapdragon Editorial Group, Inc., and Zondervan Corporation, *God's Words of Life for Women of Color: From the King James Version* (Grand Rapids, MI: Zondervan, 2002). See also this NIV Bible translation targeting women of color: *Aspire: The New Women of Color Study Bible: For Strength and Inspiration* (Grand Rapids, MI: Zondervan, 2007).

66. Michelle Clark Jenkins, *She Speaks: Wisdom From the Women of the Bible to the Modern Black Woman* (Nashville, TN: Thomas Nelson, 2013).

Tamar." The relatively short retellings are devoid of any references to sexism and racism. The enslaved and raped woman, Hagar, appears as a "handmaid"[67] who experiences God's faithfulness by rescuing her and her son, Ishmael, in the desert. She is a slave "in a foreign nation" but becomes "a free woman, with a promise from God."[68] Another biblical woman, Pharaoh's daughter in Exodus 2, is praised for overcoming "racial prejudice and injustice."[69] She rescues baby Moses, a Hebrew infant, and adopts him as a son. The lesson Jenkins derives from this story is this: "God can use each of us to carry out His plan whether we belong to Him or not."[70] Women are there to be the "helpmates" of "the men in our lives," similar to Zipporah who helped her husband Moses "when Moses had failed to circumcise their son."[71] In conclusion, Christian Right books on women in the Bible construct the notion of woman with ontological autonomy, and so differences among women are not addressed and intersectional qualifications are absent.

The Separation of Power from Knowledge

The third neoliberal strategy, as defined by Fuchs, aims to contribute to the advancement of human knowledge by separating knowledge (biblical inter-pretation) from power (hermeneutical interests). In fact, this strategy enables interpreters to hide their deep complicities with the structures of domination in the world. When biblical interpreters employ this strategy, they present their readings as innocent, unmotivated, and unshaped by theo-political interests. It is difficult to identify this third strategy in the Christian Right's interpretations because, claiming to be concerned with matters of spiritual growth and doctrinal truth, they present themselves as merely elaborating on spiritual truth about the Bible as it shines through the biblical women's stories. They characterize themselves as neutral mediators of biblical knowledge. In other words, this third neoliberal strategy emerges in a complicated fashion in Christian Right's readings because the authors, recognizing their theo-political partisanship, believe they communicate universally valid and politically innocent knowledge about the word of God.

67. Ibid., 24.
68. Ibid., 25.
69. Ibid., 55,
70. Ibid., 56.
71. Ibid., 59. Interestingly, the biographical approach also appears in the scholarly feminist literature; see, e.g. Athalya Brenner, *I am … Biblical Women Tell Their Own Stories* (Minneapolis, MN: Augsburg Fortress, 2005). The book, *Black and White Bible, Black and Blue Wife: My Story of Finding Hope after Domestic Abuse*, written by Ruth A. Tucker (Grand Rapids, MI: Zondervan, 2016), is not about race but about evangelical women's experiences with spousal abuse.

A sophisticated example for this third strategy can be found in *The IVP Women's Commentary*, edited by Catherine Clark Kroeger and Mary J. Evans.[72] The two Christian egalitarian scholars acknowledge the particular social location within which their commentary stands. Kroeger and Evans explain that their commentary serves as a "complement rather than as an alternative"[73] to other Bible commentaries that are mostly written from the "curtailed perspective" of "white, Western, classically educated, middle-class males."[74] Kroeger and Evans seek to "redress this imbalance,"[75] and so their commentary "is not written simply 'for' women as opposed to men, it is rather written 'from' women …." They acknowledge to write "unashamedly" from "a particular perspective," featuring "women's questions," but the commentary as such aims to serve "the whole church—both women and men."[76]

The editors of the commentary thus claim to provide politically innocent knowledge (interpretations) despite the acknowledgement of their hermeneutical interests (power). They assert that their commentary aims for a universal reach that embraces all of humanity. Accordingly, "this commentary doesn't just look at passages about women, it looks at *all* of Scripture from a woman's perspective."[77] In other words, Kroeger and Evans insist on universal validity. They contend that they do not "read into" the Bible, as might be suspected in light of their particular "women's" perspective; rather they present what comes "from the text." Their commentary is grounded in the deep-seated conviction that the included interpretations are theo-politically innocent; they are based in exegesis and not in eisegesis.

Ultimately, then, the commentary's editors present their biblical interpretations (knowledge) as independent from their hermeneutical interests (power). Kroeger and Evans emphasize that "Scripture is inspired by God and given for the benefit of all humanity." At the same time they acknowledge writing from a "hermeneutic of faith" that is grounded in "a conviction that the Scriptures are meant for healing rather than hurt, for affirmation of all persons, especially those who are oppressed."[78] In short, this commentary advances a complex partisan conviction that asserts hermeneutical innocence. It maintains to merely rehearse the teachings of the Bible. In this sense, it is indeed the case that the *IVP Women's Commentary* is written with a "feminist hermeneutic, albeit from a more conservative position than some other materials."[79] The volume, subscribing to "the full inspiration of the

---

72. Catherine Clark Kroeger and Mary J. Evans (eds), *The IVP Women's Commentary* (Downers Grove, IL: InterVarsity Press, 2002).

73. Ibid., xiii.

74. Ibid., xiii.

75. Ibid.

76. Ibid.

77. Ibid. (Emphasis added.)

78. Ibid., xiv.

79. Ibid., xv.

Bible and the full equality of women,"[80] references its hermeneutical interests but it claims to just describe divine truth as it is found in the Bible. Importantly, then, the commentary separates knowledge about biblical women from the politics of gender; it alleges to present the Bible as it is, not as one wishes it to be,[81] and so it advances the third neoliberal strategy. It separates knowledge from power.

Another less comprehensive volume that also illustrates the third neoliberal strategy is *Dynamic Women of the Bible*. Written by Ruth Tucker, this book contains a complicated mixture of acknowledging hermeneutical reading interests on the one hand and asserting descriptive neutrality on the other.[82] In an extensive way Tucker refers to her hermeneutical subjectivity when she elaborates on the formation of her "own worldview." She writes:

> My imagination, like all imaginations, arises out of my own worldview, one formed in the northern Wisconsin farming community in which I was raised, never far away from the country church on the corner of County H and Lewis Road. My worldview has been stretched by such diverse cultures as those in East Texas; Newark, New Jersey; Crown Point, Indiana; Kijabe, Kenya; Moscow; and Singapore, places where I set up temporary residence. For twenty-eight years, I made my home in an integrated neighborhood in Grand Rapids, Michigan, and after that in a nearby river-rat neighborhood on a floodplain in Comstock Park, where I am writing today. Add to that a slew of Asian, African, and Latino students, and you might think I am a model of diversity. Far from it. Open these pages, and a white middle-class woman is writing every line.[83]

This description of a life lived in geographically diverse neighborhoods is impressive, but Tucker does not explain how the various towns, places, and people she encountered have contributed to stretching her reading practice. How have her days spent in New Jersey, Kenya, or Singapore made any substantive difference to her reading of the Bible? She suggests that living in different places did not matter at all in the development of her "worldview."

---

80. Ibid.

81. See, e.g. the commentary on the book of Genesis that states in its second sentence: "Genesis 1–11 describes how the cosmos came into being, how marriage arose, how it happened that men dominate women and that the ground unwillingly gives its produce, how culture and the many languages began." This sentence explains neither the logic of declaring the mentioned items as self-evident nor the contested historical-literary nature of Genesis 1–11 in biblical scholarship. For a sympathetic discussion of this and other egalitarian works, see, e.g. Karen Strand Winslow, "Recovering Redemption for Women: Feminist Exegesis in North American Evangelicalism," in Susanne Scholz (ed.), *Feminist Interpretation of the Hebrew Bible in Retrospect: Social Location (vol. 3)* (Sheffield: Sheffield Phoenix Press, 2014), 269–89.

82. Ruth Tucker, *Dynamic Women of the Bible: What We Can Learn from Their Surprising Stories* (Grand Rapids, MI: Baker Books, 2014).

83. Ibid., xvi–xvii.

She believes her "worldview" is inescapably white, middle-class, and female. This position essentializes her identity which, in turn, allows Tucker to present literalist retellings bereft of her encounters with diversely located people. Stuck in essentialist and individualized identity markers, she even exclaims: "[T]here is no way I can enter into her [Missippian neighbor's] worldview or that of any other black women transplanted from Mississippi, and surely not Kenyan or Korean women."[84] Is it simply that this "college and seminary professor for some three decades" loves "lively discussions in class and the wide-ranging points of view" so that she can interpret biblical women without "making these women over into my own image?"[85] The statement about her upbringing is disturbing because her biblical interpretations are so utterly untouched by her acknowledged experiences. She prides herself to have lived in diverse neighborhoods but not to have been tainted by them. She observes "other" people with a hermeneutics of separation that she also applies to biblical women. Tucker remains detached and unmoved by them although she also believes they have somehow enriched her life. It is unclear how her twenty-eight years of living in many different places have stretched her hermeneutics beyond "the country church on the corner of County H and Lewis Road."

Like the *IVP Women's Commentary*, then, Tucker makes personal statements about her background in a nod of recognition to her own "subjectivity." She seems to believe that the purity of her subjectivity lends credence to her ability to present an objective interpretation of the biblical women's stories. In her opinion, she describes the biblical women for who they are, separated from contemporary readers by historical distance and authorial intent. Tucker also advises that contemporary expectations and rationality do not matter in the interpretation of these texts. Much in the Bible does "not make sense to a rational questioning mind," she explains, which she finds "okay" because it "is not the purpose of Scripture."[86] To this white, middle-class, female interpreter, what matters is to appreciate "the down-to-earth reality"[87] and "the symbolic dimension of these women"[88] who are "elusive women of millennia past"[89] and their stories are an enrichment "to our lives."[90]

Tucker's need to separate knowledge (biblical interpretation) from power (hermeneutical interests) is obvious in her descriptions of biblical women whom

---

84. Ibid.

85. Ibid., xvi. The back page offers the following biographical information: "Ruth A. Tucker (PhD, Northern Illinois University) has for more than three decades taught at colleges and seminaries, including Trinity Evangelical Divinity School and Calvin Theological Seminary."

86. Ibid., xiv.

87. Ibid., xiii.

88. Ibid., xiv.

89. Ibid., xviii.

90. Ibid.

she discusses mostly in pairs.[91] So, for instance, in a chapter on "Eve and Noah's Wife: Mothers of Us All," Tucker compares Eve and Ms. Noah when she claims: "Eve grabs our imaginations. She's inquisitive and feisty as the woman who stands forever as the mother of us all. Noah's wife has an entirely different role to play, but in a very significant sense, she too is the mother of us all. In fact, she is the only woman in the Bible besides Eve who could be considered as such."[92] Her literary retelling of the two women's stories avoids making references to contemporary women, giving the impression of offering a fair and unambiguous portrayal of their situations. Only a section, entitled "Questions to Think About," invites readers to make direct connections between the biblical characters and themselves, such as: "What issues and problems relevant to women today may have also confronted Eve?" and "Are you able to contemplate Noah's wife and daughters-in-law and their terrible loss of extended family members and friends in the great deluge?"[93]

The third neoliberal strategy, enabling interpreters to separate knowledge from power, is more difficult to delineate in the Christian Right's treatment of women in the Bible. As it turns out, it is hard for those authors not to acknowledge their hermeneutical interests (power) as they construct their biblical interpretations (knowledge). Being evangelical and feeling the need to affirm the inerrancy or divine inspiration of the Bible, they refer to their hermeneutical interests. However, they do not substantively connect them to their readings. They assert reading biblical texts objectively ("exegesis") and merely describing biblical content. In this sense, then, Christian Right's interpreters present their readings as innocent, unmotivated, and unshaped by their interpretive interests (power) despite their repeated acknowledgments of reading the Bible from "somewhere." In sum, in many Christian Right books on women in the Bible the third strategy appears in a more muddled fashion than in neoliberal feminist scholarship on the Bible. Christian Right's hermeneutical interests are identity markers too strong to succumb entirely to "Western and European liberalism and humanism in Reason."[94]

Asserting Women, Gender, and Sexuality as Intersectional Constructs in Feminist Biblical Studies: Concluding Comments

As shown, the three neoliberal strategies, which Fuchs identifies in academic feminist biblical scholarship, are also found in evangelical books on women in

---

91. Several chapters include more than two female characters, such as Chapter 6 on "Jochebed, Miriam, and Zipporah: Moses's Mother, Sister, and Wife" or Chapter 10 on "Delilah, Samson's Mother, and Other Nameless Women: Guile and Innocence." Chapter 14 features only one woman but she has four specified roles: "Bathsheba: Seducer, Widow, Wife, and Mother." Similarly, Chapter 19 features only "Mary: Mother and Disciple of Jesus."

92. Ibid., 2.

93. Ibid., 12.

94. Fuchs, "The Neoliberal Turn in Feminist Biblical Studies," 56.

the Bible. These works articulate women's experiences as monolithic, unified, rooted in women's biological functions and roles, and normative throughout the ages. They also attribute ontological autonomy to the category of woman, as if the concept were independent of time and space. Since the same also applies to the category of man, Christian Right's interpretations stabilize the heteronormative gender binary in the Bible and beyond. Evangelical readers pursue the third neoliberal strategy in a complex fashion. While they usually acknowledge their hermeneutical interests (power) in some way, they present their biblical interpretations (knowledge) as mere descriptions of the word of God. Still, this combination approach promotes its rehearsals of biblical content as politically detached, independent, and innocent. The three strategies have thus proven helpful in understanding basic features, characteristics, and assumptions in Christian Right interpretations of women in the Bible. They help deconstruct as a hermeneutical fallacy the Christian Right's assertion of offering a "common sense, natural, and straightforward reading of the Bible."[95]

Feminist scholars have long explained that such positivist and essentializing approaches to biblical texts do not lead to societal transformation of gender practices because they accept androcentric and heteronormative arrangements as universal and even eternal. Feminist Bible scholars must therefore be critical of these works and include discussions about historical-hermeneutical developments, feminist theories, and theo-political assumptions in their investigations of past and present ideas about woman, gender, and sexuality. Feminist Bible scholars need to engage the Bible and its interpretation history "in a self critical reexamination of liberal terms like individual rights, or equality, democracy, humanity,"[96] and to contribute to gender justice in its various intersectional manifestations.

Several observations need to be added here. It is startling to realize that Christian Right's books on women in the Bible exhibit similar hermeneutical assumptions to what Fuchs characterizes as neoliberal feminist biblical scholarship. Even the organization of the books, whether written by Christian Right's or academic authors, is often the same, featuring one or two biblical women as central to each chapter or to an entire manuscript.[97] Another striking similarity

95. Fuchs, "The Neoliberal Turn," 66.

96. Ibid., 67

Ursula Rapp, *Mirjam: Eine feministisch-rhetorische Lektüre der Mirjamtexte in der hebräischen Bibel* (BZAW 317; Berlin: Walter de Gruyter, 2002).

97. This organizational preference appears in many academic works, often with some modifications; see, e.g. Elizabeth A. McCabe (ed.), *Women in the Biblical World: A Survey of Old and New Testament Perspectives* (Plymouth and Lanham, MD: University Press of America, 2009); Tammi J. Schneider, *Mothers of Promise: Women in the Book of Genesis* (Grand Rapids, MI: Baker Acdemic, 2008); Patricia Dutcher-Walls, *Jezebel: Portraits of a Queen* (Collegeville, MN: Michael Glazier Books, 2004); Tammi J. Schneider, Sarah: Mother of Nations (New York: Continuum, 2004); Tikva Frymer-Kensky, *Reading the Women of the Bible* (New York: Schocken Books, 2002); Ursula Rapp, *Mirjam: Eine*

is the absence of feminist theories, whether in Christian Right's or academic interpretations. Essentialized ideas about women and ontological autonomy for the construct of woman dominate. Perhaps the lack of theoretical sophistication in neoliberal biblical interpretations has encouraged Christian Right's authors to appropriate the position that focuses on individual biblical women and stays disengaged from theoretical challenges to essentialism and a positivist-literalist hermeneutics.

The situation is indeed grim. Only a systematic and unrelenting stance that integrates intersectional feminist, gender, and queer theories offers a way out of the essentializing, naturalizing, and universalizing gender discourse in Christian Right's and academic works. It is simply insufficient to rehearse, retell or reimagine biblical women's lives in a literalist-positivist and essentializing fashion. The point of studying the Bible is not to naively repeat what the Bible presumably "says," whether it is articulated as history, literature, or in a sermon. Christian Right's books on biblical women demonstrate that this goal is too narrow, inadequate, and dangerous in the neoliberal era. As Elisabeth Schüssler Fiorenza puts it so well, the study of the Bible needs to be developed as "a rhetorical practice" so that it is understood as "a form of action and power" affecting "real people and situations."[98]

The entire direction of the feminist study of the Bible must thus shift. It needs to be conceptualized as a constructive-contextual democratic practice, as it takes place in this world. It is "a social-political and cultural-political practice" that takes "seriously its public responsibility, because the bible shaped and still shapes not only the church but also the cultural-political self-understanding of the American imagination."[99] It thus matters how interpreters present biblical women. If they limit biblical women's lives to motherhood, marriage, and childbirth, reinforce the gender binary, or divide biblical women into good and bad "girls," they contribute to a rhetorical practice of politically reactionary proportions. It is worrisome, to say the least, that so many books on biblical women have been written and published in the last few decades, advancing an androcentric and

---

feministisch-rhetorische Lektüre der Mirjamtexts in der hebräischen Bibel (BZAW 317; Berlin: Walter de Gruyter, 2002.); Mishael Mawari Caspi and Rachel S. Havrelock, *Women on the Biblical Road: Ruth, Naomi, and the Female Journey* (Lanham, MD: University Press of America, 1996); Alice Ogden Bellis, *Helpmates, Harlots, and Heroes: Women's Stories in the Hebrew Bible* (Louisville, KY: Westminster/John Knox, 1994); Katheryn Pfisterer Darr, *Far More Precious Than Jewels: Perspectives on Biblical Women* (Louisville, KY: Westminster/John Knox, 1991); Sharon Pace Jeansoon, *The Women of Genesis: From Sarah to Potiphar's Wife* (Minneapolis, MN: Fortress, 1990); Renita J. Weems, *Just a Sister Away: A Womanist Vision of Women's Relationships in the Bible* (San Diego, CA: LuraMedia, 1988); Mieke Bal, *Lethal Love: Feminist Literary Readings of Biblical Love Stories* (Bloomington: Indiana University Press, 1987).

98. Elisabeth Schüssler Fiorenza, *The Power of the Word: Scripture and the Rhetoric of Empire* (Minneapolis, MN: Fortress, 2007), 55.

99. Ibid.

heteronormative rhetoric about gender that is entirely divorced from feminist and genderqueer debates. It illustrates the urgency that biblical scholars, whether they are feminist, womanist, queer, or progressive in any other way, interrogate the scholarly and non-scholarly production of knowledge in biblical studies with the goal of producing alternative visions for a gender-just society.

Chapter 8

CONCLUSION

In 1967, Thomas Merton, the renowned contemplative monk and mystic, wrote that "a humanism for men only is ... nothing but a barbarous falsehood."[1] As this book has shown, feminists had to work long and hard to expand one-sided, androcentric, and heteronormative views on the Hebrew Bible. Their efforts can be traced back several centuries, but they probably struggled against this kind of "barbarous falsehood" for much longer than we currently know. Especially during the past four decades, feminist scholars have made a concerted effort to expand, broaden, and redefine what counts as valid biblical meanings, and they have explored the historical, political, cultural, and religious traditions for excluding women's and gender critical perspectives. The seven chapters of this book have introduced readers to the history of women reading the Hebrew Bible, presented four stories of biblical feminist scholars, discussed the various methods employed in feminist biblical research, described selected biblical narratives and poems on sexual violence, portrayed the emerging field of feminist postcolonial interpretations, explored genderqueer ways of reading the Bible, and analysed Christian Right's approaches to women in the Hebrew Bible. The study of the Hebrew Bible by feminist scholars has advanced to an extent that earlier generations could not have imagined.

Despite these advances, I have noticed in teaching U.S.–American under-graduate and graduate students during the past couple of decades that students are minimally exposed to feminist research in general and feminist biblical studies in particular. When they register for a course on feminism, gender, sexuality, and the Hebrew Bible, they raise questions like many other secular people. They want to know if the events described in biblical texts "really" happened. Since their Bible knowledge is limited, they ask when Abraham, Moses, or Jesus lived. Their initial question is, of course, not: "Who is Miriam, and when did she live, and why do we know so little about biblical women?"

Usually, students think they already know the answer to the last question; they assert: "Back then women were the property of men." They assume that in biblical times gender relations were patriarchal and hierarchical in contrast to what they

---

1. Thomas Merton, *Mystics and Zen Masters* (New York: Farrar, Straus, and Giroux, 1967), 119.

perceive as our advanced and gender-egalitarian ways of life. When they learn that not much if any historical information exists on biblical characters such as Moses, Miriam does not even come up anymore. When even Moses is unlikely to have existed as a historical figure, they question why the Hebrew Bible should still be taken seriously. After all, it offers so little "accurate" information on Moses, Miriam, and many other biblical characters and events that they wonder about the need to read these texts at all. This is, at least in my experience, one of the main concerns raised by today's secularized college and seminary generation.

I certainly sympathize with this sentiment, but I also disagree. The study of the Hebrew Bible and its interpretation histories offers much to contemporary understandings about society, religion and, as we have seen in the chapters of this book, gender relations. Let me briefly outline two main contributions that the feminist academic study of the Hebrew Bible has made during the past four decades.

First, feminist exegetes lead the way in understanding the interconnectedness of the Hebrew Bible to its historio-cultural and political meanings. Feminist interpreters have made important contributions to investigations of biblical texts, characters, and topics in light of contemporary concerns because they recognize that it is insufficient to locate biblical meanings only in Israelite history. In the process they have uncovered origins, causes, and effects of gender oppression, in its intersectional manifestations, in relation to socio-religious theories and practices. The study of the Hebrew Bible develops intellectual, historical, cultural, political, and religious grounding in the world, whether we are located in New York, Berlin, Harare, Hong Kong, Auckland, or Seoul. Since biblical meanings differ depending on the social locations of readers, feminist biblical scholars have been at the forefront of taking seriously this hermeneutical premise. They have opened up for public scrutiny their context-specific assumptions and interpretive goals, which has resulted in diverse interpretations of women characters such as Sarah, Ruth, or Jezebel. They have also illustrated how to make connections between gender and other social categories, and emphasized topics that the feminist movement has defined as crucial such as sexual violence. The new questions, topics, and reading strategies have led to new discoveries, and encouraged new conversations among scholars and lay interpreters. Feminist biblical studies have thus shown that a serious investigation of the Hebrew Bible has much to offer in understanding the world and people's place in it.

Second, the chapters of this book also demonstrate that feminist biblical scholars increasingly emphasize the need for reading biblical literature with global perspectives in mind and for recognizing the inter-religious and, especially within Europe, secularized settings in which we read these texts. It does not suffice anymore, if it ever did, to read the Hebrew Bible in the traditional Western white male paradigm. International contacts need to be nurtured so that new feminist biblical meanings address issues of concern to women, feminists, and queer people in not only European or North American settings. Geographic differences are also shaped by religious differences and, due to the events after 9/11, awareness about the need for interreligious dialogue has increased dramatically. To lock biblical meanings into a distant biblical past seems irresponsible when our own time demands attention to interreligious understanding and communication among gay, lesbian, straight, trans, and genderqueer people, fundamentalists, mainstream and progressives, people from the North, South, East, and West, Muslims, Jews, and Christians, Hindus, Buddhists, indigenous people, and the secular crowd. A withdrawal to the arcane disputes of biblical exegesis is not a future for feminist biblical studies. Rather, it consists in international, ecumenical, and interfaith understanding, communication, and exchange.

Despite these contributions, feminist biblical studies also face several challenges at this point in time. One of them has to do with the fact that there are still many colleges, universities, and seminaries without adequate course offerings in biblical studies. usually, one faculty member ensures that feminist biblical studies are taught at all, and the hiring of a second faculty member is viewed as duplicating rather than strengthening curricular needs. The neoliberal economic system, the increasing move toward fashioning universities and colleges like corporations, and the lack of marketability further hinder efforts to institute systemic curricular changes in the field. Most biblical scholars, feminist or not, teach in money-driven educational contexts in which biblical studies lack the economic cache of powerful markets, individual attempts notwithstanding. This situation is certainly not limited to biblical studies as it affects many disciplines in the arts and sciences. The curricular state in (feminist) biblical studies thus also reflects the conditions of higher education in a world in which money, greed, and speed rule.[2]

Another challenge has to do with the fact that Christian Right's scholars have begun to systematically counter feminist biblical research, often without explicit reference to existing scholarly feminist literature. Christian evangelicals consider the Bible as the word of God in contrast to feminist biblical scholarship. Feminist exegetes examine the Hebrew Bible as a document created by humans that has to be studied critically. Yet Christian conservative treatises have become popular, enjoying a wide reach among Christian lay audiences in the English-speaking world, especially in the United States. Chapter 7 outlines some of these developments as they have become apparent in popularized Christian right interpretations on women in the Bible. The popularity of these kinds of books are supported by the countless so-called Christian bookstores that specialize in selling Christian Right's books while they do not usually sell academic (feminist) biblical publications. This decision makes business-sense, as some of the Christian Right's authors sell thousands of their books and lots of money can be made from them. Certainly there are some feminist evangelical biblical scholars who are trying their best to bring exegetical balance and academic sophistication to their lay evangelical audiences. They attempt to foster the considerable theological diversity and variety of practiced belief among evangelicals although a succinct segment in the U.S.-American Christian Right's world has come to adhere to

---

2. For a detailed discussion, see my essay "Occupy Academic Bible Teaching: The Architecture of Educational Power and the Biblical Studies Curriculum," in Jane S. Webster and Glenn S. Holland (eds), *Teaching the Bible in the Liberal Arts Classroom* (Sheffield: Sheffield Academic Press, 2012), 28–43.

androcentric gender roles.[3] Thus, unsurprisingly, complementarian positions dominate the socio-cultural debates and their Bible readings. It is important, in my view, that feminist biblical scholars find ways to bring their feminist exegetical works to the attention of the larger public so that Christian Right interpretations are seen as only one way of interpreting biblical literature. This theo-political challenge is not limited to the North American context, as globally the numbers of conservative Christians has been growing in leaps and bounds during the past few decades. The challenge for feminist biblical scholars to be heard worldwide is thus colossal.

Yet another challenge relates to the field as a whole. The need for specialization has made scholarly conversations between researchers of the Hebrew Bible and the New Testament marginal and rare. For sure, some contacts exist, but the vastness of each field makes it almost impossible to engage both areas. At the same time the world outside of biblical studies hardly knows about this specialization and most non-evangelical undergraduate or graduate students are at a loss about the need for this division. The problem is particularly pertinent in the undergraduate and sometimes the master-level curriculum of biblical studies. Textbooks are not usually available for courses covering both the Hebrew Bible and the New Testament. This is also true for literature on feminist biblical studies. More books are needed, both covering the Christian canon of the Bible and including feminist works as an integral part of the discussions.

One more challenge confronts feminist biblical research when the goal is to sustain connections with contemporary political, cultural, and religious analysis. Nowadays, many students do not see a problem with women's status and gender in society, especially in Western countries. They insist that gender discrimination has ended and that sexism and heterosexism are problems of the past. Thus, students often enter biblical-studies classes assuming that there is not much need for feminist biblical work. Their political consciousness has to be raised before a productive conversation about women, gender, and sexuality issues in light of biblical studies makes sense. Students also need to become acquainted with feminist, gender, and queer theories that challenge biological notions of heteronormativity, and they have to learn about gender as a cultural, political, and historical construct. They have to be introduced to intersectionality as an intellectual idea linking gender and sexuality with other social categories. It is thus insufficient to teach a course on "women in the Bible," as if the study of this topic is identical with memorizing Bible content. The historical, methodological, and hermeneutical dimensions of feminist biblical work have to be included so that investigations into the biblical hermeneutics of feminism, gender, and sexuality do not deteriorate to literalist, sentimental, and theo-politically reactionary storytelling.

---

3. For a comprehensive discussion, see Karen Strand Winslow, "Recovering Redemption for Women: Feminist Exegesis in North American Evangelicalism," in Susanne Scholz (ed.), *Feminist Interpretation of the Hebrew Bible in Retrospect* (Sheffield: Sheffield Phoenix Press, 2016), 269.

What is required, then, are comprehensive and dialogical conversations about feminism, gender, and sexuality as they relate to the Bible. Feminist exegetes need to seek out feminist debates, theories, and, scholarship as they occur across academic disciplines and in society, and relate them to biblical exegesis. As the chapters of this book illustrate, feminist biblical research aims for the socio-political, economic, and religious understanding *and* transformation of androcentric, heteronormative, and hierarchical structures of domination. Much remains to be done in a time when traditional gender roles are reinforced everywhere and people's enthusiasm for questioning authority is low in academic and religious communities. Yet taken together, accomplishments and challenges promise a vibrant and compelling future for the field. Of course, what the future holds remains to be seen.

BIBLIOGRAPHY

Aichele, George (ed.). *Culture, Entertainment and the Bible*. Sheffield: Sheffield Academic Press, 2000.

Alter, Robert and Frank Kermode (eds). *The Literary Guide to the Bible*. Cambridge, MA: Harvard University Press, 1987.

Althaus-Reid, Marcella. *Indecent Theology: Theological Perversions in Sex, Gender, and Politics*. London and New York: Routledge, 2000.

Anderson, Cheryl B. *Women, Ideology, and Violence: Critical Theory and the Construction of Gender in the Book of the Covenant and the Deuteronomic Law*. London and New York: T&T Clark International, 2004.

Anderson, Cheryl B. *Ancient Laws and Contemporary Controversies: The Need for Inclusive Biblical Interpretation*. New York: Oxford University Press, 2009.

Anderson, Francis I. "Note on Genesis 30:8," *Journal of Biblical Literature* 88 (June 1969): 200.

Aspire: The New Women of Color Study Bible (NIV): For Strength and Inspiration. Grand Rapids, MI: Zondervan, 2007.

Avalos, Hector. *The End of Biblical Studies*. Amherst, NY: Prometheus, 2007.

Bach, Alice (ed.). "Reading Allowed: Feminist Biblical Criticism Approaching the Millennium," *Currents in Research* 1 (1993): 191–215.

Bach, Alice (ed.). *Women, Seduction, and Betrayal in Biblical Narrative*. Cambridge: Cambridge University Press, 1997.

Bach, Alice (ed.). *Women in the Hebrew Bible: A Reader*. New York: Routledge, 1998.

Bader, Mary Anna. *Sexual Violation in the Hebrew Bible: A Multi-Methodological Study of Genesis 34 and 2 Samuel 13*. New York: Lang, 2006.

Baker-Fletcher, Karen. "Seeking Our Survival, Seeking Our Life, and Wisdom: Womanist Approaches to the Hebrew Bible," in Susanne Scholz (ed.), *Feminist Interpretation of the Hebrew Bible in Retrospect*, 225–42. Vol. 3, Methods. Sheffield: Sheffield Academic Press, 2016.

Bal, Mieke. *Lethal Love: Feminist Literary Readings of Biblical Love Stories*. Bloomington: Indiana University Press, 1987.

Balmer, Randall. *The Making of Evangelicalism: From Revivalism to Politics and Beyond*. Waco, TX: Baylor University Press, 2010.

Barton, Mukti. "The Skin of Miriam Became as White as Snow: The Bible, Western Feminism and Colour Politics," *Feminist Theology* 27 (May 2001): 68–80.

Bauer, Angela. *Gender in the Book of Jeremiah: A Feminist-Literary Reading*. New York: Peter Lang, 1999.

Baumann, Gerlinde. *Liebe und Gewalt: Die Ehe als Metapher für das Verhältnis JHWH–Israel in den Prophetenbüchern*. Stuttgart: Verlag Katholisches Bibelwerk, 2000.

Baumann, Gerlinde. *Love and Violence: Marriage as Metaphor for the Relationship Between YHWH and Israel in the Prophetic Books*. Trans. Linda M. Maloney. Collegeville, MN: Liturgical Press, 2003.

Baumann, Gerlinde. *Gottes Gewalt im Wandel: Traditionsgeschichtliche und intertextuelle Studien zu Nahum 1,2–8*. Neukirchen-Vluyn: Neukirchener Verlag, 2005.

Baxter, J. Sidlow. *Mark These Men: A Unique Look at Selected Men of the Bible*. Grand Rapids, MI: Kregel, 1992 [1960].

Bellis, Alice Ogden. *Helpmates, Harlots, and Heroes: Women's Stories in the Hebrew Bible*. Louisville, KY: Westminster/John Knox, 1994.

Bellis, Alice Ogden. "Objective Biblical Truth versus the Value of Various Viewpoints: A False Dichotomy," *Horizons in Biblical Theology* (June 17, 1995): 25–36.

Bhabha, Homi K. *The Location of Culture*. London: Routledge, 1994.

Bible and Culture Collective. *The Postmodern Bible*. New Haven: Yale University Press, 1995.

Bird, Phyllis A. *Missing Persons and Mistaken Identities: Women and Gender in Ancient Israel*. Minneapolis, MN: Augsburg Fortress, 1997a.

Bird, Phyllis A. (ed.). *Reading the Bible as Women: Perspectives from Africa, Asia, and Latin America*. Atlanta: Scholars Press, 1997b.

Bird, Phyllis A. "Images of the Women in the Old Testament," in Rosemary Radford Ruether (eds), *Religion and Sexism: Images of Women in the Jewish and Christian Traditions*, 41–88. Eugene: Wipf and Stock Publishers, 1998. Originally published in 1974.

Bird, Phyllis A. "What Makes a Feminist Reading Feminist? A Qualified Answer," in Harold C. Washington, Susan Lochrie, and Pamela Thimmes (eds), *Escaping Eden: New Feminist Perspectives on the Bible*, 124–31. New York: New York University Press, 1999.

Blenkinsop, Joseph. *Isaiah 1–39*. New York: Doubleday, 2000.

Bly, Robert. *Iron John: A Book about Men*. Reading, MA: Addison-Wesley, 1990.

Blyth, Caroline. *The Narrative of Rape in Genesis 34: Interpreting Dinah's Silence*. New York: Oxford University Press, 2010.

Boer, Roland. "Yahweh as Top: A Lost Targum," in Ken Stone (ed.), *Queer Commentary and the Hebrew Bible*, 75–105. Cleveland: The Pilgrim Press, 2001.

Boswell, John. *Christianity, Social Tolerance, and Homosexuality*. Chicago: University of Chicago, 1980.

Bounds, Edward M. *Bible Men of Prayer*. Grand Rapids, MI: Zondervan, 1964 [1921].

Bousquet, Marc. *How the University Works: Higher Education and the Low-Wage Nation*. New York: New York University Press, 2008.

Brenner, Athalya. *Colour Terms in the Old Testament*. Sheffield: JSOT Press, 1982.

Brenner, Athalya. *Israelite Woman: Social Role and Literary Type in Biblical Narrative*. Sheffield: JSOT Press, 1985.

Brenner, Athalya. "Female Social Behaviour: Two Descriptive Patterns Within the 'Birth of the Hero' Paradigm," *Vetus Testamentum* 36 (3) (1986): 204–21.

Brenner, Athalya. *Ahavat Rut (in Hebrew)*. Tel Aviv: HaKibbutz HaMeu'chad Press, 1988.

Brenner, Athalya. *Song of Songs*. Sheffield: JSOT Press, 1989.

Brenner, Athalya. (ed.). *A Feminist Companion to Genesis*. Sheffield: Sheffield Academic Press, 1993a.

Brenner, Athalya. (ed.). *A Feminist Companion to Judges*. Sheffield: Sheffield Academic Press, 1993b.

Brenner, Athalya. (ed.). *A Feminist Companion to Ruth*. Sheffield: Sheffield Academic Press, 1993c.

Brenner, Athalya. (ed.). *A Feminist Companion to the Song of Songs*. Sheffield: Sheffield Academic Press, 1993d.

Brenner, Athalya. (ed.). *Genesis: A Feminist Companion to the Bible (Second Series)*. Sheffield: Sheffield Academic Press, 1993e.

Brenner, Athalya. (ed.). *A Feminist Companion to Samuel to Kings*. Sheffield: Sheffield Academic Press, 1994a.

Brenner, Athalya. "On Prophetic Propaganda and the Politics of 'Love'," in Fokkelien van Dijk-Hemmes and Athalya Brenner (eds), *Reflections on Theology and Gender*, 87–105. Kampen: Kok Pharos Publishing House, 1994b.

Brenner, Athalya. (ed.). *A Feminist Companion to Esther. Judith, and Susannah*. Sheffield: Sheffield Academic Press, 1995a.

Brenner, Athalya. (ed.). *A Feminist Companion to the Latter Prophets*. Sheffield: Sheffield Academic Press, 1995b.

Brenner, Athalya. (ed.). *A Feminist Companion to the Hebrew Bible in the New Testament*. Sheffield: Sheffield Academic Press, 1996a.

Brenner, Athalya. (ed.). *A Feminist Companion to Wisdom Literature*. Sheffield: Sheffield Academic Press, 1996b.

Brenner, Athalya. "The Hebrew God and His Female Complements," in Timothy K. Beal and David M. Gunn (eds), *Reading Bibles, Writing Bodies; Identity and The Book*, 56–71. London and New York: Routledge, 1997a.

Brenner, Athalya. *Intercourse of Knowledge: On Gendering Desire and "Sexuality" in the Hebrew Bible*. Leiden and New York: Brill, 1997b.

Brenner, Athalya. "'My' Song of Songs," in Athalya Brenner and Carole Fontaine (eds), *A Feminist Companion to Reading the Bible: Approaches, Methods, and Strategies*, 567–79. Sheffield: Sheffield Academic Press, 1997c.

Brenner, Athalya. (ed.). *Exodus and Deuteronomy: A Feminist Companion to the Bible (Second Series)*. Sheffield: Sheffield Academic Press, 1998.

Brenner, Athalya. (ed.). *Judges: A Feminist Companion to the Bible (Second Series)*. Sheffield: Sheffield Academic Press, 1999a.

Brenner, Athalya. (ed.). *Ruth and Esther: A Feminist Companion to the Bible (Second Series)*. Sheffield: Sheffield Academic Press, 1999b.

Brenner, Athalya. "Ruth as a Foreign Worker and the Politics of Exogamy," in Athalya Brenner (ed.), *Ruth and Esther: A Feminist Companion to the Bible (Second Series)*, 158–62. Sheffield: Sheffield Academic Press, 1999c.

Brenner, Athalya. (ed.). *Samuel and Kings: A Feminist Companion to the Bible (Second Series)*. Sheffield: Sheffield Academic Press, 2000a.

Brenner, Athalya. (ed.). *The Song of Songs: A Feminist Companion to the Bible (Second Series)*. Sheffield: Sheffield Academic Press, 2000b.

Brenner, Athalya. (ed.). *Prophets and Daniel: A Feminist Companion to the Bible (Second Series)*. Sheffield: Sheffield Academic Press, 2002.

Brenner, Athalya. (ed.). *Are We Amused? Humour about Women in the Biblical Worlds*. London: T&T Clark, 2003.

Brenner, Athalya. "Some Reflections on Violence against Women and the Images of the Hebrew Bible," in Jane Schaberg, Alice Bach and Esther Fuchs (eds), *On the Cutting Edge: The Study of Women in Biblical Worlds: Essays in Honor of Elisabeth Schüssler Fiorenza*. New York and London: Continuum, 2004.

Brenner, Athalya. *I am … Biblical Women Tell Their Own Stories*. Minneapolis, MN: Augsburg Fortress, 2005a.

Brenner, Athalya. "Epilogue: Babies and Bathwater on the Road," in Caroline Vander Stichele and Todd Penner (eds), *Her Master's Tools? Feminist and Postcolonial Engagements of Historical-Critical Discourse*, 333–8. Atlanta, GA: Society of Biblical Literature, 2005b.

Brenner, Athalya. *The Israelite Woman: Social Role and Literary Type in Biblical Narrative*; Cornerstone Series. London: Bloomsbury, 2015.

Brenner, Athalya and Fokkelien van Dijk-Hemmes (eds). *Reflections on Theology and Gender*. Kampen, The Netherlands: Kok Pharos Publishing House, 1994.

Brenner, Athalya and Fokkelien van Dijk-Hemmes. *On Gendering Texts: Female & Male Voices in the Hebrew Bible*. Leiden: Brill, 1996.

Brenner, Athalya and Carole Fontaine (eds). *Wisdom and Psalms: A Feminist Companion to the Bible (Second Series)*. Sheffield: Sheffield Academic Press, 1998.

Brenner, Athalya and Yehuda T. Radday (eds). *On Humour and the Comic in the Hebrew Bible*. Sheffield: Sheffield Academic Press, 1990.

Brenner, Athalya and Carole Fontaine (eds). *A Feminist Companion to Reading the Bible: Approaches, Methods and Strategies*. Sheffield: Sheffield Academic Press, 2001.

Brenner, Athalya and Jan Willem van Henten *Recycling Biblical Figures: Papers Read at a NOSTER Colloquium in Amsterdam, 12–13, 1997*. Leiden: Deo Publishing, 1999.

Brenner, Athalya and Jan Willem van Henten (eds). *Bible Translation on the Threshold of the Twenty-First Century: Authority, Reception, Culture and Religion*. London: Sheffield Academic Press, 2002.

Briggs, Sheila. "Can an Enslaved God Liberate? Hermeneutical Reflections on Philippians 2:6-11," in Katie Geneva Cannon and Elisabeth Schüssler Fiorenza (eds), *Interpretation for Liberation*, 137–53. Semeia 47; Atlanta, GA: Scholars Press, 1989.

Brooten, Bernadette. "Jüdinnen zur Zeit Jesu: Ein Plädoyer für Differenzierung." *Theologische Quartalschrift* 161 (4) (1981): 280–5.

Brooten, Bernadette. *Women Leaders in the Ancient Synagogue*. Chico, CA: Scholars Press, 1982.

Brown, Michael Joseph. "The Womanization of Blackness," in *Blackening of the Bible: The Aims of African American Biblical Scholarship*, 89–119. Harrisburg, PA: Trinity, 2004.

Butler, Judith. *Gender Trouble: Feminism and the Subversion of Identity*. London: Routledge, 1999.

Byron, Gay L. "The Challenge of 'Blackness' for Rearticulating the Meaning of Global Feminist New Testament Interpretation," in Kathleen O'Brien Wicker, Althea Spencer Miller, and Musa W. Dube (eds), *Feminist New Testament Studies: Global and Future Perspectives*, 85–102. New York: Palgave Macmillan, 2005.

Calvin, John. *Genesis*, trans. John King. Carlisle, PA: The Banner of Truth Trust, 1992.

Camp, Claudia. *Wise, Strange, and Holy: The Strange Woman and the Making of the Bible*. Sheffield: Sheffield Academic Press, 2000.

Camp, Claudia V. and Carole R. Fontaine (eds), "Women, War, and Metaphor: Language and Society in the Study of the Hebrew Bible." *Semeia* 61 (1993).

Cannon, Katie Geneva. "The Emergence of Black Feminist Consciousness," in Letty M. Russell (ed.), *Feminist Interpretation of the Bible*, 30–40. Philadelphia: Westminster, 1985.

Cannon, Katie Geneva. *Katie's Canon: Womanism and the Soul of the Black Community*. New York: Continuum, 1995.

Carroll, Robert P. *The Book of Jeremiah: A Commentary*. Philadelphia: Westminster, 1986.

Caspi, Mishael Mawari and Rachel S. Havrelock. *Women on the Biblical Road: Ruth, Naomi, and the Female Journey*. Lanham, MD: University Press of America, 1996.

Chakravarti, Uma (ed.). *Thinking Gender, Doing Gender: Feminist Scholarship and Practice Today*. New Delhi: Orient Blackswan, 2016.

Chu, Julie Li-Chuan. "Returning Home: The Inspiration of the Role Dedifferentiation in the Book of Ruth for Tiwanese Women," *Semeia* 78 (1997): 47–53.

Claussen, Dane S. *The Promise Keepers: Essays on Masculinity and Christianity*. Jefferson, NC: McFarland, 2000.

Clements, E. *Jeremiah*. Atlanta: John Knox, 1988.

Clifford, Anne M. *Introducing Feminist Theology*. Maryknoll, NY: Orbis Books, 2001.

Clifford, Richard J. and Roland E. Murphy. "Genesis," in Raymond E. Brown, Joseph A. Fitzmyer, and Roland E. Murphy (eds), *The New Jerome Biblical Commentary*, 8–43. Eaglewood Cliffs, NJ: Prentice Hall, 1990.

Clines, David J. A. "David the Man: The Construction of Masculinity in the Hebrew Bible," in *Interested Parties: The Ideology of Writers and Readers of the Hebrew Bible*, 212–43. JSOT Supplement, 205; Sheffield: Sheffield Academic Press, 1995.

Clines, David J. A. "Ecce vir, or, Gendering the Son of Man," in J. Cheryl Exum and Stephen Moore (eds), *Biblical Studies/Cultural Studies: The Third Sheffield Colloquium*, 352–75. Sheffield: Sheffield University Press, 1998.

Clines, David J. A. "He-Prophets: Masculinity as a Problem for the Hebrew Prophets and Their Interpreters," in Alastair G. Hunter and Phillip R. Davies (eds), *Sense and Sensitivity: Essays on Reading the Bible in Memory of Robert Carroll*, 311–28. London: Sheffield Academic Pres, 2002.

Clines, David J. A. "Paul, the Invisible Man," in Stephen D. Moore and Janice Capel Anderson (eds), *New Testament Masculinities*, 181–92. Atlanta, GA: Society of Biblical Literature, 2003.

Clines, David J. A. "Being a Man in the Book of the Covenant," in J. Gordon McConville and Karl Möller (eds), *Reading the Law: Studies in Honour of Gordon J. Wenham*, 3–9. New York and London: T&T Clark, 2007.

Clines, David J. A. "Dancing and Shining at Sinai: Playing the Man in Exodus 32–34," in Ovidiu Creangă (ed.), *Men and Masculinity in the Hebrew Bible and Beyond*, 54–63. Sheffield: Sheffield Phoenix Press, 2010a.

Clines, David J. A. "Final Reflections on Biblical Masculinity," in Ovidiu Creangă (ed.), *Men and Masculinity in the Hebrew Bible and Beyond*, 234–9. Sheffield: Sheffield Phoenix Press, 2010b.

Collins, John. *The Bible after Babel: Historical Criticism in a Postmodern Age*. Grand Rapids: Eerdmans, 2005.

Creangă, Ovidiu (ed.). *Men and Masculinity in the Hebrew Bible and Beyond*. Sheffield: Sheffield Phoenix Press, 2010.

Creangă, Ovidiu and Peter-Ben Smit (eds). *Biblical Masculinities Foregrounded*. Sheffield: Sheffield Phoenix Press, 2014.

Culler, Jonathan. "What is Cultural Studies?," in Mieke Bal (ed.) *The Practice of Cultural Analysis: Exposing Interdisciplinary Interpretation*, 335–47. Stanford: Stanford University Press, 1999.

Daly, Mary. *The Church and the Second Sex*. New York: Harper & Row, 1968.

Daly, Mary. *Beyond God the Father: Toward a Philosophy of Women's Liberation*. Boston: Beacon, 1973.

Darr, Katheryn Pfisterer. *Far More Precious than Jewels: Perspectives on Biblical Women*. Louisville: Westminster John Knox Press, 1991.

Day, Peggy L. (ed.). *Gender and Difference in Ancient Israel*. Minneapolis, MN: Fortress Press, 1989.

Day, Peggy L. "Biblical Studies and Women's Studies," in Klaus K. Klostermaier and Larry W. Hurtado (eds), *Religious Studies: Issues, Prospects and Proposals*, 197–209. Atlanta: Scholars Press, 1991.

De Lauretis, Teresa. "Queer Theory: Lesbian and Gay Sexualities: An Introduction," *differences* 3 (2) (1991): iii–xviii.

Dietrich, Walter and Ulrich Luz (eds). *The Bible in a World Context: An Experiment in Contextual Hermeneutics*. Grand Rapids: Eerdmans, 2002.

Donaldson, Laura E. *Decolonizing Feminisms: Race, Gender, and Empire Building*. Chapel Hill: University of North Carolina Press, 1992.

Donaldson, Laura E. "The Sign of Orpah: Reading Ruth through Native Eyes," in Athalya Brenner (ed.), *Ruth and Esther: A Feminist Companion to the Bible (Second Series)*, 130–44. Sheffield: Sheffield Academic Press, 1999.

Donaldson, Laura E. and Kwok Pui-Lan (eds). *Postcolonialism, Feminism & Religious Discourse*. New York and London: Routledge, 2002.

Douglas, Kelly Brown. "Marginalized People, Liberating Perspectives: A Womanist Approach to Biblical Interpretation," *ATR* 83 (Winter 2001): 41–7.

Drinkwater, Gregg, Joshua Lesser, and David Shneer (eds). *Torah Queeries: Weekly Commentaries on the Hebrew Bible*. New York: New York University Press, 2009.

Dube, Musa W. "The Unpublished Letters of Orpah to Ruth," in Athalya Brenner (ed.), *Ruth and Esther: A Feminist Companion to the Bible (Second Series)*, 145–50. Sheffield: Sheffield Academic Press, 1999.

Dube, Musa W. *Postcolonial Feminist Interpretation of the Bible*. St Louis: Chalice, 2000.

Dube, Musa W. (ed.). *Other Ways of Reading: African Women and the Bible*. Atlanta and Geneva: Society of Biblical Literature/WCC Publications, 2001a.

Dube, Musa W. "Divining Ruth for International Relations," in Musa W. Dube (ed.), *Other Ways of Reading: African Women and the Bible*, 179–95. Atlanta and Geneva: Society of Biblical Literature/WCC Publications, 2001b.

Duggan, Lisa. "The New Homonormativity: The Sexual Politics of Neoliberalism," in Russ Castronovo and Dana D. Nelson (eds), *Materializing Democracy: Toward a Revitalized Cultural Politics*, 175–94. Durham, NC: Duke University Press, 2002.

Dutcher-Walls, Patricia. *Jezebel: Portraits of a Queen*. Collegeville, MN: Michael Glazier Books, 2004.

Eilberg-Schwartz, Howard. *God's Phallus and Other Problems for Men and Monotheism*. Boston: Beacon Press, 1994.

Ellwood, Gracia Fay. "Rape and Judgement," *Daughters of Sarah* 11 (1985): 9–13.

Elvey, Anne F. *An Ecological Feminist Reading of the Gospel of Luke: A Gestational Paradigm*. Lewiston: Edwin Mellen, 2005.

Eng, David L., Judith Halberstam, and Jose Estaban Munoz, "What's Queer about Queer Studies Now? Introduction," *Social Text* 23 (3–4) (Fall–Winter 2005): 1–17.

Engelken, Karen. *Frauen im Alten Israel: Eine begriffsgeschichtliche und sozialrechtliche Studie zur Stellung der Frau im Alten Testament*. BWANT 130. Stuttgart: W. Kohlhammer, 1990.

Engelken, Karen. "pilaegaes," in G. Johannes Botterweck, Helmer Ringgren, and Hans-Josef Fabry (eds), *Theologisches Wörterbuch zum Alten Testament*, 586–90. Vol. 6. Stuttgart: W. Kohlhammer, 1987.

Eshkenazi, Tamara Cohn and Andrea L. Weiss (eds). *The Torah: A Women's Commentary*. New York: WRJ/URJ Press, 2008.

Esser, Annette and Luise Schottroff (eds). *Feminist Theology in a European Context*. Kampen: Kok Pharos, 1993.

Eugene, Toinette M. "A Hermeneutical Challenge for Womanists: The Interrelation between the Text and Our Experience," in Gayle G. Koontz and Willar Swartley (eds), *Perspectives on Feminist Hermeneutics*, 20–8. Elkhart, IN: Institute for Mennonite Studies, 1987.

Evans, Debra. *Six Qualities of Women of Character: Life-Changing Examples of Godly Women*. Grand Rapids, MI: Zondervan, 1996.

Evans, Debra. *Women of Courage: Inspiring Stories of Faith, Hope, and Endurance*. Grand Rapids, MI: Zondervan, 1999.

Evans, Mary, Clare Hemmings, Marsha Henry, Hazel Johnsteon, Sumi Madhok, Ania Plomien, and Sadie Wearing (eds), *The SAGE Handbook of Feminist Theory*. Thousand Oaks, CA: Sage, 2014.

Exum, J. Cheryl. "'Mother in Israel': A Familiar Figure Reconsidered," in Letty Russell (ed.), *Feminist Interpretation of the Bible*, 73–85. Philadelphia: Westminster Press, 1985.

Exum, J. Cheryl. *Fragmented Women: Feminist (Sub)versions of Biblical Narratives*. Valley Forge, PA: Trinity Press International, 1993a.

Exum, J. Cheryl. "The (M)other's Place," in *Fragmented Women: Feminist (Sub)versions of Biblical Narratives*. Valley Forge, PA: Trinity Press International, 1993b.

Exum, J. Cheryl. *Plotted, Shot, and Painted: Cultural Representations of Biblical Women*. Sheffield: Sheffield Academic Press, 1996a.

Exum, J. Cheryl. "Bathsheba Plotted, Shot, and Painted," in *Plotted, Shot, and Painted: Cultural Representations of Biblical Women*. Sheffield: Sheffield Academic Press, 1996b.

Exum, J. Cheryl. (ed.). *Beyond the Biblical Horizon: The Bible and the Arts*. Leiden: E. J. Brill, 1999.

Exum, J. Cheryl. "Feminist Study of the Old Testament," in Andrew D. H. Mayes (ed.), *Text in Context: Essays by Members of the Society for Old Testament Study*, 86–115. Oxford: Oxford University Press, 2000.

Exum, J. Cheryl and David J. A. Clines (eds). *The New Literary Criticism and the Hebrew Bible*. Valley Forge, PA: Trinity Press International, 1993.

Exum, J. Cheryl and Stephen D. Moore. "Biblical Studies/Cultural Studies," in J. Cheryl Exum and Stephen D. Moore (eds), *Biblical Studies/Cultural Studies*, 19–45. Sheffield: Sheffield Academic Press, 1998.

Fewell, Danna Nolan and David M. Gunn, *Gender, Power and Promise: The Subject of the Bible's First Story*. Nashville, TN: Abingdon, 1993.

Fischer, Irmtraud. "Genesis 12–50: Die Ursprungsgeschichte Israels als Frauengeschichte," in Luise Schottroff and Marie-Theres Wacker (eds), *Kompendium Feministische Bibelauslegung*, 1–15. 2nd edn. Gütersloh: Gütersloher Verlagshaus, 1998.

Fontaine, Carole R. *With Eyes of Flesh: The Bible, Gender, and Human Rights*. Sheffield: Sheffield Phoenix, 2008.

Fox, Everett. *The Five Books of Moses: Genesis, Exodus, Leviticus, Numbers, Deuteronomy*. New York: Schocken Books, 1995.

Foucault, Michel. *The Order of Things: An Archaeology of the Human Sciences*. New York: Random House, 1970.

Foucault, Michel. *The History of Sexuality: An Introduction (vol. 1)*. Trans. Robert Hurley. New York: Random House, 1978.

Fretheim, Terence E. "The Books of Genesis," in Leander E. Keck, William Marcellus, Terence E. Fretheim, and Walter C. Kaiser (eds), *The New Interpreter's Bible*, 321–674. Vol. 1. Nashville: Abingdon, 1994.

Frymer-Kensky, Tikva. *In the Wake of the Goddess: Women, Culture, and the Biblical Transformation of Pagan Myth*. New York: Macmillan, 1993.

Frymer-Kensky, Tikva. *Reading the Women of the Bible*. New York: Schocken, 2002.

Frymer-Kensky, Tikva. "Goddesses: Biblical Echoes," in *Studies in Bible and Feminist Criticism*. Philadelphia: The Jewish Publication Society, 2006.

Fuchs, Esther. "The Literary Characterization of Mothers and Sexual Politics in the Hebrew Bible," in Adela Yarbro Collins (ed.), *Feminist Perspectives on Biblical Scholarship*, 117–36. Atlanta: Scholars Press, 1985.

Fuchs, Esther. *Sexual Politics in the Biblical Narrative: Reading the Hebrew Bible as a Woman*. Sheffield: Sheffield Academic Press, 2000a.

Fuchs, Esther. "The Biblical Mother: The Annunciation and Temptation Type-Scenes," in *Sexual Politics in the Biblical Narrative: Reading the Hebrew Bible as a Woman*. Sheffield: Sheffield Academic Press, 2000b.

Fuchs, Esther. "Prophecy and the Construction of Women: Inscription and Erasure," in Athalya Brenner (ed.), *Prophets and Daniel: A Feminist Companion to the Bible (Second Edition)*, 54–69. Sheffield: Sheffield Press, 2001.

Fuchs, Esther. "Men in Biblical Feminist Scholarship." *JFSR* 19 (2) (Fall 2003): 93–114.

Fuchs, Esther. "Points of Resonance," in Jane Schaberg, Alice Bach and Esther Fuchs (eds), *On the Cutting Edge: The Study of Women in Biblical Worlds*, 1–20. New York: Continuum, 2004.

Fuchs, Esther. *Feminist Theory and the Bible: Interrogating the Sources*. Feminist Studies and Sacred Texts Series. Lanham, MD: Lexington Books, 2016a.

Fuchs, Esther. "The Neoliberal Turn in Feminist Biblical Studies," in *Feminist Theory and the Bible: Interrogating the Sources*, 55–70. Feminist Studies and Sacred Texts; Lanham, MD: Lexington Books, 2016b.

Furnish, Victor Paul. *The Moral Teaching of Paul*. Rev. 3rd edn. Nashville, TN: Abingdon, 2009.

Gafney, Wilda C. M. "A Black Feminist Approach to Biblical Studies," *Encounter* 67 (Autumn 2006): 391–403.

Gafney, Wilda C. M. *Womanist Midrash: A Reintroduction to the Women of the Torah and the Throne*. Louisville, KY: Westminster John Knox Press, 2017.

Gane, Roy E., Nicholas P. Miller, and H. Peter Swanson (eds). *Homosexuality, Marriage, and the Church: Biblical, Counseling, and Religious Liberty Issues*. Berrien Springs, MI: Andrews University Press, 2012.

George, Elizabeth. *The Remarkable Women of the Bible and Their Message for Your Life Today*. Eugene: Harvest House, 2003.

George, Jim. *10 Minutes to Knowing the Men and Women of the Bible*. The Bare Bones Bible Series; Eugene, OR: Harvest House Publishers, 2010.

Gilmour, Michael J. *Tangled Up in the Bible: Bob Dylan & Scripture*. New York: Continuum, 2004.

Giroux, Henry A. *Neoliberalism's War on Higher Education*. Chicago: Haymarket Books, 2014.

Goldingay, John. "Hosea 1–3, Genesis 1–4, and Masculist Interpretation," *Horizons in Biblical Theology* 17 (1995): 37–44.

Goldstein, Elyse. *ReVisions: Seeing Torah Through a Feminist Lens*. Woodstock, VT: Jewish Lights Publishing, 1998.

Goodloe, Amy. "Lesbian-Feminism and Queer Theory: Another 'Battle of the Sexes'?"; originally published at Lesbian.org in 1994; republished in 2014. Available online: http://amygoodloe.com/papers/lesbian-feminism-and-queer-theory-another-battle-of-the-sexes/ (accessed December 12, 2016).

Gordon, Cynthia. "Hagar: A Throw-away Character among the Matriarchs?" in Kent H. Richards (ed.), *Society of Biblical Literature 1985 Seminar Papers*, 271–7. Cambridge, MA: Society of Biblical Literature, 1985.

Gössmann, Elisabeth. "History of Biblical Interpretation by European Women," in Elisabeth Schüssler Fiorenza (ed.), *Searching the Scripture: A Feminist Introduction*, 29–32. New York: Crossroad, 1993.

Grady, J. Lee. *Fearless Daughters of the Bible: What You Can Learn from 22 Women Who Challenged Tradition, Fought Injustice and Dared to Lead*. Bloomington, MN: Chosen Book, 2012.

Grant, Jacquelyn. "Black Theology and the Black Woman," in James H. Cone and Gayraud S. Wilmore (eds), *Black Theology*, 323–38. Vol. 1. Maryknoll, NY: Orbis, 1993.

Grenholm, Christina and Daniel Patte (eds). *Gender, Tradition, and Romans: Shared Ground, Uncertain Borders*. New York: T&T Clark, 2005.

Grimes, Jessica. "Reinterpreting Hagar's Story." *Lectio difficilior: European Electronic Journal of Feminist Exegesis* 1 (2004). Available online: http://www.lectio.unibe. ch/04_1/Grimes.Hagar.htm (accessed December 12, 2016).

Grohmann, Marianne. "Feministische Theologie und jüdisch-christlicher Dialog," http:// www.jcrelations.net/Feministische+Theologie+und+christlich-j%FCdischer+Dialog.12 73.0.html?&L=3 (accessed December 12, 2016).

Guest, Deryn. *When Deborah Met Jael: Lesbian Biblical Hermeneutics*. London: SCM Press, 2005a.

Guest, Deryn, Robert E. Goss, Mona West, and Thomas Bohache (eds). *The Queer Bible Commentary*. London: SCM Press, 2005b.

Guest, Deryn. "Judges," in Deryn Guest, Robert E. Goss, Mona West, and Thomas Bohache (eds), *The Queer Bible Commentary*, 167–89. London: SCM Press, 2006.

Guest, Deryn. *Beyond Feminist Biblical Studies*. Sheffield: Sheffield Phoenix Press, 2012.

Gunkel, Hermann. *Genesis*. Trans. Mark E. Biddle. Macon, GA: Mercer University Press, 1997.

Gunn, David M. "Bathsheba Goes Bathing in Hollywood: Words, Images, and Social Locations." *Semeia* 74 (1996): 75–102.

Gunn, David M. *Judges*. Oxford: Blackwell, 2005.

Haddox, Susan E. *Metaphor and Masculinity in Hosea*. Studies in Biblical Literature 141. New York: Peter Lang, 2011.

Haddox, Susan E. "Masculinity Studies of the Hebrew Bible: The First Two Decades." *Currents in Biblical Research* 14 (2) (February 2016): 176–206.

Haddox, Susan E. "Is There a Biblical Masculinity? Masculinities in the Hebrew Bible." *Word & World* 31 (1) (Winter 2016): 5–14.

Halperin, David M. *Saint Foucault: Towards a Gay Hagiography*. New York and Oxford: Oxford University Press, 1995.

Hamilton, Victor P. *The Book of Genesis: Chapters 18–50*. Grand Rapids: Eerdmans, 1995.

Harcourt, Wendy (ed.). *The Palgrave Handbook of Gender and Development: Critical Engagements in Feminist Theory and Practice*. New York: Palgrave Macmillan, 2016.

Harrison, Beverly W. "Review of *In Memory of Her*, by Schüssler Fiorenza." *Horizons* 11 (1984): 150–3.

Harrisville, Roy A. and Walter Sundberg. *The Bible in Modern Culture: Baruch Spinoza to Brevard Childs*. 2nd edn. Grand Rapids: Eerdmans, 2002.

Hedwig-Jahnow-Forschungsprojekt (ed.). *Körperkonzepte im Ersten Testament: Aspekte einer feministischen Anthropologie*. Stuttgart: W. Kohlhammer, 2003.

Herbison, Donna. *Through My Eyes: Women of the Bible*. Bloomington: Authorhouse, 2015.

Higgs, Liz Curtis. *Bad Girls of the Bible, and What We Can Learn from Them*. Colorado Springs, CO: WaterBrook Press, 2013 [2007, 1999].

Higgs, Liz Curtis. *It's Good to Be Queen: Becoming as Bold, Gracious, and Wise as the Queen of Sheba*. Colorado Springs, CO: WaterBrook Press, 2015.

Hill, Renee L. "Who Are We for Each Other? Sexism, Sexuality and Womanist Theology." in James H. Cone and Gayraud S. Wilmore (eds), *Black Theology: A Documentary History*, 345–51. Vol. 2. Maryknoll, NY: Orbis, 1992.

Holladay, William L. *Jeremiah: A Commentary on the Book of the Prophet Jeremiah Chapters 1–25*. Philadelphia: Fortress Press, 1986.

hooks, bell. *Feminist Theory: From Margin to Center*. Cambridge: South End Press, 2000.

Hornsby, Theresa. "Capitalism, Masochism and Biblical Interpretation," in Teresa J. Hornsby and Ken Stone (eds), *Bible Trouble: Queer Reading at the Boundaries of Biblical Scholarship*, 137–56. Atlanta, GA: Society of Biblical Literature Atlanta, 2011.

Howell, Maxine. "Towards a Womanist Pneumatological Pedagogy and Re-reading the Bible from British Black Women's Perspectives," *Black Theology* 7 (2009): 86–99.

Huber, Elaine C. "They Weren't Prepared to Hear: A Closer Look at *The Women's Bible*." *Andover Newton Quarterly* 16 (March 1976): 271–6.

Hurley, James B. *Man and Woman in Biblical Perspective*. Grand Rapids, MI: Zondervan, 1981.

Isasi-Diaz, Ada Maria. *En la lucha: In the Struggle: A Hispanic Women's Liberation Theology*. Minneapolis, MN: Fortress, 1993.

Isasi-Diaz, Ada Maria. *Mujerista Theology: A Theology for the Twenty-First Century*. Maryknoll, NY: Orbis, 1996.

Isasi-Diaz, Ada Maria. "The Bible and *Mujerista* Theology," in Susan Brooks Thistlethwaite and Mary Potter Engel (eds), *Lift Every Voice: Constructing Christian Theologies from the Underside*, 267–75. Maryknoll, NY: Orbis, 1998.

Jahnow, Hedwig. "Die Frau im Alten Testament," in Hedwig-Jahnow Projekt (ed.), *Feministische Hermeneutik und Erstes Testament: Analysen und Interpretationen*, 30–47. Stuttgart: Kohlhammer, 1994. Originally published in *Die Frau* 21 (1914): 352–8, 417–26.

James, Carolyn Custis. *The Gospel of Ruth: Loving God Enough to Break the Rules*. Grand Rapids, MI: Zondervan, 2008.

Jeansonne, Sharon Pace. *The Women of Genesis: From Sarah to Potiphar's Wife*. Minneapolis, MN: Fortress Press, 1990a.

Jeansonne, Sharon Pace. "Rebekah: The Decisive Matriarch," in *The Women of Genesis: From Sarah to Potiphar's Wife*. Minneapolis, MN: Fortress Press, 1990b.

Jeffreys, Sheila. "The Queer Disappearance of Lesbian Sexuality in the Academy," *Women's Studies International Forum* 17 (5) (1994): 459–72.

Jenkins, Michelle Clark. *She Speaks: Wisdom From the Women of the Bible to the Modern Black Woman*. Nashville, TN: Thomas Nelson, 2013.

Jenkins, Philip. *The New Faces of Christianity: Believing the Bible in the Global South*. New York: Oxford University Press, 2006.

Jenkins, Philip. "Believing in the Global South," *First Things* (December 2006). Available online: http://www.firstthings.com/article/2006/12/believing-in-the-global-south (accessed December 12, 2016).

Jenkins, Philip. *The Next Christendom: The Coming of Global Christianity*. 3rd edn. Oxford and New York: Oxford University Press, 2011.

Jobling, J'Annine. *Feminist Biblical Interpretation in Theological Context*. Hampshire: Ashgate, 2002.

Jones-Warsaw, Koala. "Towards a Womanist Hermeneutic: A Reading of Judges 19–21," *JITC* 22 (1) (1994): 172–86.

Junior, Nyaha. *An Introduction to Womanist Biblical Interpretation*. Louisville, KY: Westminster John Knox Press, 2015.

Junior, Nyaha. "Womanist Biblical Interpretation," in Linda Day and Carolyn Pressler (eds), *Engaging the Bible in a Gendered World*, 37–46. Louisville and London: Westminster John Knox Press, 2006.

Kaiser, Otto. *Isaiah 1–12: A Commentary*. 2nd edn. Philadelphia: Westminster, 1983.

Kaltenbach, Caleb and Matthew Vines. "Debating Bible Verses on Homosexuality" *New York Times* (8 June 2015). Available online: http://www.nytimes.com/interactive/2015/06/05/us/samesex-scriptures.html?_r=0 (accessed on December 12, 2016).

Katz, Jonathan. *The Invention of Heterosexuality*. Chicago and London: University of Chicago Press, 1995.

Keel, Othmar and Silvia Schroer. *Schöpfung. Biblische Theologien im Kontext altorientalischer Religionen*. Göttingen: Vandenhoeck & Ruprecht, 2002.

Keel, Othmar and Silvia Schroer. *EVA—Mutter alles Lebendigen. Frauen- und Göttinnenidole aus dem Alten Orient*. Fribourg 2004.

Kemp, Jonathan. "A Queer Age: Or, Discourse Has a History," *Graduate Journal of Social Science* 6 (1) (2009): 3–23.

Kern, Kathi. *Mrs. Stanton's Bible*. Ithaca and London: Cornell University Press, 2001.

Kimmel, Michael S. *The Politics of Manhood: Profeminist Men Respond to the Mythopoetic Men's Movement (and the Mythopoetic Leaders Answer)*. Philadelphia: Temple University Press, 1995.

Kirk-Duggan, Cheryl A. *Pregnant Passion: Gender, Sex, and Violence*. Atlanta, GA: SBL Press, 2003.

Klagsbrun, Francine. "Ruth and Naomi, Rachel and Leah," in Judith A. Kates and Gail Twersky Reimer (eds), *Reading Ruth: Contemporary Women Reclaim a Sacred Story*. New York: Ballantine Books, 1994.

Klein, Michael L. "Not to be Translated in Public," *Journal of Jewish Studies* 39 (1) (Spring 1988): 80–91.

Köstenberger, Andreas J. *God's Design for Man and Woman: A Biblical-Theological Survey*. Wheaton, IL: Crossway, 2014.

Kroeger, Catherine Clark. and Mary J. Evans (eds). *The IVP Women's Commentary*. Downers Grove, IL: InterVarsity Press, 2002.

Krondorfer, Björn. "Introduction," in Björn Krondorfer (ed.), *Men and Masculinities in Christianity and Judaism: A Critical Reader*, xi–xxi. London: SCM Press, 2009.

Krondorfer, Björn. "Biblical Masculinity Matters," in Ovidiu Creangă and Peter-Ben Smit (eds), *Biblical Masculinity Foregrounded*, 286–96. Sheffield: Sheffield Phoenix Press, 2014.

Kvam, Kristen E., Linda S. Schearing and Valerie H. Ziegler (eds). *Eve & Adam: Jewish, Christian and Muslim Readings on Genesis and Gender*. Bloomington, IN: Indiana University Press, 1999.

Kwok, Pui-Lan. "Racism and Ethnocentrism in Feminist Biblical Interpretation," in Elisabeth Schüssler Fiorenza (ed.), *Searching the Scriptures: A Feminist Introduction*, 101–16. New York: Crossroad, 1993.

Kwok, Pui-Lan. *Introducing Asian Feminist Theology*. Cleveland: Pilgrim, 2000.

Kwok, Pui-Lan. *Discovering the Bible in the Non-Biblical World*. Eugene, OR: Wipf and Stock, 2003.

Kwok, Pui-Lan. *Postcolonial Imagination and Feminist Theology*. Louisville: Westminster John Knox Press, 2005.

Laffey, Alice L. *An Introduction to the Old Testament: A Feminist Perspective*. Philadelphia: Fortress, 1988.

Lee, Dorothy. *Flesh and Glory: Symbol, Gender, and Theology in the Gospel of John*. New York: Crossroad, 2002.

Lee, Yeong-Mee. *Isaiah's Theology of Salvation with Special Attention to the Female Imagery of Zion*. (In Korean) Seoul: Malgunulim, 2004.

Leneman, Helen. "Portrayals of Power in the Stories of Delilah and Bathsheba: Seduction in Song," in Leonard Jay Greenspoon and Bryan F. Le Beau (eds), *Sacred Text, Secular Times: The Hebrew Bible in the Modern World*, 227–43. Omaha, NE: Creighton University Press, 2000.

Lings, K. Renato. "The 'Lyings' of a Woman: Male-Male Incest in Leviticus 18.22?" *Theology & Sexuality* 15 (2) (2009): 231–50.

Lockyer, Herbert. *All the Kings and Queens of the Bible: Tragedies and Triumphs of Royalty in Past Ages*. Grand Rapids, MI: Zondervan, 1961.

Lockyer, Herbert. *All the Books and Chapter of the Bible' Combination of Bible Study and Daily Meditation Plan*. Grand Rapids, MI: Zondervan, 1966.

Lockyer, Herbert. *All the Women of the Bible: The Life and Times of All the Women of the Bible*. Grand Rapids, MI: Zondervan, 1967.

Lockyer, Herbert. *All the Holy Days and Holidays or, Sermons on All National and Religious Memorial Days*. Grand Rapids, MI: Zondervan, 1968.

Lockyer, Herbert. *All the Children in the Bible*. Grand Rapids, MI: Zondervan, 1970.

Lockyer, Herbert. *All the Messianic Prophecies of the Bible*. Grand Rapids, MI: Zondervan, 1973.

Lockyer, Herbert. *All the Divine Names and Titles in the Bible: A Unique Classification of All Scriptural Designations of the Three Persons of the Trinity*. Grand Rapids, MI: Zondervan, 1975.

Lockyer, Herbert. *All the Men of the Bible: A Portrait Gallery and Reference Library of More than 3000 Biblical Characters*. Grand Rapids, MI: Zondervan, 1988 [1958].

Lockyer, Herbert. *All About the Holy Spirit*. Peabody, MA: Hendrickson Publishers, 1995 [1949].

Lockyer, Herbert. *All About the Second Coming*, ed. Herbert Lockyer, Jr. Peabody, MA: Hendrickson Publishers, 1997.

Lockyer, Herbert. *All the Music of the Bible: An Exploration of Musical Expression in Scripture and Church Hymnody*. Peabody, MA: Hendrickson Publishers, 2004.

Long, Philips V. (ed.). *Israel's Past in Present Research: Essays on Ancient Israelite Historiography*. Winona Lake, IN: Eisenbrauns, 1999.

Lorde, Audre. "The Master's Tools Will Never Dismantle the Master's House," in *Sister Outsider: Essays and Speeches*, 110–14. Berkeley: Crossing Press, 2007. Originally published in 1984.

Low, Katherine. "Space for Women and Men: Masculinity Studies in Feminist Biblical Interpretation," in Susanne Scholz (ed.), *Feminist Interpretation of the Hebrew Bible in Retrospect*, 345–63, Vol. 3, Method. Sheffield: Sheffield Phoenix Press, 2016.

Macartney, Clarence Edward. *Great Women of the Bible*. New York and Nashville: Abingdon, 1942.

Macias, Kathi. *Mothers of the Bible Speak to Mothers of Today*. Birmingham, AL: New Hope Publishers, 2009.

Marble, Annie Russell. *Women of the Bible: Their Services in Home and State*. New York and London: The Century Co., 1923.

Marchal, Joseph A. "Queer Studies and Critical Masculinity Studies in Feminist Biblical Studies," in Elisabeth Schüssler Fiorenza (ed.), *Feminist Biblical Studies in the Twentieth Century: Scholarship and Movement*, 261–80. Bible and Women: An Encyclopædia of Exegesis and Cultural History 9.1. Atlanta: Society of Biblical Literature, 2014.

Manona, Ncumisa. "The Presence of Women in Parables: An Afrocentric Womanist Perspective," *Scriptura* 81 (2002): 408–21.

Martin, Clarice J. "Womanist Interpretation of the New Testament: The Quest for Holistic and Inclusive Translation and Interpretation," *JFSR* 6 (1990): 41–61.

Martin, Clarice J. "Womanist Biblical Interpretation," in John H. Hayes (ed.), *Dictionary of Biblical Interpretation*, 655–8. Nashville, TN: Abingdon, 1999.

Masenya, Madipoane J. "African Womanist Hermeneutics: A Suppressed Voice from South Africa Speaks," *JFSR* 11 (1995): 149–55.

Mbuwayesango, Dora R. "How Local Divine Powers Were Suppressed: A Case of Mwari of the Shona," in Musa W. Dube (ed.), *Other Ways of Reading: African Women and the Bible*, 63–77. Atlanta and Geneva: Society of Biblical Literature/WCC Publications, 2001.

McCabe, Elizabeth A. (ed.). *Women in the Biblical World: A Survey of Old and New Testament Perspectives*. Plymouth and Lanham, MD: University Press of America, 2009.

McKinlay, Judith E. "A Son is Born to Naomi: A Harvest for Israel," in Athalya Brenner (ed.), *Ruth and Esther: A Feminist Companion to the Bible (Second Series)*, 151–7. Sheffield: Sheffield Academic Press, 1999.

McKinlay, Judith E. *Reframing Her: Biblical Women in Postcolonial Focus*. Sheffield: Sheffield Phoenix Press, 2004.

Merton, Thomas. *Mystics and Zen Masters*. New York: Farrar Straus, and Giroux, 1967.

Meyers, Carol. *Discovering Eve: Ancient Israelite Women in Context*. New York: Oxford University Press, 1988.

Meyers, Carol, Toni Craven and Ross S. Kraemer (eds). *Women in Scripture: A Dictionary of Named and Unnamed Women in the Hebrew Bible, the Apocryphal/Deuterocanonical Books and New Testament* Grand Rapids: Eerdmans, 2000.

Milne, Pamela J. "Toward Feminist Companionship: The Future of Feminist Biblical Studies and Feminism," in Athalya Brenner and Carole Fontaine (eds), *A Feminist Companion to Reading the Bible: Approaches, Methods, and Strategies*, 39–60. Sheffield: Sheffield Academic Press, 1997.

Milne, Pamela J. "Minimalists on Parade: An Academic Conference in Rome Highlighted the Positions of Scholars Who Think the Bible Has Little or No Reliable History." *Biblical Archaeology Review* 31 (1) (January–February 2005): 16–17.

Mitchell, Joan L. *Beyond Fear and Silence: A Feminist-Literary Reading of Mark*. New York: Continuum, 2001.

Mitchem, Stephanie Y. *Introducing Womanist Theology*. Maryknoll, NY: Orbis, 2002.

Mohanty, Chandra Talpade. "Under Western Eyes: Feminist Scholarship and Colonial Discourses." *Feminist Review* 30 (Autumn 1988): 60–88.

Moore, Russell D. and Andrew T. Walker. *The Gospel & Same-Sex Marriage*. Gospel for Life; Nashville, TN: B&H Books, 2016.

Moore, Stephen D. (ed.). *In Search of the Present: The Bible Through Cultural Studies*. Semeia 82; Atlanta: Society of Biblical Literature, 1998.

Moore, Stephen D. *God's Beauty Parlor and Other Queer Spaces in and Around the Bible*. Stanford: Stanford University Press, 2001.

Moore, Stephen D. "O Man, Who Art Thou …? Masculinity Studies and New Testament Studies," in Stephen D. Moore and Janice Capel Anderson (eds), *New Testament Masculinities*, 1–22. Atlanta, GA: Society of Biblical Literature, 2003.

Moore, Stephen D. "Gigantic God: Yahweh's Body," in *The Bible in Theory: Critical and Postcolonial Essays*, 201–20. Atlanta, GA: SBL, 2010.

Moore, Stephen D. "Final Reflections on Biblical Masculinity," in Ovidiu Creangă (ed.), *Men and Masculinity in the Hebrew Bible and Beyond*, 240–55. Sheffield: Sheffield Phoenix Press, 2010.

Mosala, Itumelung J. *Biblical Hermeneutics and Black Theology in South Africa*. Grand Rapids: Eerdmans, 1989.

Muilenburg, James. "Form Criticism and Beyond," *Journal of Biblical Literature* 88 (1969): 1–18.

Nadar, Sarojini. "A South African Indian Womanist Reading of the Character of Ruth," in Musa W. Dube (ed.), *Other Ways of Reading: African Women and the Bible*, 159–75. Atlanta and Geneva: Society of Biblical Literature/WCC Publications, 2001.

Nelson, Cary, Paula A. Treichler and Lawrence Grossberg. "Cultural Studies: An Introduction," in Lawrence Grossberg, Cary Nelson, and Paula Trichler (eds), *Cultural Studies*, 1–22. New York: Routledge, 1992.

Newsom, Carol A. and Sharon H. Ringe (eds). *Women's Bible Commentary with Apocrypha*. Louisville: Westminster John Knox Press, 2012 [1998, 1992].

Nicol, George G. "Genesis xxix.32 and xxv.22a Reuben's Reversal," *Journal of Theological Studies* 31 (1980): 536–9.

O'Brien, Julia M. *The Aesthetics of Violence in the Prophets*. New York: T&T Clark, 2010.

Oduyoye, Mercy Amba. *Introducing African Women's Theology*. Cleveland: Pilgrim, 2001.

Ollenburger, Ben C. "The History of Israel Contested and Revised," *Modern Theology* 16 (4) (October 2000): 529–40.

Olson, Dennis T. "Untying the Knot? Masculinity, Violence, and the Creation-Fall Story of Genesis 2–4," in Linda Day and Carolyn Pressler (eds), *Engaging the Bible in a Gendered World: An Introduction to Feminist Biblical Interpretation in Honor of Katharine Doob*, 71–86. Louisville and London: Westminster John Knox, 2006.

Once-A-Day Men and Women of the Bible Devotional, Paperback: 365 Insights from Scripture's Most Memorable People (365 Insights from Scripture's Most Memorable People). Grand Rapids, MI: Zondervan, 2012.

Parvey, Constance F. "Theology and Leadership of Women in the New Testament," in Rosemary Radford Ruether (ed.), *Religion and Sexism: Images of Women in the Jewish and Christian Traditions*, 117–49. Eugene: Wipf and Stock Publishers, 1998.

Penney, James. *After Queer Theory: The Limits of Sexual Politics*. London: Pluto Press, 2014.

Petermann, Ina J. "'Schick die Fremde in die Wüste!' Oder: Sind die Sara-Hagar-Erzählungen aus Genesis 16 und 21 ein Beispiel (anti-) rassistischer Irritation aus dem Alten Israel?" in Silvia Wagner, Gerdi Nützel and Martin Kick (eds), *(Anti-) Rassistische Irrationen: Biblische Texte und interkulturelle Zusammenarbeit*, 137–50. Berlin: Alektor Verlag, 1994.

Pitzele, Peter. "The Myth of the Wrestler," in *Our Fathers'" Wells: A Personal Encounter with the Myths of Genesis*. San Francisco: HarperSanFrancisco, 1995.

Plaskow, Judith. "Christian Feminism and Anti-Judaism," *Cross Currents* 28 (1978): 306–9.

Plaskow, Judith. "Movement and Emerging Scholarship: Feminist Biblical Scholarship I the 1970s in the United States," in *Feminist Bible Studies in the Twentieth Century: Scholarship and Movement*. 21–34. Bible and Women 9.1. Atlanta, GA: SBL Press, 2014.

Polich, Laurie. *Creative Bible Lessons from the Old Testament: 12 Character Studies on Surprisingly Modern Men & Women*. Grand Rapids, MI: Youth Specialties/Zondervan, 2005.

Poorman, Sue, and Lawrence O. Richards. *Women of the Bible: The Live and Times of Every Woman of the Bible*. Nashville, TN: Thomas Nelson, 2003.

Provan, Iain, V. Philips Long, and Tremper Longman III (eds). *Biblical History of Israel*. Louisville: Westminster John Knox Press, 2003.

Puar, Jasbir K. *Terrorist Assemblages: Homonationalism in Queer Times*. Durham, NC: Duke University Press, 2007.

Puar, Jasbir K. "Rethinking Homonationalism," *International Journal Middle Eastern Studies* 45 (2013): 336–9.

Punt, Jeremy. "Dealing with Empire and Negotiating Hegemony: Developments in Postcolonial Feminist Hebrew Bible Criticism," in Susanne Scholz (ed.), *Feminist Interpretation of the Hebrew Bible in Retrospect*, 278–303. Vol. 3, Method. Sheffield: Sheffield Phoenix Press, 2016.

Ramban (Nachmanides). *Commentary on the Torah: Genesis*, trans. Charles B. Chavel. New York: Shilo, 1971.

Rapp, Ursula. *Mirjam: Eine feministisch-rhetorische Lektüre der Mirjamtexts in der hebräischen Bibel*. BZAW 317; Berlin: Walter de Gruyter, 2002.

Rashkow, Ilona N. *Taboo or Not Taboo: Sexuality and Family in the Hebrew Bible*. Minneapolis, MN: Fortress, 2000.

Rich, Adrienne. "Compulsory Heterosexuality and Lesbian Existence," in *Blood, Bread, and Poetry: Selected Prose 1979-1985*, 23–75. London: W. W. Norton, 1986.

Rotenberg, Mordechai. "The 'Midrash' and Biographic Rehabilitation," *Journal for the Scientific Study of Religion* 25 (1) (1986): 41–55.

Rusche, Helga. *They Lived By Faith: Women in the Bible*. Baltimore: Helicon, 1963.

Russell, Letty M. and Shannon J. Clarkson. *Dictionary of Feminist Theologies*. Louisville: Westminster John Knox Press, 1996.

Said, Edward W. *Orientalism*. New York: Vintage, 1979.

Said, Edward W. *Culture and Imperialism*. New York: Knopf, 1993.

Sakenfeld, Katharine Doob. "Old Testament Perspectives: Methodological Issues," *JSOT* 22 (1982): 13–20.

Sandys-Wunsch, John. *What Have They Done to the Bible: A History of Modern Biblical Interpretation*. Collegeville, MN: Liturgical Press, 2005.

Sarna, Nahum M. *Genesis*. The JPS Torah Commentary Series. Philadelphia: JPS, 1989.

Schaberg, Jane. *The Illegitimacy of Jesus: A Feminist Theological Interpretation of the Infancy Narratives*. San Francisco: Harper & Row, 1987.

Schäfer, Axel R. *Countercultural Conservatives: American Evangelicalism from the Postwar Revival to the New Christian Right*. Madison: University of Wisconsin Press, 2011.

Scholz, Susanne. "Sodom and Gomorrah (Genesis 19:1-29) on the Internet," *Journal of Religion and Society* 1 (1999). Available online: www.creighton.edu/JRS

Scholz, Susanne. *Rape Plots: A Feminist Cultural Study of Genesis 34*. New York: Lang, 2000.

Scholz, Susanne (ed.). *Biblical Studies Alternatively: An Introductory Anthology*. Upper Riversaddle, NJ: Prentice Hall, 2003.

Scholz, Susanne. "Gender, Class, and Androcentric Compliance in the Rapes of Enslaved Women in the Hebrew Bible." *Lectio difficilior: European Electronic Journal of Feminist Exegesis* 1 (2004), http://www.lectio.unibe.ch/04_1/Scholz.Enslaved.htm (accessed December 12, 2016).

Scholz, Susanne. "Back Then it Was Legal: The Epistemological Imbalance in Readings of Biblical and Ancient Near Eastern Rape Legislation," *Journal of Religion and Abuse* 7 (3) (December 2005): 5–35. Also published in *The Bible and Critical Theory* 1 (4) (December 2005a). Available online: http://publications.epress.monash.edu/toc/bc/1/4

Scholz, Susanne. "The Christian Right's Discourse on Gender and the Bible," *Journal of Feminist Studies in Religion* 21 (1) (Spring 2005b): 83–104.

Scholz, Susanne. *Sacred Witness: Rape in the Hebrew Bible*. Minneapolis, MN: Fortress Press, 2010.

Scholz, Susanne. "Feminist Scholarship of the Old Testament," *Oxford Bibliographies Online Research Guides* (2012a). Available online: http://www.oxfordbibliographies. com/view/document/obo-9780195393361/obo-9780195393361-0020.xml (accessed December 12, 2016)

Scholz, Susanne. "Occupy Academic Bible Teaching: The Architecture of Educational Power and the Biblical Studies Curriculum," in Jane S. Webster and Glenn S. Holland (eds), *Teaching the Bible in the Liberal Arts Classroom*, 28–43. Sheffield: Sheffield Academic Press, 2012b.

Scholz, Susanne. (ed.). "A Commentary upon Feminist Commentary: A Report from the Feminist Biblical Trenches," *lectio difficilior: European Electronic Journal for Feminist Exegesis* (2014). Available online: http://www.lectio.unibe.ch/e/index_e.html.

Scholz, Susanne. (ed.). *Feminist Interpretation of the Hebrew Bible in Retrospect*. Vols 1–3; Sheffield: Sheffield Phoenix Press, 2016 [2014, 2013].

Schottroff, Luise, Silvia Schroer, and Marie-Theres Wacker. *Feminist Interpretation: The Bible in Women's Perspective*. Minneapolis, MN: Fortress Press, 1998.

Schottroff, Luise and Marie-Theres Wacker (eds). *Von der Wurzel getragen: Christlich-feministische Exegese in Auseinandersetzung*. New York: Brill, 1996.

Schottroff, Luise and Marie-Theres Wacker (eds). *Kompendium Feministische Bibelauslegung*. Gütersloh: Chr. Kaiser/Gütersloher Verlagshaus, 1999.

Schottroff, Luise and Marie-Theres Wacker (eds). *Feminist Biblical Interpretation: A Compendium of Critical Commentary on the Books of the Bible and Related Literature*. Trans. Lisa E. Dahill, Everett R. Kalin, Nancy Lukens, Linda M. Maloney, Barbara Rumscheidt, Martin Rumscheidt, and Tina Steiner. Grand Rapids, MI and Cambridge: William B. Eerdmans, 2012.

Schroeder, Joy A. *Deborah's Daughters: Gender Politics and Biblical Interpretation*. Oxford and New York: Oxford University Press, 2014.

Schroer, Silvia and Thomas Staubli. *Die Körpersymbolik der Bibel*. Gütersloh: Gütersloher Verlagshaus, 2005.

Schroer, Silvia. *Die Weisheit hat ihr Haus gebaut. Studien zur Gestalt der Sophia in den biblischen Schriften*. Mainz: Matthias Grünewald Verlag, 1996.

Schroer, Silvia. "Diachronic Sections," in Luise Schottroff, Silvia Schroer, and Marie-Theres Wacker (eds), *Feminist Interpretation: The Bible in Women's Perspective*, 102–45. Minneapolis, MN: Fortress Press, 1998.

Schüssler Fiorenza, Elizabeth. (ed.). *In Memory of Her: A Feminist Theological Reconstruction of Christian Origins*. New York: Crossroad, 1983.

Schüssler Fiorenza, Elizabeth. "Transforming a Legacy," in Elisabeth Schüssler (ed.) *Searching the Scripture: A Feminist Introduction*, 2–8. New York: Crossroad, 1993.

Schüssler Fiorenza, Elizabeth (ed.). *The Power of the Word: Scripture and the Rhetoric of Empire*. Minneapolis, MN: Augsburg Fortress, 2007.

Schüssler Fiorenza, Elizabeth (ed.). *Democratizing Biblical Studies: Toward an Emancipatory Educational Space*. Louisville, KY: Westminster John Knox, 2009.

Schüssler Fiorenza, Elizabeth (ed.). *Feminist Biblical Studies in the 20th Century*. The Bible and Women—An Encyclopaedia of Exegesis and Cultural History, 9.1. Atlanta, GA: SBL Press, 2014.

Schneider, Laurel C. "Queer Theory," in A. K. M. Adam (ed.), *Handbook of Postmodern Biblical Interpretation*, 206–12. St. Louis: Chalice Press, 2000.

Schneider, Tammi J. *Sarah: Mother of Nations*. New York: Continuum, 2004.

Schneider, Tammi J. *Mothers of Promise: Women in the Book of Genesis*. Grand Rapids, MI: Baker Academic, 2008.

Schneiders, Sandra M. *Women and the Word*. New York: Paulist, 1986.

Scroggs, Robin. *The New Testament and Homosexuality*. Philadelphia: Fortress Press, 1983.

Sedgewick, Eve. *Epistemology of the Closet*. Berkeley and Los Angeles, CA: University of California Press, 1990.

Sedgewick, Eve. "Gender Criticism," in Stephen Greenblatt and Giles Gunn (eds), *Redrawing the Boundaries: The Transformation of English and American Literary Studies*, 271–301. New York: Modern Language Association of America, 1992.

Segovia, Fernando F. "'And They Began to Speak in Other Tongues': Competing Modes of Discourse in Contemporary Biblical Criticism," in Fernando F. Segovia and Mary Ann Tolbert (eds), *Reading from this Place: Social Location and Biblical Interpretation in the United States, vol. 1*, 1–32. Minneapolis, MN: Fortress Press, 1995a.

Segovia, Fernando F. "Cultural Studies and Contemporary Biblical Criticism: Ideological Criticism as Mode of Discourse," in Fernando F. Segovia and Mary Ann Tolbert (eds), *Reading from this Place: Social Location and Biblical Interpretation in Global Perspective, vol. 2*, 1–17. Minneapolis, MN: Fortress Press, 1995b.

Segovia, Fernando F. *Interpreting Beyond Border*. Sheffield: Sheffield Academic Press, 2000.

Seifert, Elke. *Töchter und Väter im Alten Testament: Eine ideologiekritische Untersuchung zur Verfügungsgewalt von Vätern über ihre Töchter*. Neukirchen-Vluyn: Neukirchener Verlag, 1997.

Shanks, Hershel (ed.). "The Search for History in the Bible," *Biblical Archaeology Review* 26 (2) (March–April 2000): 25–51.

Sherwood, Yvonne M. *The Prostitute and the Prophet: Hosea's Marriage in Literary-Theoretical Perspective*. Sheffield: Sheffield Academic Press, 1996.

Sherwood, Yvonne M. *A Biblical Text and Its Afterlives: The Survival of Jonah in Western Culture*. Cambridge: Cambridge University 2000.

Shields, Mary E. "Multiple Exposures: Body Rhetoric and Gender in Ezekiel 16," in Athalya Brenner (ed.), *Prophets and Daniel: A Feminist Companion to the Bible (Second Series)*, 137–53. New York: Sheffield Academic Press, 2001.

Siegele-Wenschkewitz, Lenore (ed.). *Verdrängte Vergangenheit, die uns bedrängt: Feministische Theologie in der Verantwortung für die Geschichte*. München: Kaiser Verlag, 1988.

Snapdragon Editorial Group, Inc. and Zondervan Corporation. *God's Words of Life for Women of Color: From the King James Version*. Grand Rapids, MI: Zondervan, 2002.

Spangler, Ann. *Dreams: True Stories of Remarkable Encounters with God*. Grand Rapids, MI: Zondervan, 1997.

Spangler, Ann. *Les femmes de la Bible: une année d'études bibliques sur les femmes dans l'Écriture*. Nîmes: Vida éd, 2004a.

Spangler, Ann. *Praying the Names of God: A Daily Guide*. Grand Rapids, MI: Zondervan, 2004b.

Spangler, Ann. *Mütter im Buch der Bücher: ein Andachtsbuch*. Asslar, Gerth Medien, 2007a.

Spangler, Ann. *Sheng jing zhong de nv ren*, with Jean Syswerda. Trans. Wanlan He. Taibei: Dao sheng chu ban she, 2007b.

Spangler, Ann. *Madres de la Biblia*. Miami, FL: Editorial Vida, 2008.

Spangler, Ann. *The Names of God*. Grand Rapids, MI: Zondervan, 2009.

Spangler, Ann. *Women of the Bible: Eve to Pricilla*. Grand Rapids, MI: Zondervan, 2010.

Spangler, Ann. *Frauen im Buch der Bücher: ein Andachtsbuch für das ganze Jahr*. Assler: Gerth Medien, 2012.

Spangler, Ann. *Wicked Women of the Bible*. Grand Rapids, MI: Zondervan, 2015.

Spangler, Ann and Wendy Bello. *Dulces palabras de Dios, con amor, para ti: una guía diaria*. Miami, FL: Editorial Vida, 2011.

Spangler, Ann and LaVonne Neff. *The Names of God Bible*. Grand Rapids, MI: Revell, 2011.

Spangler, Ann. and Jean E. Syswerda. *Women of the Bible: A One-Year Devotional Study of Women in Scripture*. Grand Rapids, MI: Zondervan, 1999.

Spangler, Ann and Jean E. Syswerda. *Prayer through the Eyes of Women of the Bible*. Grand Rapids, MI: Inspirio, 2000.

Spangler, Ann and Jean E. Syswerda. *Blessings and Promises through the Eyes of Women of the Bible*. Grand Rapids, MI: Inspirio, 2001.

Spangler, Ann and Jean E. Syswerda. *Women of the Bible: 52 Bible Studies for Individuals and Groups*. Grand Rapids, MI: Zondervan, 2002 [1999].

Spangler, Ann and Jean E. Syswerda. *Mothers of the Bible: A Devotional*. Grand Rapids, MI: Zondervan, 2006.

Spangler, Ann and Robert D. Wolgemuth. *Fathers in the Bible: A Devotional*. Grand Rapids, MI: Zondervan, 2006.

Spangler, Ann and Robert D. Wolgemuth. *Men of the Bible: A One-Year Devotional Study of Men in Scripture*. Grand Rapids, MI: Zondervan, 2007 [2002].

Spangler, Ann and Robert D. Wolgemuth. *Padres de la Biblia*. Miami, FL: Vida, 2008.

Speiser, Ephraim A. *Genesis: Introduction, Translation, and Notes*. The Anchor Bible Commentary. Garden City, NY: Doubleday, 1964.

Spivak, Gayatri Chakravarty. "Can the Subaltern Speak?" in Cary Nelson and Larry Grossberg (eds), *Marxism and the Interpretation of Culture*, 271–313. Chicago: University of Illinos Press, 1988.

Spivak, Gayatri Chakravarty. *Death of a Discipline*. New York: Columbia University Press, 1993.

St. Clair, Raquel A. "Womanist Biblical Interpretation," in Brian K. Blount (ed.), *True to Our Native Land: An African American New Testament Commentary*, 54–62. Minneapolis, MN: Fortress, 2007.

St. Clair, Raquel A. *Call and Consequences: A Womanist Reading of Mark*. Minneapolis, MN: Fortress, 2008.

Stanton, Elizabeth Cady. *The Women's Bible*. Boston: Northeastern University Press, 1993.

Steger, Manfred B. and Ravi K. Roy. *Neoliberalism: A Very Short Introduction*. Oxford and New York: Oxford University Press, 2010.

Stichele, Caroline Vander and Todd Penner (eds). *Her Master's Tools? Feminist and Postcolonial Engagements of Historical-Critical Discourse*. Atlanta: Society of Biblical Literature, 2005.

Stichele, Caroline Vander and Todd Penner. *Contextualizing Gender in Early Christian Discourse: Thinking Beyond Thecla*. London: T&T Clark, 2009.

Stone, Ken. "Homosexuality and the Bible or Queer Reading? A Response to Martti Nissinen," *Theology & Sexuality* 14 (2001a): 107–18.

Stone, Ken. "Queer Commentary and Biblical Interpretation: An Introduction," in Ken Stone (ed.), *Queer Commentary and the Hebrew Bible*, 116–39. Cleveland: The Pilgrim Press, 2001b.

Stone, Ken. "'You Seduced Me, You Overpowered Me, and You Prevailed': Religious Experience and Homoerotic Sadomasochism in Jeremiah," in Lisa Isherwood (ed.), *Patriarchs, Prophets and Other Villains*, 101–9. London and Oakville: Equinox, 2007.

Strauss, Ed. *Bible Prayers for Fathers: A Devotional.* Barbour Books, 2016.

Sudlow, Elizabeth Williams. *Career Women of the Bible.* New York: Pageant Press, 1951.

Sugirtharajah, R. S. *Asian Biblical Hermeneutics and Postcolonialism: Contesting the Interpretations.* Maryknoll, NY: Orbis Books, 1998a.

Sugirtharajah, R. S. *The Postcolonial Bible.* Sheffield: Sheffield Academic Press, 1998b.

Sugirtharajah, R. S. (ed.). *Vernacular Hermeneutics.* Sheffield: Sheffield Academic Press, 1999.

Sugirtharajah, R. S. *The Bible and the Third World: Precolonial, Colonial, and Postcolonial Encounters.* Cambridge and New York: Cambridge University Press, 2001.

Sugirtharajah, R. S. *Postcolonial Criticism and Biblical Interpretation.* Oxford and New York: Oxford University Press, 2002.

Surin, Kenneth. "Culture/Cultural Studies," in A. .K. M. Adam (ed.), *Handbook of Postmodern Biblical Interpretation*, 49–54. St Louis: Chalice Press, 2000.

Syswerda, Jean E. *Women of the Bible: 52 Bible Studies for Individuals and Groups.* Grand Rapids, MI: Zondervan, 2002.

Tamez, Elsa. *Bible of the Oppressed.* Maryknoll, NY: Orbis Books, 1982.

Tamez, Elsa. *Against Machismo: Interviews with Male Latin American Liberation Theologians.* Yorktown Heights, NY: Meyer-Stone Books, 1987.

Tamez, Elsa. "Women's Rereading of the Bible," in Virginia Fabella and Mercy Amba Oduyoye (eds), *With Passion & Compassion.* Maryknoll, NY: Orbis, 1988.

Tamez, Elsa. *Through Her Eyes: Women's Theology from Latin America.* Maryknoll, NY: Orbis, 1989.

Tamez, Elsa. *The Scandalous Message of James: Faith Without Works is Dead.* New York: Crossroad, 1990.

Tamez, Elsa. *Amnesty By Grace: Justification by Faith from a Latin American Perspective.* Nashville: Abingdon Press, 1993.

Tamez, Elsa. "The Woman Who Complicated the History of Salvation," in John S. Pobee and Bärbel von Wartenberg-Potter (eds), *New Eyes for Reading: Biblical and Theological Reflections By Women From the Third World*, 5–17. Geneva: World Council of Churches, 1996.

Tamez, Elsa. *When the Horizons Close: Rereading Ecclesiastes.* Maryknoll, NY: Orbis, 2000.

Tamez, Elsa. "An Ecclesial Community: Women's Visions and Voices," *Ecumenical Review* 53 (1) (January 2001): 5763.

Tamez, Elsa. "Reading the Bible Under a Sky Without Stars," in Walter Dietrich and Ulrich Luz (eds), *The Bible in a World Context*, 57–63. Grand Rapids: Eerdmans, 2002.

Tamez, Elsa. "Living Ecumenically: An Absolute Necessity: Reflections from Academic Experience," *Ecumenical Review* 75 (5) (January 2005): 12–18.

Thimmes, Pamela. "What Makes a Feminist Reading Feminist? Another Perspective," in Harold C. Washington, Susan Lochrie, and Pamela Thimmes (eds), *Escaping Eden: New Feminist Perspectives on the Bible*, 132–40. New York: New York University Press, 1999.

Thompson, Thomas L. "The Role of Faith in Historical Research," *Scandinavian Journal of the Old Testament* 19 (1) (2005): 111–34.

Tischler, Nancy M. *Men and Women of the Bible: A Reader's Guide.* Westport, CT: Greenwood Press, 2002.

Tolbert, Mary Ann. *The Bible and Feminist Hermeneutics.* Chico, CA: Scholars Press, 1983.

Trible, Phyllis. "Studies in the Book of Jonah" [microform]. (Unpublished Ph.D. thesis; Columbia University, New York, 1963).

Trible, Phyllis. "Depatriarchalizing in Biblical Interpretation," *Journal of the American Academy of Religion* 41 (March 1973a): 30–48.

Trible, Phyllis. "Eve and Adam: Genesis 2–3 Reread," *Andover Newton Quarterly* (March 13, 1973b): 251–8.

Trible, Phyllis. *God and the Rhetoric of Sexuality.* Philadelphia: Fortress Press, 1978.

Trible, Phyllis. "The Effects of Women's Studies on Biblical Studies," *JSOT* 22 (1982): 3–71.

Trible, Phyllis. *Texts of Terror: Literary-Feminist Readings of Biblical Narratives.* Philadelphia: Fortress Press, 1984.

Trible, Phyllis. "Subversive Justice: Tracing the Miriamic Traditions," in Walter J. Harrelson, Douglas A. Knight, and Peter J. Paris (eds), *Justice and the Holy*, 99–109. Atlanta: Scholars Press, 1989a.

Trible, Phyllis. "Five Loaves and Two Fishes: Feminist Hermeneutics and Biblical Theology," *Theological Studies* 50 (2) (1989b): 279–95.

Trible, Phyllis. "Genesis 22: The Sacrifice of Sarah," in Jason P. Rosenblatt and Joseph C. Sitterson (eds), *"Not in Heaven": Coherence and Complexity in the Biblical Narrative*, 170–91. Bloomington: University of Indiana Press, 1991.

Trible, Phyllis. "If the Bible's so Patriarchal, How Come I Love It?" *Bible Review* 8 (October 1992a): 44–7, 55.

Trible, Phyllis. "The Pilgrim Bible," in Sarah Cunningham (ed.), *We Belong Together: Churches in Solidarity with Women*, 15–17. New York: Friendship, 1992b.

Trible, Phyllis. "Treasures Old and New: Biblical Theology and the Challenge of Feminism," in Francis Watson (ed.), *Open Text: New Directions for Biblical Studies?*, 32–56. London: SCM Press, 1993.

Trible, Phyllis. *Rhetorical Criticism: Context, Method, and the Book of Jonah.* Minneapolis, MN: Fortress Press, 1994.

Trible, Phyllis. "Eve and Miriam: From the Margins to the Center," in Hershel Shanks (ed.), *Feminist Approaches to the Bible: Symposium at the Smithsonian Institution*, 5–24. Washington, DC: Biblical Archaeological Society, 1995.

Trible, Phyllis. "Exegesis For Storytellers and Other Strangers," *Journal for Biblical Literature* 114 (1) (1995): 3–19.

Trible, Phyllis. "Not a Jot, Not a Tittle: Genesis 2–3 after Twenty Years," in Kristen E. Kvam, Linda S. Schearing and Valarie H. Ziegler (eds), *Eve and Adam: Jewish, Christian, and Muslim Readings on Genesis and Gender*, 439–44. Bloomington: Indiana University Press, 1999a.

Trible, Phyllis. "Bible in the Round," in Margaret A. Farley and Serene Jones (eds), *Liberating Eschatology: Essays in Honor of Letty M. Russell*, 47–54. Louisville: Westminster John Knox, 1999b.

Trible, Phyllis. "Take Back the Bible," *Review and Expositor* 97 (Fall 2000): 425–31.

Trible, Phyllis and B. Diane Lipsett (eds), *Faith and Feminism: Ecumenical Essays.* Louisville, KY: Westminster John Knox, 2014.

Trible, Phyllis and Letty M. Russell (eds.). *Hagar, Sarah, and Their Children: Jewish, Christian, and Muslim Perspectives*. Louisville: Westminster John Knox Press, 2006.

Tucker, Gene M. *Isaiah*. The New Interpreter's Bible. Vol. 6. Nashville: Abingdon Press, 2001.

Tucker, Ruth A. *Dynamic Women of the Bible: What We Can Learn from Their Surprising Stories*. Grand Rapids, MI: Baker Books, 2014.

Tucker, Ruth A. *Black and White Bible, Black and Blue Wife: My Story of Finding Hope after Domestic Abuse*. Grand Rapids, MI: Zondervan, 2016.

Unterman, Isaac. *The Five Books of Moses: The Book of Genesis: Profoundly Inspiring Commentaries and Interpretations Selected from the Talmudic-Rabbinic Literature*. New York: Bloch, 1973.

Von Rad, Gerhard. *Genesis: A Commentary*. Philadelphia: Westminster, 1972.

Wacker, Marie-Theres. *Weltordnung und Gericht: Studien zu 1 Henoch 22*. Forschung zur Bible. Vol. 45. Würzburg: Echter Verlag, 1982.

Wacker, Marie-Theres. (ed.). *Der Gott der Männer und die Frauen*. Düsseldorf, 1988a.

Wacker, Marie-Theres. "Matriarchale Bibelkritik-ein antijudaistisches Konzept," in Leonore Siegele-Wenschkewitz (ed.), *Verdrängte Vergangenheit, die uns bedrängt: Feministische Theologie in der Verantwortung für die Geschichte*, 181–242. München: Kaiser, 1988b.

Wacker, Marie-Theres. (ed.). *Theologie feministisch: Disziplinen, Schwerpunkte, Richtungen*. Patmos, Düsseldorf, 1988c.

Wacker, Marie-Theres. "God as Mother? On the Meaning of a Biblical God-Symbol for Feminist Theology," in Anne E. Carr and Elisabeth Schüssler Fiorenza (eds), *Motherhood: Experience, Institution, Theology*, 103–11. Edinburgh: T&T Clark, 1989.

Wacker, Marie-Theres. "Feministisch-theologische Blicke auf die neuere Monotheismus-Diskussion: Anstöße und Fragen," in Georg Braulik, Marie-Theres Wacker, and Erich Zenger (eds), *Der eine Gott und die Göttin*, 17–48. Freiburg: Herder, 1991.

Wacker, Marie-Theres. "Feminist Theology and Anti-Judaism: The Status of the Discussion and the Context of the Problem in the Federal Republic of Germany," *Journal of Feminist Studies in Religion* 61 (1992): 51–75.

Wacker, Marie-Theres. "Kosmisches Sakrament oder Verpfändung des Körpers? 'Kultprostitution' im biblischen Israel und im hinduistischen Indien," *Biblische Notizen* 61 (1992): 51–75.

Wacker, Marie-Theres. "Spuren der Göttin im Hoseabuch," in Walter Dietrich and Martin A. Klopfenstein (eds), *Gott allein? JHWH-Verehrung und biblischer Monotheismus im Kontext der israelitischen und altorientalischen Religionsgeschichte*, 229–48. Freiburg, Schweiz and Göttingen: Universitätsverlag/Vandenhoeck & Ruprecht, 1994.

Wacker, Marie-Theres. *Figurationen des Weiblichen im Hosea-Buch*. Freiburg: Herder, 1995.

Wacker, Marie-Theres. "Gendering Hosea 13," in Bob Becking and Meindert Dijkstra (eds), *On Reading Prophetic Texts: Gender-Specific and Related Studies in Memory of Fokkelien van Dijk-Hemmes*, 265–82. Leiden and New York: Brill, 1996.

Wacker, Marie-Theres. "Gottes Groll, Gottes Güte und Gottes Gerechtigkeit im Joel-Buch," in Ruth Scoralick (ed.), *Das Drama der Barmherzigkeit Gottes*, 107–24. Stuttgart: Katholisches Bibelwerk, 2000.

Wacker, Marie-Theres. "Rizpa oder: Durch Trauer-Arbeit zur Versöhnung (Anmerkungen zu 2 Sam. 21, 1–14)," in Klaus Kiesow and Thomas Meurer (eds), *Textarbeit: Studien zu Texten und ihrer Rezeption aus dem Alten Testament und der Umwelt Israels (Festschrift für Peter Weimar)*, 545–67. Münster: Ugarit Verlag, 2003.

Wacker, Marie-Theres and Erich Zenger (eds). *Der eine Gott und die* Göttin: *Gottesvorstellungen des biblischen Israel im Horizont feministischer Theologie*. Freiburg: Herder, 1991.

Walker, Alice. *In Search of Our Mother's Gardens: Womanist Prose*. San Diego: Harcourt Brace Jovanovich, 1983.

Washington, Harold C., Susan Lochrie, and Pamela Thimmes (eds). *Escaping Eden: New Feminist Perspectives on the Bible*. New York: New York University Press, 1999.

Weems, Renita J. *Just a Sister Away: A Womanist Vision of Women's Relationships in the Bible*. San Diego, CA: LuraMedia, 1988.

Weems, Renita J. "Do You See What I See? Diversity in Interpretation," *Church & Society* 82 (September–October 1991): 28–43.

Weems, Renita J. "Womanist Reflections on Biblical Hermeneutics," in James H. Cone and Gayraud S. Wilmore (eds), *Black Theology: A Documentary History*, 216–24. Vol. 2. Maryknoll, NY: Orbis, 1992b.

Weems, Renita J. "The Hebrew Women Are Not Like the Egyptian Women: The Ideology of Race, Gender and Sexual Reproduction in Exodus 1," *Semeia* 59 (1992a): 25–34.

Weems, Renita J. *Battered Love: Marriage, Sex, and Violence in the Hebrew Prophets*. Minneapolis, MN: Augsburg Fortress, 1995.

Weems, Renita J. "Re-reading for Liberation: African American Women and the Bible," in Silvia Schroer and Sophia Bietenhard (eds), *Feminist Interpretation of the Bible and the Hermeneutics of Liberation*, 19–32. London and New York: Sheffield Academic Press, 2003.

Wenig, Margaret Moers. "Male and Female God Created Them: Parashat Bereshit (Genesis 1:1–6:8)," in Gregg Drinkwater, Joshua Lesser, and David Shneer (eds), *Torah Queeries: Weekly Commentaries on the Hebrew Bible*, 11–18. New York and London: New York University Press.

West, Gerald O. "And the Dumb Do Speak: Articulating Incipient Readings of the Bible in Marginalized Communities," in J. W. Rogerson, Margaret Davies, M. Daniels and R. Carroll (eds), *The Bible in Ethics: The Second Sheffield Colloquium*, 174–92. Sheffield: Sheffield Academic Press, 1995.

West, Gerald O. and Musa W. Dube Shomana (eds.). *"Reading With": An Exploration of the Interface Between Critical and Ordinary Readings of the Bible: African Overtures*. Atlanta: Scholars Press, 1996.

West, Gerald O. and Musa W. Dube Shomana (eds). *The Bible in Africa: Transactions, Trajectories, and Trends*. Leiden: Brill, 2000.

West, Mona. "Reading the Bible as Queer Americans: Social Location and the Hebrew Scriptures," *Theology & Sexuality* 10 (March 1999): 28–42.

Westbrook, Raymond. "The Female Slave," in Victor H. Matthews a.o. (eds), *Gender and Law in the Hebrew Bible and the Ancient Near East*, 214–38. Sheffield: Sheffield Academic Press, 1998.

Westermann, Claus. *Genesis 12–36: A Commentary*. Trans. John J. Scullion. Minneapolis: Augsburg, 1985.

Williams, Delores S. "The Color of Feminism: Or, Speaking the Black Woman's Tongue," *JRT* 43 (1986): 42–58.

Williams, Delores S. *Sisters in the Wilderness: The Challenge of Womanist God-Talk*. Maryknoll, NY: Orbis Books, 1993a.

Williams, Delores S. "Womanist Theology: Black Women's Voices," in James H. Cone and

Gayraud S. Wilmore (eds), *Black Theology: A Documentary History*, 265–72. Vol. 2. Maryknoll, NY: Orbis, 1993b.

Wilson, Stephen M. *Making Men: The Male Coming-of-Age Theme in the Hebrew Bible*. Oxford: Oxford University Press, 2015.

Wimbush, Vincent L. "The Bible and African Americans: An Outline of an Interpretative History," in Cain Hope Felder (ed.), *Stony the Road We Trod: African American Biblical Interpretation*, 81–97. Minneapolis, MN: Fortress, 1991.

Winslow, Karen Strand. "Recovering Redemption for Women: Feminist Exegesis in North American Evangelicalism," in Susanne Scholtz (ed.), *Feminist Interpretation of the Hebrew Bible in Retrospect*, 269–89, Vol. 2, Social Locations. Sheffield: Sheffield Academic Press, 2014.

Wittig, Monique. *The Straight Mind and Other Essays*. New York: Harvester Wheatsheaf, 1992.

Wolde, Ellen J. "Does "Innâ Denote Rape? A Semantic Analysis of a Controversial Word," *Vetus Testamentum* 52 (4) (2002): 528–44.

Wolgemut, Robert. *The Father's Plan: A Bible Study for Dads*. Nashville, TN: Thomas Nelson, 2010.

Wolgemut, Robert. *NIV, Dad's Devotional Bible*. Grand Rapids, MI: Zondervan, 2016.

Yamada, Frank M. *Configurations of Rape in the Hebrew Bible*. New York: Lang, 2008.

Yee, Gale A. (ed.). *Judges & Method: New Approaches in Biblical Studies*. Minneapolis, MN: Fortress, 1995.

Yee, Gale A. *Poor Banished Children of Eve: Woman as Evil in the Hebrew Bible*. Minneapolis, MN: Augsburg Fortress, 2003.

Yoo, Yani. "Han-Laden Women: Korean 'Comfort Women' and Women in Judges 19–21," *Semeia* 78 (1997): 37–46.

INDEX OF PRIMARY TEXTS

INDEX OF AUTHORS

CPSIA information can be obtained
at www.ICGtesting.com
Printed in the USA
LVHW020137030221
678155LV00009B/111